LEAVING
COLLEGE

LEAVING COLLEGE

Rethinking the Causes and Cures of Student Attrition

Vincent Tinto

SECOND EDITION

The University of Chicago Press
Chicago and London

The University of Chicago Press, Chicago 60637
The University of Chicago Press, Ltd., London
© 1987, 1993 by The University of Chicago
All rights reserved. Published 1993.
Paperback edition 2012
Printed in the United States of America

21 20 19 18 17 16 15 14 13 12   7 8 9 10 11

ISBN-13: 978-0-226-80449-1 (cloth)
ISBN-13: 978-0-226-00757-1 (paper)
ISBN-10: 0-226-80449-6 (cloth)
ISBN-10: 0-226-00757-X (paper)

Library of Congress Cataloging-in-Publication Data

Tinto, Vincent.
    Leaving college : rethinking the causes and cures of student
attrition / Vincent Tinto.—2nd edition.
        p. cm.
    Includes biographical references (p.) and index.
    1. College dropouts—United States. 2. College attendance—United
States. I. Title.
LC148.15.T56 1993
378.1'69—dc20   93-28582
                                                      CIP

To Pat, Katie, and Gabby Tinto

Contents

Preface ―
to Second Edition

Once the concern of several "enlightened" institutions, the goal of enhanced student retention has become, since the first edition of this book, a common part of institutional and state planning. This growing acceptance of the importance of student retention has been reflected in an explosion of research and policy reports seeking to better understand and address the forces that shape student retention in higher education.

This explosion of research has served to refine, supplement, and, in some cases, challenge our understanding of the complex forces shaping student retention. It has given rise to a much needed debate in both research and policy circles about the adequacy of past theory and the effectiveness of existing programs to enhance student retention on campus.

The intent of this edition is to take a look back on recent evidence and to ask to what degree our past understandings should be changed to better reflect our current body of knowledge and experience. It seeks to resynthesize, where necessary, and to extend, where appropriate, our work to new areas of inquiry and policy that were only touched upon in the first edition. This has thus become a considerably revised and expanded second edition. Indeed some sections of the book have been almost completely rewritten and other sections added where before there was only passing reference.

Several immediate changes will be evident to readers of the first edition. Chapter 2 on the scope and patterning of student departure has been totally rewritten. It now utilizes more recent data (e.g., the High School and

Beyond Study of the activities of 1980 high school graduates) and a wider range of data (e.g. the American College Testing Program data on institutional rates of attrition) to explore what we know about student departure in higher education. This makes it possible to ask whether and in what manner rates of departure have changed over the past twenty years.

Chapter 3 on the roots of individual departure from institutions of higher education has been revised to include virtually all the important research done since 1987. This has led to substantially revised sections on the experience of older students and of students of color in higher education and on the nature of attrition in commuting and two-year institutions.

Chapter 4, which speaks to a theory of student departure, has been refined in a number of areas to more clearly address how that theory can be applied both to the experience of students of color and adult students and to the situation facing commuting institutions and two-year colleges. In this respect, the revisions to the model clarify the role of multiple college communities in student retention and the ways in which external communities influence the individual's experience within college.

Equally important, chapter 4 now speaks to the critical relationship between the experience of the classroom and student learning and persistence. It looks at the growing body of research on the effect of student experience on learning and persistence and posits the view that involvement in the smaller communities of the classroom is important not only in its own right but also for subsequent involvement in the larger communities of the college. In this manner, the theory has been expanded to explicitly include the role of classrooms in the process of student persistence. In so doing, this edition seeks to correct an imbalance in past conversations about student attrition, an imbalance created by the insistence that attrition is largely a reflection of what goes on outside the classroom and therefore a matter primarily for those in student affairs.

The following chapter on policy, chapter 5, has also been completely rewritten and expanded. It draws upon the wealth of recent information to expand our treatment of programs and provide an increased range of specific examples of programs in different institutional contexts. The conclusion, chapter 6, has been only slightly revised, in keeping with the need to more explicitly recognize the importance of the classroom to the broader issue of student retention.

There are now two appendixes. The first, on assessment, has been revised in a number of areas to address recent developments in program assessment and the new federal requirement on the reporting of retention data. The second, on doctoral persistence, is entirely new to this edition. It proposes the broad outlines of a theory of doctoral persistence that draws on our model of undergraduate persistence and on recent research on doctoral persistence.

At the same time, it speaks to the types of research studies that would have to be carried out for us to move to a fully articulated theory.

Finally, the revised edition represents the closing of a circle. Since the first edition of the book, I have learned much from the many dedicated faculty, staff, and administrators I have met during visits to campuses and speeches at various conferences, workshops, and retreats. Their comments and reactions, as much as the formal research, has been instrumental to the thinking that went into this edition of the book. In this way, this edition represents my attempt to capture their expertise and close the circle between research and policy so that each informs the other. Equally important, it also represents the closing of a circle of writing and reflection, a closing statement about an issue to which I have given much of my time during the past eighteen years.

Vincent Tinto
Syracuse, New York

Acknowledgments

I am indebted to numerous individuals and institutions for having freely given of their time and resources so that this book could be completed.

For the first edition, my own institution, Syracuse University, was particularly supportive. The administration at that time, especially Volker Weiss and Dean Hal Herber, willingly provided additional resources and grants during various stages in the development of the manuscript. Without their support, the book would not have been possible. My colleagues and friends in the School of Education and in my program, Cultural Foundations of Education, especially Gerald Grant, Thomas Green, and Emily Robertson, were outstandingly supportive and mercifully tolerant of my tendency to forget things while working on the book. Their patience and good humor were much appreciated.

Much of the first draft of the work was completed while I was on sabbatical leave at Stanford University. Dean Myron Aiken and Henry Levin of the School of Education graciously provided the office facilities and library resources so important to the development of the manuscript. Their support, together with that of the Institute of Finance and Governance, made the sabbatical year both productive and pleasurable.

I had detailed and helpful comments on various portions of the manuscript of the first edition from Phyllis Bader-Borel, State University of New York at Albany; Janet Edwards, State University of New York at Plattsburgh; James Murtha, City University of New York; Ernie Pascarella, the University of

Illinois at Chicago; Pat Terenzini, now of the Pennsylvania State University; and John Weidman, the University of Pittsburgh.

Several of my students also aided the work. Diane Lebo Wallace, a graduate student in Cultural Foundations of Education at Syracuse University, assisted in both the development and writing of the manuscript. A talented writer, she spent countless hours trying to teach an old dog new tricks on how to write well. Barry Lentz, also a graduate student in Cultural Foundations of Education, lent a patient ear to my questions and concerns. He and other students, many of whom were members of my class on student retention, aided immeasurably in the refinement of the manuscript by continually forcing me to clarify my ideas and concerns.

The second edition of the book benefited as well from a great variety of people who, in many cases unknowingly, helped me rethink afresh issues that I too easily came to take for granted. The many researchers whose work I referred to and the many faculty, staff, administrators, and students with whom I spoke during my many visits to campuses and conferences were instrumental to the revisions found in this edition. It is their work and experience that are reflected here. Several individuals, in particular Anne Goodsell and Pat Russo, graduate students at Syracuse University, and William Tierney of Pennsylvania State University were especially helpful in getting me to appreciate the power of qualitative methods to reveal truths that are frequently overlooked in quantitative studies of retention. Their thoughts, particularly those on issues of diversity, were very important to my own thinking on this subject. So also must I acknowledge the contributions of John Bean of Indiana University, Alberto Cabrera of the State University of New York at Albany, and Amaury Nora of the University of Illinois at Chicago. Their recent work was most useful to my rethinking sections of the book. Finally, parts of this edition, especially those dealing with classrooms and student learning, have benefited greatly from my work with the National Center on Postsecondary Teaching, Learning, and Assessment. A five-year, 5.9-million-dollar project funded by the U.S. Department of Education's Office of Educational Research and Improvement (OERI), the Center has served as a meeting place for a variety of ideas and arguments about the interconnectedness of student experience in college. It has also provided funding that has enabled me to explore the impact of college learning communities upon student persistence and learning in both four- and two-year colleges.

Acknowledgment must also go to my editor, John Tryneski, to Jo Ann Kiser, manuscript editor for the second edition, and to the several anonymous reviewers whose critical and careful reading provided valuable feedback on matters of both substance and clarity. My editor, a person of much wisdom and grace, knew when to prod and when to leave alone. I will forever be grateful for his trust. And I will forever be spoiled.

One person's support and caring can never be fully repaid. The late Burton Blatt, past Dean of the School of Education at Syracuse University, was a source of continuing good will, kindness, and encouragement. His gentle yet firm caring will not be forgotten. I only regret that he could not read the completed work.

Finally, to my wife, Patricia Price Tinto, and my children, Eda Katharine and Gabrielle Clare, I owe special thanks. They wisely forced me not to lose sight of the importance of people in my life by keeping me true to one simple and enduring truth, namely that what I expect of institutions in their treatment of students I should also expect of myself in my relations with other people.

—1—

Introduction

The Dimensions and Consequences of Student Departure from Higher Education

More students leave their college or university prior to degree completion than stay. Of the nearly 2.4 million students who in 1993 entered higher education for the first time, over 1.5 million will leave their first institution without receiving a degree. Of those, approximately 1.1 million will leave higher education altogether, without ever completing either a two- or a four-year degree program.

The consequences of this massive and continuing exodus from higher education are not trivial, either for the individuals who leave or for their institutions. For individuals the occupational, monetary, and other societal rewards of higher education are in large part conditional on earning a college degree.[1] For example, men ages twenty-five and older with one to three years of college report a median annual income in 1989 of $31,308. College graduates of the same age report an median income of $38,565, a difference of slightly more than 23 percent (U.S. Office of Education 1991, table 357).

This is not to say that those who attend and fail to obtain a degree have not benefited from higher education. As with the process of trial and error in the job market, college education may lead individuals to discover their likes and dislikes and uncover the occupations that are compatible with their interests and abilities. Nevertheless, it is commonly recognized that a college degree, especially a four-year degree, is an important certificate of occupational entry without which access to prestigious positions in society becomes measurably more difficult.

For institutions, the consequences of high rates of student departure, though measured in different terms, are of no less concern. It is a concern sparked by the belated recognition that the long awaited decline in the size of the college-going population, especially among high school graduates, has finally arrived. Though the most recent projections of total enrollments indicate an upswing beyond 1996 (U.S. Department of Education 1991), the experience of greatly reduced financial resources has led institutions to appreciate, as they had never before, the necessity of retaining as many of their students as possible.

The experience of shrinking enrollments varies considerably among institutions of higher education. While some institutions, most notably the prestigious private colleges and universities, continue to gain enrollments, many smaller and less prestigious public and private colleges, two- and four-year, have undergone dramatic declines. Some institutions, primarily the smaller tuition-driven colleges, have teetered on the brink of financial collapse. Indeed, many have closed their doors in recent years with many more predicted to follow suit.

In response, institutions have invested in recruitment campaigns to increase the number of applicants. Some have done so with notable success. But as more institutions have come to utilize sophisticated marketing techniques to recruit students, the value of doing so has diminished markedly.[2] College marketing campaigns no longer produce the much-publicized gains in enrollments that once characterized the student recruitment scene. They no longer offer the hope of insuring institutional survival in the coming years.

Little wonder, then, that institutions have come to view the retention of students as the only reasonable course of action left to insure their survival, and that a growing number have turned their energies in that direction with a renewed passion. Armed with recent research findings and reports of successful retention practices, institutions have rushed headlong into the fray. Not infrequently they have enlisted the services of the recently enlarged army of retention consultants who offer promise of a quick and easy solution.

The Limits of Our Understanding of Student Departure

But the path to enhanced student retention is not an easy or a smooth one. Successful retention efforts are difficult to mount, if only because of our continuing inability to make sense of the variable character of student departure. Despite the extensive body of literature which speaks to the question, there is still much we do not know about its longitudinal character and the complex interplay of forces which give rise to it. Furthermore, much of what we think we know is wrong or at least misleading. A good deal of the literature is filled with stereotypical portraits of those student dropouts. For instance, dropouts have been frequently portrayed as having a distinct personality profile or as lacking in a particularly important attribute needed for college completion. As a consequence, we have been given the mistaken view that student dropouts are different or deviant from the rest of the student population. Such stereotypes are reinforced by a language, a way of talking about student departure which labels individuals as failures for not having completed their course of study in an institution of higher education. In this regard, the label dropout is one of the more frequently misused terms in our lexicon of educational descriptors. It is used to describe the actions of all leavers regardless of the reasons or conditions which mark their leaving. But leavers often do not think of themselves as failures. Many see their actions as quite positive steps toward goal fulfillment. Indeed, it is often the case that such departures are an important part of the process of discovery which marks individual social and intellectual maturation.

Our knowledge of successful forms of action is no less limited. Despite having acquired information from a variety of successful retention programs (e.g., Beal and Noel 1980; Adelman 1984), we have yet to distinguish those attributes of successful programs that are institution-specific from those that are more generally essential. Though we have a sense of what sorts of actions seem to work, we are not yet able to tell administrators how and why different actions work on different campuses for different types of students. More importantly, we have not been able to tell institutional officials what procedures they should follow to initiate successful retention programs suited to their own needs and resources. Up till now, our advice has been quite general and descriptive, rather than explanatory in nature. Consequently, it has frequently been wrong or at least seriously misleading.

What we have yet to do and what we clearly need to do is to produce a viable synthesis of what we know about the character and causes of student departure and the nature of successful retention programs. We need to develop a theory of student departure which clearly explains the longitudinal process of student leaving from institutions of higher education while capturing the complexity of behaviors that underlie that phenomenon. And we must do so in a fashion that leads to concrete answers to the questions administrators ask about enhancing student retention.

The Goals and Structure of the Book

To answer those questions, this book focuses on two distinct but related goals. First, it attempts to give order to the extensive body of research on student departure by proposing a theory of departure from institutions of higher education which focuses on the role institutions play in influencing the social and intellectual development of their students. Drawn from studies of suicide and of rites of passage to community membership, that theory will provide a view of student leaving and institutional action which stresses both the limits of institutional action and the unique responsibility institutions share in the education of their students.

Second, the book intends to show what can be done to increase student retention in higher education. But rather than offer a specific solution to that problem—that is, a series of discrete steps which will lead to increased retention—it proposes a course of action, a way of thinking about student dropout, that can be employed in a variety of settings to confront the phenomenon of student departure. In this respect, the work represents an extended discourse on the character of problem solving in higher education as it pertains to the problem of student dropout. It will focus on the logical procedures educators should employ, what they should know about, and the considerations they should take into account as they go about the task of formulating specific actions to retain more of their students to degree completion.

My hope is that educators will have a more complete and a more complex view of the phenomenon we so casually label as dropout, and that they will have at their disposal a more refined set of intellectual tools or procedures which can be applied to the task of student retention as it occurs in specific institutional settings. In the final analysis, the key to successful student retention lies with the institution, in its faculty and staff, not in any one formula or recipe. It resides in the ability of faculty and staff to apply what is known about student retention to the specific situation in which the institution finds itself.

In considering this goal, I will argue that our view of student dropout has been blurred by a number of stereotypes and misconceptions we have long held about it. I will argue that the term "dropout," if it is to be used at all, should be strictly limited to a very narrow range of student departures, namely, to those situations where the implied notion of failure can be reasonably applied to both the individual and the institution. Moreover I will posit the view that retention should not be the ultimate goal of institutional action, though it may be a desirable outcome of institutional efforts. Instead, institutions and students would be better served if a concern for the education of students, their social and intellectual growth, were the guiding principle of institutional action. When that goal is achieved, enhanced student retention will naturally follow. Though student retention is the immediate focus of this book, the character of a student's education and the environments which support that education will serve as its underlying theme.

Thus, I will reason that the first step institutions should take in confronting the problem of student dropout is the specification of institutional educational goals. Institutions must first be able to determine the goals of their actions before they can hope to detail what those actions might be. They must come to a decision as to the character of their educational mission and therefore to an understanding of the purposes for which students are to be admitted and retained within the institution. Only when that decision is made can institutions reasonably direct the actions they take with regard to student retention. Goal clarification enables educators to come to grips with the thorny question of which types of departure among which types of students are to be the object of institutional action and which are to be considered the natural outcome of institutional functioning. As we will demonstrate in chapter 3, student leaving arises from a great variety of sources and takes on a range of different forms. Some have to do with academic difficulties, others do not. A large proportion of departures occur even when individuals are meeting the minimum academic standards of the institution. As a consequence, the actions taken to respond to one form of departure may differ from those required to treat another form. More importantly, actions which may be beneficial in one case may prove counterproductive in another. There are limits to what institutions can do to retain students. Difficult choices have to be made, choices which cannot be reasonably made without prior decisions about the goals of institutional existence.

Chapter 2 will concern itself with a description of what we currently know about the scope and character of student departure from higher education. It will report recent evidence about the movements of students into and out of institutions of higher education over the past ten years. The following chapter, chapter 3, will present a broad-ranging synthesis of research on the multiple causes of student leaving. This synthesis will serve in turn as the foundation for the building in chapter 4 of a theory of student departure from college. Drawn from the work of Emile Durkheim and Arnold Van Gennep, this theory will argue that colleges and universities are like other human communities; that student departure, like departure from human communities generally, necessarily reflects both the attributes and actions of the individual and those of the other members of the community in which that person resides. Decisions to withdraw are more a function of what occurs after entry than of what precedes it. They are reflections of the dynamic nature of the social and intellectual life of the communities which are housed in the institution, in particular of the daily interaction which occurs among its members. Student departure may then serve as a barometer of the social and intellectual health of institutional life as much as of the experiences of students in the institution.

I will argue in chapter 5 that the key to successful institutional action on behalf of student retention centers not only on the goal of education but also on the institution's ability to provide settings for that education to occur. It requires a commitment born of the reciprocal obligation institutions and individuals accept when an individual is admitted to a higher educational community. In this sense, the discussion of the principles of successful retention action will be a discussion of the nature of educational commitment and of the obligations that commitment imposes alike on students and institutions of higher education.

In conclusion, I will argue in chapter 6 that there are answers to the questions educators pose regarding student retention. But those answers, like so many others, lead to another series of questions that only educators can answer, questions regarding the nature of educational communities and the educational obligations they entail. If there is a secret to successful retention, it lies in the willingness of institutions to involve themselves in the social and intellectual development of their students. That involvement and the commitment to students it reflects is the primary source of students' commitment to the institution and of their involvement in their own learning.

Two appendixes conclude the book. The first appendix (Appendix A) includes a series of comments about the character of effective assessment of student retention and its utilization in broader programs of student retention. Though institutions can and should learn from the experiences of other colleges and universities, it remains for each institution to discern for itself the particular events which shape student departure from its campus. To that end, I will argue that effective assessment must be sensitive to the broad range of student experiences and the longitudinal character of student passage through the institution. More importantly, it must enable the institution to capture the quality of those experiences as they are understood by the student. Assessment must, in this sense, be grounded in the common experience of students as they pass through the institution.

The second appendix (Appendix B) applies the theory of undergraduate leaving to the question of doctoral persistence. After reviewing the rather limited research on doctoral persistence, the appendix shows how the theory developed in chapter 4 can be modified to explain the longitudinal process of doctoral persistence. Particular attention is paid to the differing stages that mark progress toward a doctoral degree and the manner in which the forces that shape persistence vary from stage to stage. Finally, attention is turned toward the need for new research and institutional policies designed to enhance completion of doctoral degrees in the United States.

—2—

The Scope and Patterning of Student Departure from Higher Education

Before we attempt to explain student departure, we must first describe its occurrence in higher education. In this instance, we will focus on two specific questions of description. First, we will ask what percentage of entering students complete their college degree programs within a six-year period. What proportion of those students complete their degrees within their first institution and what proportion transfer to another institution? To what degree do those proportions change when one extends the time period beyond six years? Second, we will inquire as to the degree to which rates of student departure vary for different groups of students and types of institutions. Do rates of departure vary for students of different sex, race, social origins, and ability? How do they vary for institutions of different levels (two- and four-year) and selectivity?

As we describe these patterns, we will extend our conversation in several directions. First, we will inquire about the rates of departure that mark the first year of college. Specifically, we will explore data that speak to the question of how persistence to the second year of college varies among institutions of different levels and selectivity. Then, we will extend our view to institutional rates of degree completion and ask how those rates vary among public and private four- and two-year institutions and among institutions of differing selectivity. Next, we will compare those data to data from earlier sources and ask whether these rates have changed over the past twenty years. The same question will then be asked of data that describe system rates of

7

degree completion;, that is, the rate at which the system writ large produces degrees. Finally, we will turn our attention to what we know about the variation in rates of degree completion among students of differing attributes, specifically race, ability, and social status.

In describing the scope and patterning of student departure, we will continually distinguish between the departure of persons from individual institutions (*institutional departure*) and departure from the wider system (*system departure*). These, as we will see, are quite different not only in character but also in scope and variability among different segments of the college student population.[1]

Not all student departures from institutions of higher education lead to withdrawal from the broader system of higher education. Though all institutional leavers are similar from the perspective of the institution from which they leave, many of those leaving transfer to other institutions of higher education (*immediate transfer*). Some of the latter persons eventually earn their college degrees, though it may take them more than four or five years to do so. From the perspective of the system, those persons are counted as completers. Of course, not all institutional leavers immediately transfer to other institutions. Many leave higher education altogether (*system departure*), whereas others temporarily withdraw from the system (*stopouts*). Among the latter group of students, some return to their initial institution (*institutional stopouts*) and others enroll in another institution (*delayed transfer*). In the latter case, some students may delay their return for many years. As adults, they sometimes restart their studies anew as freshmen despite having earned some credits previously.

The Entry of Individuals into Higher Education

Before we talk of departure, we must first speak of entry. Patterns of entry are necessarily related, in time, to eventual patterns of departure. There are many different paths into the collegiate system. It is currently estimated, for instance, that nearly 77 percent of all first-time entrants begin their college careers at the start of the fall semester. Another 20 percent will enter sometime after that point, many at the beginning of the following semester. The remainder will enter their institutions in the summer prior to the start of the academic year.[2]

But of all entrants to higher education in a given academic year, approximately 17 percent will not enroll in degree-credit programs. Many will be part-time students who take a variety of courses unrelated to any coherent degree program. Such participation is more common within the two-year sector, especially in the community colleges, than in the four-year sector. But even in the latter, institutions have been moving to increase the numbers of individuals who begin their college careers on a part-time basis, often without regard to specific degree programs. Pressing economic needs have led many more institutions to stretch their entry net wider in an effort to capture an increasing number and diversity of students.

Such diversity of college entry makes the estimation of rates of student departure, institutional and systemic, a very difficult task. Though an institution may keep quite accurate records of student entry, such data are difficult to obtain on either a state or a national level. Sometimes those data are not reported. Other times they are not provided in a form amenable to standardization across different institutions (e.g., institutions may employ very different definitions of departure or use different groups to draw their estimates). But even when the data are obtainable, one is still left with the problem of determining if and when departure has occurred. This is an especially difficult problem among those persons whose participation is part-time and not directly related to a given degree program. The understandable tendency of institutions is to keep such participants "on the books" until it is unmistakably clear that they will not return. As a result, institutions are likely to somewhat underestimate the extent of student departure in any given year.

For these and other reasons, most observers of student departure have tended to concentrate upon the behaviors of those persons who start their college careers in recognized degree programs. Past research has thus somewhat underestimated the total scope of student departure within the higher educational enterprise and, at the same time, has understated the diversity of pathways individuals employ to earn their college degrees and the length of time they take to eventually do so. Be that as it may, we will have to make do with such partial descriptions. Until more accurate data are available on the entire range of student movements, we will have to take our estimates of aggregate rates of student departure as precisely that: estimates, which may somewhat misrepresent the scope and patterning of student participation in higher education.

Composition of the College Entrant Pool

The great majority of new college students are members of the high school graduating class of the preceding spring. Among a recent national sample of fall 1990 freshmen, 92.4 percent reported themselves as having graduated from high school in the preceding spring (Astin, Korn, and Berz 1990). This is somewhat lower than similar data of the fall 1982 freshman, where 94.0 percent reported themselves as very recent high school graduates (Astin, Hemond, and Richardson 1982). Not surprisingly, the percentage of 1990 freshmen who are recent high school graduates is highest in the universities (98.1 percent) and lowest in the two-year colleges (85.0 percent).[3]

But increasingly some members of an entering class are adults who either had begun their college careers for the first time after many years of educational inactivity or had renewed a college career that had been started some years earlier. Until recently, and especially in the late 1940s and early 1950s, many such entrants were members of the armed forces who took advantage of the educational benefits of the G.I. Bill. Increasingly, they are older women who wish to avail themselves of opportunities for higher education after years of family responsibilities that kept them close to home, or older men who see additional education as a route to job change.

In 1976, students twenty-five years of age and older made up 24.3 percent of all undergraduate students. In 1989 that figure increased to 30.3 percent. The great bulk of those enrollments are part-time, with students twenty-five years of age and older making up 66.6 percent of all part-time enrollments in 1989 (U.S. Department of Education, *The Condition of Education,* 1991). Indeed, much of the growth of enrollments generally over that period has been in part-time attendance, and a majority of those students work while attending college.

It follows then that adult participation in higher education as a proportion of full-time attendance is considerably smaller. In 1989, adults (as we have defined them above) made up 10.7 percent of all full-time undergraduate enrollments (U.S. Department of Education, *The Condition of Education,* 1991), and in the fall of 1990 constituted only 2.7 percent of all first-time, full-time freshmen (Astin, Korn, and Berz 1991). This difference between total and first-time, full-time enrollments indicates that a disproportionate number of adult learners in higher education are enrolled on a part-time basis often unrelated to degree programs and/or have returned to college some years after having first enrolled for a degree program.

It should also be noted that in both the two- and the four-year sectors numbers of new students will in fact be individuals who have transferred either from other institutions in the same sector or from institutions in the other sector. For any individual institution such transfers may be an important and often quite sizable component of the entering student body in any given year. For our present purposes, though these transfer students are new to the institution, they are not regarded as new to the system of higher education.

Finally, the remaining members of any college-entering cohort are persons from other nations. Though the number of these entrants is increasing —in 1988 361,200 students were from foreign nations (up from 252,600 a decade earlier) (U.S. Department of Education, *Digest of Education Statistics,* 1991)—they will not be part of our present discussion. Once more this is the case not because their departure is any less important than that of other students. Rather, it reflects the paucity of reliable information on their movements within higher education.

Variation in Immediate and Delayed Entry to College among
Different Groups of Students

Diversity of patterns of college entry is also apparent among students of different gender, race, ability, and social class. Among members of the high school class of 1980 a greater proportion of females, whites, and persons of higher ability and social status origins entered college than of males and persons of either black or Hispanic origins (U.S. Department of Education, *The Condition of Education*, 1991). And among those who delayed their entrance to college, students were more likely to be male than female, non-white than white, and of lower socioeconomic origins.

Not surprisingly, late entrants were also more likely to enter the two-year college sector. Whereas only 31.6 percent of immediate entrants went to two-year colleges, slightly over 70 percent of delayed entrants did so. The tendency of delayed entrants to favor two-year colleges was more noticeable among females than males, among blacks and Hispanics than among whites, and among persons of lower ability than those of higher ability. Understandably, delayed entrants and adult entrants, whether immediate or delayed, are more likely than regular entrants to be enrolled part-time and to be employed, full- or part-time, while enrolled (Eckland and Henderson 1981, p.21). For those persons, college participation is a concurrent part of one's employment, not a prelude to it.

It should be observed that our interest in differences in patterns of immediate and delayed entrance and of full- and part-time attendance is more than merely academic. It bears directly on the issue of eventual persistence. Students who delay entry to college and/or who attend part-time are, on the average, much less likely to obtain their undergraduate degrees than are students who begin immediately after high school (Carroll 1989). For instance, it is estimated that delayed entrants who enter less than four-year institutions and who enroll part-time are *five times* less likely than immediate full-time four-year entrants to obtain a four-year degree (Carroll 1989, p. 29).

Composition of the College Student Population

Differences in patterns of college entry result in observable differences in the composition of the college population. In addition to the already noted "aging" of the student body, it is apparent that college students are becoming more female. Today, as contrasted to twenty years ago, females comprise the single largest segment of the college student population. In 1990, for instance, females made up 53.8 percent of all first-time, full-time fall freshmen (Astin, Korn, and Berz 1990) and at least 54.3 percent of all enrollments in higher education (U.S. Department of Education, *Digest of Educational Statistics*, 1991). These increases reflect both the larger number of females in the high school graduating cohort and the fact that a somewhat larger percentage of female high school graduates go on to college immediately after graduation—61.6 percent and 59.6 percent of female and male 1988 high school graduates respectively.

The college population is also becoming more diverse. Though it is evident that college students are, as a group, of higher ability and from higher social status backgrounds than are high school seniors generally, this is less true today than it was twenty years ago. The same can be said of the racial diversity of the student body, though the patterning of these gains has been uneven. For students of color generally, percentage enrollment in higher education has increased from 15.4 percent in 1976 to 18.4 percent in 1988. But whereas Hispanics and Asian or Pacific islander enrollments have increased over that period from 3.5 and 1.8 percent to 5.2 and 3.8 percent respectively, enrollments of black, non-Hispanic students has declined somewhat, from 9.4 percent to 8.7 percent (U.S. Department of Education, *The Condition of Education,* 1991).

These figures do not mean, however, that the *number* of black students in higher education has declined. It has not. In fact the number of blacks over that period has increased somewhat, from 1,033,000 in 1976 to 1,129,000 in 1988 (U.S. Department of Education, *Digest of Educational Statistics,* 1991, table 194). What these data reveal is that the *proportionate* participation of blacks has declined somewhat as the rates of participation of other minority groups have increased.

College Participation: Some Observations
The diversity of first-time college entries leads us to consider a number of commonly held misconceptions about the nature of college participation. First, we have tended to underestimate the proportion of high school graduates who eventually enter the higher educational enterprise (Kolstad 1981). By ignoring delayed entrance (both full- and part-time) we have tended to underestimate overall collegegoing by at least 10 percent. In the process, we have also painted a picture of first-time enrollments which has tended to be racially, socially, and intellectually more selective than is actually the case. By so doing, we have inadvertently distorted the image one obtains of the role two-year colleges play in the careers of many high school graduates.

The diversity of modes of college entry should also make us pause as we approach the task of trying to describe patterns of student departure from higher education. Clearly the task of completely describing those departures is more complex than is commonly recognized. A complete description would require, at a minimum, that we fully map out the movements of both regular and delayed entrants over an extended period of time. Given the scale, complexity, and costs of attempting to do so, it is not surprising that researchers have focused almost entirely on the college careers of persons who enter college for the first time in any given year in degree-credit programs rather than on those of any given high school graduating cohort and/or of those who enter in non-degree-credit programs.

In the present instance, we will do the same. We will seek to describe the extent and character of the departure of students from college who enter higher education for degree credit within a given year of entry. We will do so, however, with the understanding that this is but one part, albeit the major part, of the overall picture of student departure from higher education.[4]

The Scope of Departure from Higher Education

In attempting to map out the scope of student departure from higher education, we will draw on four different sources. In two instances we will use data from the National Longitudinal Survey of the educational activities of the high school graduating class of 1972 (hereafter referred to as NLS) and from the High School and Beyond studies of the educational activities of the high school graduating class of 1980 (hereafter referred to as HSB). In doing so, we will make the not unreasonable assumption that, as regards completion and departure, these students' college experiences—especially the experiences of the 1980 cohort—are not untypical of most recent college-going cohorts.

Our third source of data comes from the American College Testing Program survey of institutions (henceforth referred to as ACT). These are self-reported data that have been collected every year for the past ten years. Unlike the NLS and HSB surveys, which were designed to be representative of high school seniors generally and were administered to individual students, the ACT surveys come from institutions that have chosen to participate in the ACT program. These tend to be somewhat smaller colleges located primarily in the Midwest and the South. Though not entirely representative of all institutions of higher education across the country, especially those in the East and West, they do capture a large enough spectrum of institutions to give us a reasonable portrait of institutional behaviors over the past decade.

The fourth source of data comes from the recent *Survey of Retention at Higher Education Institutions* (Chaney and Farris 1991)—hereafter referred to as HES. Drawn from a survey of 428 colleges and universities, these data capture a reasonably representative picture of retention among full-time students who either began bachelor's degree programs in fall 1984 or fall 1988 or began associate degree programs in fall 1987.

As we have indicated, these last two sources are unlike the NLS and HSB data files in that they are not derived from survey questionnaires administered to individuals but are the result of institutional self-reports that focus on first-time, full-time student entering cohorts. Consequently, they are likely to underestimate overall attrition somewhat, if only because institutions tend to understate part-time and non-degree enrollments. Nevertheless, they do provide a useful benchmark for changes in institutional rates of persistence over the past decade that cannot be obtained elsewhere.

Student Departure in the First Year of College

We begin our study of departure with the first year of college. We do so because the first year proves, as we shall see in later chapters, to be an especially important year in the process of persistence. The character of one's experience in that year does much to shape subsequent persistence. By the same token, the largest proportion of institutional leaving occurs in that year and prior to the beginning of the second year. For this reason alone, as we shall see in chapter 5,the first year has become a special object of institutional policy aimed at reducing student attrition.

We turn first to the most recent ACT data, drawn from institutional reports of first-year persistence of the fall 1990 entering class (American College Testing Program 1992). For that very recent cohort, first-year attrition from four and two-year institutions was reported to be 26.8 and 44.0 percent respectively (table 2.1). Among four-year institutions, freshman to sophomore year attrition was higher in the public sector (28.3 percent) than in the private sector (24.0 percent). Among two-year colleges, first-year attrition was reported at 47.9 and 27.4 percent among public and private institutions respectively.

It is worth noting again that first-year leaving represents a very sizable part of all institutional leaving, that a majority of all leaving takes place in the first year. For the four- and two-year institutions reporting to ACT in 1992, first-

Table 2.1 Institutional Rates of First-Year Attrition for
Full-Time and All Entering Students (1992 ACT Survey)

Institution Type	Full-Time Entrants
Four-year public	28.3
Four-year private	24.0
Four-Year Total	26.8
Two-year public	47.9
Two-year private	27.4
Two-Year Total	44.0

Source: American College Testing Program, 1992.

year attrition represented 53.3 and 67.7 percent respectively of all *institutional leavers*. Little wonder then that institutional concern with attrition centers on the first year.

Because these data are reported for full-time, first-time students only, they necessarily underestimate somewhat first-year institutional leaving among all entering students, some of whom are part-time, nonmatriculated, or transfers from other institutions. Because we have no reliable national data that track such students over the first year, we are not sure how much higher rates of first-year attrition actually are, but we can make a reasonable guess. We do know, for instance, that the proportion of first-time students who are part-time is roughly 28.8 percent overall.[5] We also know that among all enrolled students, part-time enrollments have sometimes outnumbered full-time enrollments. In 1989, for instance, part-time enrollments represented 41.6 percent of total undergraduate enrollment, and in public and private institutions was 45.7 and 23.7 percent respectively (U.S. Department of Education 1990, tables 14–16). Among public and private four-year institutions part-time enrollments made up 30.9 and 30.6 percent respectively of all enrollments, and among public and private two-year colleges 65.7 and 39.1 percent (U.S. Department of Education, *Digest of Education Statistics*, 1991, table 167). If we now assume, just for the sake of argument, that part-time and nonmatriculated students are twenty percent more likely to leave before their second year of college, we can estimate from table 2.1 the first-year attrition rates given in table 2.2 below.[6]

FIRST-YEAR ATTRITION AND INSTITUTIONAL SELECTIVITY

The ACT data also enable us to separate out rates of first-year attrition among first-time, full-time students as a function of institutional selectivity. Here institutional selectivity is measured by the average entering SAT scores of beginning full-time students (table 2.3).

Table 2.2 Estimated Institutional Rates of First-Year Attrition for All Entering Students (1992 ACT Survey)

Institution Type	All Entrants
Four-year public	30.0
Four-year private	25.4
Four-Year Total	28.5
Two-year public	54.2
Two-year private	29.6
Two-Year Total	49.6

Source: American College Testing Program, 1992.

Table 2.3 Institutional Rates of First-Year Attrition
among Full-time Students by Institutional Selectivity

Institution Selectivity		Mean (%)
Highly selective	SAT > 1100	8.0
Selective	SAT 931–1099	17.5
Traditional	SAT 801–930	26.4
Liberal	SAT 700–800	32.9
Open	SAT < 700	45.5

Source: American College Testing Program, 1992.

It is quite apparent that higher selectivity is associated with lower rates of first-year attrition among beginning full-time students. For instance, the most selective institutions lose only 8.0 percent of their beginning full-time students before the start of the second year whereas open-enrollment institutions lose 45.5 percent of their full-time students.

It should be noted, however, that there is, within any category of selectivity, a wide range of institutional rates of first-year attrition. Though highly selective institutions, as a group, have the lowest rate of first-year attrition, not all institutions in that group have lower rates of attrition than do all institutions in the next lower category of selectivity.

The point of making this observation is to remind the reader that student attributes such as those measured by selectivity do not entirely explain differences between institutional rates of first-year attrition. As we will see in later chapters, a more complete analysis of rates of institutional departure must also refer to institutional climate and the patterns of interaction among students, faculty, and staff that mark the life of the institution.

CHANGES IN FIRST-YEAR ATTRITION OVER TIME

If we now look at the ACT data files for selected years since 1983, we can ask how rates of first-year institutional attrition for full-time students have changed since they were first reported in 1983 (table 2.4). Looking at table 2.4 we find that with the possible exception of changes in the public two-year sector, there is no clear trend in the data to suggest that overall rates of first-year institutional attrition across the nation are declining.

Interestingly, these estimates are not very different from those recently reported by the HES survey of the 1988 entering class (Chaney and Farris 1991) and those reported over twenty years ago in the NLS survey of 1972 high school graduates (U.S. Department of Education 1977). According to the HES data (not shown), among first-time full time students in the four-year sector who began college in fall 1988, 23.4 percent left college prior to the start of

Table 2.4 Institutional Rates of First-Year Attrition by Institutional
Type and Control: ACT Surveys of Institutions 1983–1992

	1992	1990	1986	1983
Four-year public	28.3	28.6	29.6	29.1
Four-year private	24.0	23.8	24.0	23.4
Four-Year Total	26.8	26.9	27.5	27.1
Two-year public	47.9	47.7	47.0	46.0
Two-year private	27.4	29.4	30.8	30.0
Two-Year Total	44.0	44.0	43.7	43.2

Source: American College Testing Program, 1983, 1986, 1990, 1992.

their second year. The two-year sector figure was 42.4 percent. These figures represent 47.4 and 63.3 percent of all leavers respectively. Among four-
year institutions, rates of first-year leaving were higher in the public sector
than they were in the private sector (24.2 and 21.7 percent respectively).
Data from the ACT data files for the same entering class, that is fall 1988,
yield first-year attrition rates of 26.9 and 44.0 percent for four- and two-year
institutions generally (table 2.4, 1990 survey). First-year attrition was reported to be 28.6 and 23.8 percent among public and private four-year institutions and 47.7 and 29.4 percent among public and private two-year
colleges.

The NLS survey of 1972 high school graduates are based on individual,
rather than institutional, reports. As a result, they are less likely to underestimate rates of attrition. In these data, 27.8 percent of all four-year and 40.7
percent of all two-year entrants (full- and part-time) left their first institution
prior to the start of the second year (see Tinto 1987, tables 2.3 and 2.4).
Given that the NLS data include part-time as well as full-time students, they
add further weight to the notion that overall rates of institutional first-year
attrition, certainly in the four-year sector, have not changed considerably
over the past twenty years.

When one looks at changes in rates of first-year attrition as a function of
institutional selectivity, however, one notices a somewhat more complex
picture of first-year attrition (table 2.5). Despite the overall stability in rates
of attrition, first-year attrition has declined somewhat in all but the least selective institutions. This is especially apparent among the most selective institutions, where attrition rates have declined nearly twenty percent between
1983 and 1992. Among the least selective institutions, many of whom are
two-year institutions, first-year attrition has increased to a high of 45.5 percent in 1992.

Of course, not all institutional departures leave higher education. Some
transfer to continue their higher education elsewhere. Here the early 1972

Table 2.5 Institutional Rates of First-Year Attrition by Institutional Selectivity: 1983–1992 (ACT Surveys)

·Institutional Selectivity		1992	1990	1986	1983
Highly selective	SAT > 1100	8.0	11.2	11.6	10.0
Selective	SAT 931–1099	17.5	19.5	20.2	18.0
Traditional	SAT 801–930	26.4	30.9	29.7	29.0
Liberal	SAT 700–800	32.9	41.6	40.6	39.0
Open	SAT < 700	45.5	41.4	42.3	41.0

Source: American College Testing Program, 1983, 1986, 1990, 1992.

NLS data document the extent to which first-year departure results in *system departure* (see Tinto 1987, tables 2.3 and 2.4). Among four-year entrants, 11.3 percent transfer before their second year, whereas among two-year entrants 9.3 percent do so (40.6 and 22.9 percent respectively of leavers in each sector). In other words, when we refer to *system departure,* only 16.5 and 31.4 percent of four- and two-year entrants left higher education before the start of their second year. Unfortunately, we do not have more recent national data that allow us to easily disentangle first-year transfers from system departures. It is safe to say, however, that we can expect similar, if not somewhat increased, proportions of transfers in the succeeding several years.[7]

Student Departure from Institutions of Higher Education and Rates of College Completion

INSTITUTIONAL RATES OF COMPLETION

Having described institutional departure in the first year of college and its change over time, we now turn to the broader issue of degree completion in higher education. As before, we will focus on institutional rates of degree completion, that is the rate at which individuals who begin their programs in a particular college or university complete their degrees within a given time frame in that college or university. Only later will we speak to what is known about rates of system completion and therefore about degree completion that occurs via transfer between institutions of higher education.

We begin our inquiry with data from the ACT files and therefore with information about rates of institutional degree completion among full-time students. According to the most recent ACT data (table 2.6), those drawn from freshmen entering college in 1986, barely half or 50.2 percent of all new full-time four-year college entrants are reported to earn their bachelor's degree in their institution of initial registration *within five years of entry* (American College Testing Program 1992). Among two-year colleges, de-

Table 2.6   Institutional Rates of Degree Completion
by Institutional Type and Control (1986 Entrants)

Institution Type	Completion Rate
Four-year public	46.7
Four-year private	57.6
Four-Year Total	50.2
Two-year public	38.7
Two-year private	64.3
Two-Year Total	43.4

Source: American College Testing Program, 1992.

Table 2.7   Institutional Rates of Degree Completion
among Public and Private Four-Year Institutions by
Selectivity (1986 Entrants)

Institution Selectivity		Public	Private
Highly selective	SAT > 1100	66.2	82.3
Selective	SAT 931–1099	52.2	66.3
Traditional	SAT 801–930	45.1	55.3
Liberal	SAT 700–800	40.1	44.9
Open	SAT < 700	38.2	43.1
Total		46.7	57.6

Source: American College Testing Program, 1986.

gree completion *within three years* of initial registration was reported to be
43.4 percent among full-time students. We see also that degree completion
was less frequent among public institutions than among private ones.

Among four-year institutions degree completion rates were understandably higher in more selective institutions, public and private (table 2.7). In
each category of selectivity, private rates of degree completion were higher
than those among public institutions. Interestingly, the difference in rates of
degree completion between public and private institutions increased with selectivity and was greatest in the most selective institutions.

CHANGES IN INSTITUTIONAL RATES OF DEGREE
COMPLETION OVER TIME

If we now extend our time frame to include the earliest ACT data, those
drawn from the entering class in fall 1977 (American College Testing Program 1983) as well as those from the entering classes of 1980 and 1984
(American College Testing Program 1986, 1990), we note that while rates of
two-year degree completion appear to have declined only slightly, if at all,

Table 2.8 Institutional Rates of Completion from 1983 to 1992
by Institutional Type and Control (ACT Surveys)

Institution Type	1992	1990	1986	1983
Four-year public	46.7	47.9	48.4	52.6
Four-year private	57.6	57.4	58.4	59.6
Four-Year Total	50.2	51.1	51.6	54.8
Two-year public	38.7	38.6	37.9	40.0
Two-year private	64.3	66.4	64.0	64.0
Two-Year Total	43.4	43.9	43.1	44.1

Source: American College Testing Program, 1983, 1986, 1990, 1992.

over that period, rates of four-year degree completion declined noticeably (table 2.8).

It is interesting to note that the very recently released NCAA study of graduation rates of Division I colleges—namely the larger universities and colleges that qualify as Division I athletic institutions—reported a six-year graduation rate of 53 percent for the fall 1984 entering class (Cage 1992). Given the extra year allowed for graduation in that report, the ACT estimate of 51.1 percent for the same entering cohort is very similar.

As a way of further extending our time frame and also checking the accuracy of these estimates, we can refer to the 1972 NLS survey that followed individual high school seniors beyond high school. Estimates drawn from those data yield an estimated rate of institutional four-year degree completion of 59.3 percent among students entering four-year colleges and universities full-time after high school.[8] This is well within range of the ACT estimates in table 2.8. More importantly, it further reinforces the notion that institutional rates of four-year degree completion have declined over the past fifteen years.

CONSIDERING THE ROOTS OF CHANGING INSTITUTIONAL
RATES OF DEGREE COMPLETION

What are the possible roots of this apparent decline in rates of institutional degree completion? Many changes in college-going have occurred over those years, any one or combination of which may explain the decline of rates of institutional completion. As we have seen above, the mix of students attending higher education has changed. Among other things, the proportion of students in four-year institutions attending part-time has increased from 26.7 percent in 1970 to 31.4 in 1989. At the same time the proportion of students who work while going to college has also increased. And many more are delaying their entry to college to some years after high school. It is

Table 2.9 Changing Rates of Institutional Degree Completion by Selectivity (Public)

Institution Selectivity	1992	1990	1986	1983
Highly selective SAT > 1100	66.2	62.7	66.1	66.1
Selective SAT 931–1099	52.2	52.7	53.5	56.6
Traditional SAT 801–930	45.1	47.4	52.2	54.4
Liberal SAT 700–800	40.1	42.1	43.7	47.9
Open SAT < 700	38.2	40.5	41.7	44.1
Total Public	46.7	47.9	48.4	52.6

Source: American College Testing Program, 1983, 1986, 1990, 1992.

Table 2.10 Changing Rates of Institutional Degree Completion by Selectivity (Private)

Institution Selectivity	1992	1990	1986	1983
Highly selective SAT > 1100	82.3	81.1	80.0	79.1
Selective SAT 931–1099	66.3	66.6	66.1	66.4
Traditional SAT 801–930	55.3	56.0	56.7	59.1
Liberal SAT 700–800	44.9	46.3	50.3	51.3
Open SAT < 700	43.1	44.1	47.8	47.4
Total Private	57.6	57.8	58.4	59.6

Source: American College Testing Program, 1983, 1986, 1990, 1992.

also the case that the academic credentials of college-bound high school seniors, as measured by the combined Scholastic Aptitude Test scores, has declined from 948 in 1970 to 903 in 1988 (U.S. Office of Education, *Digest of Education Statistics,* 1991, table 124). Not surprisingly, the same period has seen an increase in the numbers of entering college students requiring some form of remediation. Just as important, financial aid has shrunk overall and been increasingly shifted toward loans and away from grants (Mortenson 1991).

These changes alone could have brought about greater declines in persistence than are observed in these data. The absence of more sizable declines, for instance in first-year attrition, is itself a noteworthy finding. A particularly telling piece of information, in this regard, can be gleamed from the ACT data on institutional rates of four-year degree completion as a function of institutional selectivity over the past ten years (tables 2.9 and 2.10). In both public and private sectors, the decline in rates of institutional completion is more noticeable among less selective institutions, especially among those whose SAT selectivity is below 930. Not surprisingly, these institutions, both public and private, have felt a disproportionate burden of the changing mix of student participation. In this regard, it is striking that rates of four-year degree completion among the most selective institutions, those that have experienced little relative change in student participation, either have remained steady or have even increased somewhat over time—a gain of 3.2 percent among the most selective private institutions.

The latter fact, namely that the most selective private and public institutions have improved or at least kept steady their rates of institutional completion over time, reflects something other than changing student mix. As we shall argue in chapter 5, it also mirrors a growing movement among institutions to establish programs to address the roots of student departure. It is a movement whose consequences are only now beginning to be felt.

In this context it bears repeating that differences in rates of completion between categories of institutions need not apply equally well for all institutions in those categories. For example, though it has been estimated that the average rate of institutional departure from four-year colleges is approximately 50 percent (of full-time entrants), the departure rate for individual four-year colleges ranges from a high of over 80 percent to as low as a reported 7 percent of entering students over a five-year period (Astin 1975). Private nonsectarian four-year colleges and prestigious Catholic women's colleges tend to have the lowest rates of departure. As a group, their mean rate of departure was only 13 percent. Just below that group are the prestigious universities, both public and private, and the prestigious private Protestant colleges. Their average rate of departure was reported to be only 18 and 19 percent respectively. On the other end of the four-year college spectrum were found a number of urban state colleges that have traditionally served as jumping-off points for transfer to the large public universities. These institutions tend to report rates of departure which cluster about the mean for the four-year sector as a whole. Some of the better-known report five-year rates of departure of less than 30 percent whereas others report rates as high as 65 percent.

The point here is really quite simple, namely, that institutional rates of departure are necessarily a reflection of the particular attributes and circumstances of an institution. Though the sharing of a common attribute, such as four-year status and selectivity, may imply a commonality of circumstances, only institution-specific studies of departure can provide insight into the circumstances which lead to a given rate of departure from a particular institution.

SYSTEM RATES OF DEGREE COMPLETION

So far we have concentrated on institutional rates of degree completion. As a result, our picture of degree completion is quite narrow. This is the case because completion via continuous institutional persistence is only one of a number of paths to degree attainment. Among any group of college entrants, some students obtain their degrees via transfer while others take more than five years to complete their degrees. And while most of those transfers come from other four-year institutions, some come from two-year colleges. To gauge therefore the character of degree completion as an attribute of the higher education *system,* one has to consider these completions as well.

Unfortunately data to estimate *system completion* is more difficult to obtain. Such data cannot rely on institutional reports such as those reported above, but must come from a national study of student persistence derived from individual reports of behavior. Here we have only two sources of information from which to draw, namely the NLS studies of the high school graduating class of 1972 and the HSB studies of the high school graduating class of 1980. For presentation purposes, the results of these studies are presented in figure 2.1 and 2.2.

Data from the NLS study of the activities of the 1972 high school graduating class indicate that 61.9 percent of those students entered college by 1978 (fig. 2.1). Of those entrants, a total of 38.7 percent obtained their bachelor's and 12.8 percent obtained two-year or lesser degrees within six years of high school graduation. In other words, a grand total of 51.5 percent of all college goers had earned some type of postsecondary degree six years after high school.

Sixteen years after high school, the percentage of college entrants earning four- and two-year or lesser degrees rose to 41.0 and 17.7 percent respectively (Eagle and Carroll 1988b). Thus, a total of 58.7 percent of all 1972 graduates who entered college sometime after high school obtained some type of postsecondary degree within sixteen years of high school graduation. Though most obtained their degrees from their first institution, many eventually earned their degrees via transfer between institutions. According to NLS

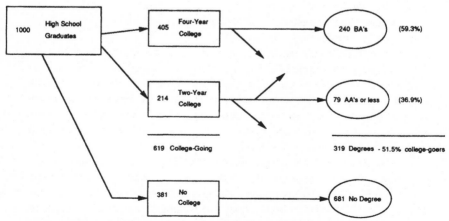

Fig. 2.1. Postsecondary attainments of 1972 high school graduates (six years after graduation).

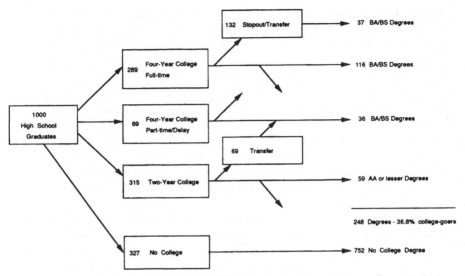

Fig. 2.2. Postsecondary attainments of 1980 high school graduates (six years after graduation).

estimates, approximately thirty percent of all B.A.'s and A.A.'s or lesser degrees earned over that period will have been obtained via transfer.[9]

The HSB study of the 1980 high school graduates reveals a somewhat different picture (fig. 2.2). By 1986, 46.8 percent of all college goers had obtained some type of degree.[10] This represents an apparent decline of approximately five percent from the 1972 cohort. At the same time, the relative mix of four- and two-year degree attainment changed. Relative to the 1972 cohort, an increasing proportion of students earned A.A. or lesser degrees. Among the 1980 cohort, 28.1 percent had earned B.A. degrees while 18.6 percent had earned A.A. or lesser degrees within six years of high school graduation.

What appears to be a marked decline in system completion rates proves, however, to partially reflect changing patterns of college participation over that period. Relative to the 1972 graduates, more students from the 1980 cohort went on to college, especially to two-year colleges, and more remained enrolled without degrees after six years. Furthermore, after six years, nearly the same proportion of both groups either had obtained their degrees or remained enrolled in college.

If these findings prove applicable to more recent cohorts, as one has reason to believe, it then follows that underlying the changing rates of system degree completion over six years is a changing flow of students to four- and two-year institutions after high school and a changing rate at which students progress through the system either within their original institutions or within the system via transfer. In addition to the changes in student behaviors noted above, more students are choosing to enter the two-year sector after high school and a greater proportion are progressing more slowly through the system (*Digest of Education Statistics*, 1991).

These observations suggest that over the long-term, that is over sixteen years, both system and therefore institutional rates of degree completion have not changed as much as our earlier analysis indicated. Indeed, they may have remained relatively steady. What has changed is the manner and rate at which individuals progress. Apparent changes in institutional and systemic effectiveness may actually be a reflection of these individual changes. In passing, it might also be observed that the rate of four-year degree completion appears not to have changed substantially over the last one hundred years. Though some variations have occurred over time, the observed rate of degree completion today is very nearly the same as that estimated at the turn of the century (Tinto and Lentz 1986).[11]

THE DEPARTURE OF STUDENTS FROM HIGHER EDUCATION: SOME OBSERVATIONS

Though student departures amount to a very sizable proportion of any entering cohort, it should be observed that researchers and policy analysts have generally overestimated the extent of student departure from higher education. The reasons for such overestimation are varied. It is the case, for instance, that until recently we have been unable to accurately track the detailed movements of individuals through the higher educational enterprise. Only with the recent NLS and HSB data have we been able to develop a nationally representative profile of sufficient detail to trace the flow of persons in and out of the system. Though we have had a number of detailed institutional studies of departure, these have been too few and far between to provide a reliable estimate of the national scope of student movements.

Past limitations in the study of departure have led researchers to focus primarily on the movements of those students who enter higher education and via continuous enrollment complete their college degrees in the "standard" four-year period. In so doing researchers have unavoidably underestimated the extent of eventual degree completion. We now know that many students require more than four years to complete their degree programs. About half of such "delayed" completions are the result of persons' requiring more than four years of continuous enrollment to earn their degrees. Many, but not all, reflect the effect of transfer upon time to degree completion. Others are the consequence of the fact that an increasing number of individuals attend college on a part-time basis and/or are employed at least part-time while going to college. Still others are "stopouts" who, after leaving college, re-enter at a

later time to complete their degrees. But many others simply mirror the fact
that some four-year degree programs are in fact programs of more than four
years' duration.

The net result of such extended and varied forms of participation is to increase the numbers of persons who eventually complete their college degrees. For some institutions the extent of that increase can be quite
substantial. For example, long-term follow-up studies of male entrants to the
University of Illinois in 1952 and to the University of Wisconsin in 1964
indicate that the proportion of entering students who eventually complete
their bachelor's degrees increases from 41 and 45 percent respectively after
the standard four years to 69 and 71 percent after ten and seven years respectively (Eckland 1964a, 1964b; Campbell 1980). In both cases about half of
the delayed graduates had been in continuous attendance but had taken
longer than "expected" to graduate. The remaining half were persons who
after departing had re-enrolled to complete their degrees.

More striking still are the results of a long-term study of retention in the
City University of New York system (Lavin, Murtha, and Kaufman 1984).
After four years, only 34 percent of regularly admitted students and 16 percent of open admission students had graduated from senior college. After
five years, those figures rose to 53 and 32 percent respectively, and after nine
years to 61 and 42 percent respectively. Among community college entrants,
only 12 percent of regularly admitted students and but 3 percent of open admission students completed their degree programs on time. After five years
those figures rose to 43 and 25 percent respectively, and after nine years to 45
and 27 percent respectively.

Though these cases may be somewhat unusual relative to the national average, they serve to caution us against premature judgments about the extent
and the diversity of paths by which individuals eventually earn their college
degrees. We should not underestimate the tenacity of some individuals. Nor
should institutions unnecessarily limit the options individuals have in completing their degree programs. If anything, those options might be increased.
The so-called standard path to college completion may soon be the exception
rather than the rule. These observations also hold, in part, for a second form
of mis-estimation, namely, the underestimation of the proportion of any cohort of high school graduates who eventually enter and complete a college
degree. This arises, in part, from the just noted tendency of researchers to
understate the degree of college completion of recent cohorts of college entrants. It also mirrors the underestimation of the proportion of high school
graduates who delay their entry into higher education one or more years beyond high school graduation. It is now estimated that at least 8 percent of the
1972 high school graduating class and nearly 15 percent of the 1980 high
school graduating class had delayed their entry to college between one and

six years after leaving high school.[12] Presumably that figure has further increased since 1980.[13]

The point of making these observations goes beyond the mere noting of the understandable shortcomings of past assessments of the extent of departure from higher education. Given the complexity and diversity of individual movements in and through the system, it would not have been surprising had we erred even more in our judgments. The intent of these observations is rather to suggest that in thinking about the character and causes of student departure and the sorts of actions which might constitute effective institutional policy for student retention we should not underestimate the ability of people to eventually obtain their college degrees. Nor should we minimize the diversity of behaviors which lead individuals to leave and eventually to return to complete their college degree programs.[14] Though the models and figures we have drawn have a necessary order to them, the odysseys many individuals take to degree completion are long drawn out affairs with many intermediate stops.

Group Differences in Rates of Degree Completion

So far we have centered our attention on institutional and system rates of completion for the college-going cohort generally. Now we turn our attention to differences within that cohort. Specifically, we now ask how rates of degree completion within higher education vary among different groups of students, specifically among persons of different sex, race, ability, and social class. In this instance, we will refer to the 1980 HSB studies and the data they provide on rates of system degree completion among persons of different attributes.

As we do so, two important caveats are called for. First, it must be noted that the 1980 HSB data describing variations in departure among different types of individuals in fact describe system, not institutional, departure. We must remember that though a given type of student has, a higher rate of system departure than do other students, it does not follow that this applies equally well to institutional departure or in each and every institution of higher education. Only institution-specific studies can determine whether this is the case. Nevertheless, as the patterns of system departure noted here follow those reported in several recent multi-institution studies of departure, for instance of black and white students of different attributes (Pascarella and Chapman 1983; Nettles et al. 1984), they may be taken to be broadly indicative of the differences which mark those groups' departure from institutions of higher education generally.

Second, these data, whether on institutional or on system departure, are aggregate data which describe the behavior of groups of individuals and institutions. They do not describe the behavior of each and every group member. Similarly, though differences in rates of system departure among groups of students may be indicative of broad differences in the character of their experiences in higher education, only knowledge of the experiences of individuals within specific institutional settings will tell us of the unique character of individual departure from institutions of higher education. Broad surveys of rates of institutional and system departure such as those reported here provide only a limited understanding of that process. Nevertheless, they do afford us a useful map of individual (and institutional) variation upon which we can later build a model which explains the variability of student departure among different types of institutions. It is in this vein that we employ these data.

To begin our inquiry, we first look at the percentages of students of differing attributes in the 1980 high school graduating cohort who went on to postsecondary education prior to 1986 (table 2.11). Several differences among those students are immediately evident. Among the 1980 high school graduates going on to college (70.8 percent), more females than males and more whites than blacks and Hispanics entered college by 1986. Overall, a greater proportion of high school graduates entered four-year colleges and universities (37.7 percent) than entered two-year colleges (33.1 percent). This was true for all groups except students of Hispanic origin. They entered two-year colleges at almost twice the rate that they entered four-year institutions (40.5 and 20.9 percent respectively).

If we now look at the rates at which the college-going members of the 1980 high school graduating class earned postsecondary degrees by 1986 (table 2.12), we see that some of the above differences carry over to degree completion. Females were more likely than males to earn a degree after having begun postsecondary education, and whites were more likely than either Hispanics or blacks to earn a degree. Noticeably, Hispanics were the most likely to earn an associate degree or less and the least likely to earn a bache-

Table 2.11 Rates of College Participation among 1980 High School Graduates by Sex and Race

Category	Percent Going to College	Two-Year Colleges	Four-Year Colleges
Total	70.8	33.1	37.7
Male	69.1	31.3	37.8
Female	72.4	35.0	37.4
Hispanic	61.4	40.5	20.9
Black	68.3	32.0	36.3
White	71.4	32.8	38.6

Source: Eagle and Carroll (1988a).

Table 2.12   Rates of Degree Completion Six Years after High School among Students Who Entered Higher Education by 1986, by Sex and Race

Category	Percent Going to College	Total Degrees	AA Degree or Less	BA/BS Degree
Total	70.8	44.2	17.7	26.5
Male	69.1	42.3	15.7	26.6
Female	72.4	45.9	19.4	26.5
Hispanic	61.4	35.0	24.0	11.0
Black	68.3	30.1	15.3	14.8
White	71.4	46.7	17.6	29.1

Source: Eagle and Carroll (1988b, pp. 29–31, tables 2a and 2b).

lor's degree. Slightly more than 68 percent of all Hispanic college degree recipients earned the A.A. degree or less, whereas only about 38 percent of white degree recipients did so.

It might be recalled, in this context, that there has been a shift in patterns of college-going generally that has led a greater share of college goers to enter higher education via the two-year sector (figs. 2.1 and 2.2). For instance, while a greater share of 1980 high school graduates went on to college than did the 1972 graduating class, a greater proportion of those entrants entered two-year institutions than was the case in 1972. Not surprisingly, the shift toward two-year colleges has been particularly evident among students of Hispanic origins. In 1972, approximately 31 percent of Hispanic degree recipients earned an associate degree or less, whereas in 1980, over 68 percent did so.[15]

To get a more detailed picture of group patterns of degree attainment, one that includes measures of ability and socioeconomic background as well as ethnicity, we now turn to the data from the 1980 HSB studies of six-year persistence among students who entered a four-year college full-time immediately after high school.

We begin by looking at patterns of six-year persistence among students of differing ability (table 2.13), differing socioeconomic status backgrounds (table 2.14), and ethnicity (table 2.15). It should be noted, in these and the following tables, that the category "persisters" pertains to everyone who, as of 1986, was either still enrolled in a four-year college via continuous attendance or had enrolled again after having stopped out sometime after first entry to college. Completers and departers, of course, are persons who have either obtained their four-year degrees or dropped out without having earned a four-year degree.

As to the relationship between ability and persistence, and that between socioeconomic status and persistence, it is not surprising that persons of

Table 2.13 Six-Year Persistence Rates for Students Entering Four-Year Colleges Full Time Immediately after High School, by Ability

Persistence Status	All Students	Lowest Quartile	Second Quartile	Third Quartile	Highest Quartile
Completers	45.7	17.6	33.4	41.2	57.5
Persisters	12.3	16.3	11.2	14.3	11.5
Departers	42.0	66.1	55.4	44.5	31.0

Source: Porter (1990, table A–23).

Table 2.14 Six-Year Persistence Rates for Students Entering Four-Year Colleges Full Time Immediately after High School, by Socioeconomic Status

Persistence Status	All Students	Lowest Quartile	Second Quartile	Third Quartile	Highest Quartile
Completers	45.7	30.1	33.9	48.1	55.4
Persisters	12.3	12.0	13.3	11.6	11.1
Departers	42.0	57.9	52.8	40.3	33.5

Source: Porter (1990, table A–20).

higher ability and of higher socioeconomic status are more likely to complete a four-year degree within six years. Nor is it surprising that differences in rates of degree completion between highest and lowest quartiles of ability were greater than that between highest and lowest quartiles of socioeconomic status. As was evident in the 1972 NLS studies (Tinto 1987, table 2.6) and in other studies (Astin 1975, Manski and Wise 1983), the likelihood of eventually earning a college degree, especially a four-year degree, is more strongly associated with measures of individual ability than with socioeconomic status.[16]

Among persons of different ethnicity (table 2.15), white students were considerably more likely, indeed almost twice as likely, to earn a four-year degree by 1986 as were black or Hispanic students. But among Hispanic students, at least, some of that difference was due to the fact that more of those students were still enrolled than were white students. Over an extended time period, then, one would expect the gap in four-year degree completion between Hispanic and white students to diminish somewhat. Though it may diminish as well for black students, it is unlikely to shrink more than a few percentage points.

Of course, a good deal of these differences in rates of four-year degree completion can be attributed to differences between students of color and white students in their average measures of tested ability (table 2.16) and

Table 2.15 Six-Year Persistence Rates for Students
Entering Four-Year Colleges Immediately after
High School, by Ethnicity

Ethnicity	Completers	Persisters	Departers
Hispanic	25.3	21.3	53.4
Black	25.8	13.8	60.4
White	48.8	11.9	39.3
Total	45.7	12.3	42.0

Source: Porter (1990, table A–24).

Table 2.16 Six-Year Persistence Rates for Students Entering
Four-Year Colleges Full Time Immediately after High School,
by Ethnicity and Ability Test Score

	Completers	Persisters	Departers
Hispanic Students			
Lowest quartile	9.1*	16.6*	74.3
Second quartile	23.2	20.2*	56.7
Third quartile	25.5	24.0	50.5
Highest quartile	44.8	24.0*	31.2
Black Students			
Lowest quartile	17.2	12.6*	70.2
Second quartile	29.2	18.6	52.2
Third quartile	35.1	10.1*	54.8
Highest quartile	26.2*	12.5*	61.3
White Students			
Lowest quartile	20.2*	19.1*	60.7
Second quartile	35.5	8.3*	56.2
Third quartile	43.4	13.8	42.8
Highest quartile	58.7	11.2	30.1

Note: An asterisk (*) indicates unweighted N less than 30.
Source: Derived from Porter (1990, table A–24).

their socioeconomic backgrounds (table 2.17). Looking, for the moment, only at degree completers and excluding the several cases where the unweighted Ns are too small (less than 30) for reliable estimates, it is quite apparent that differences in rates of four-year degree completion between persons of different ethnicity but of similar ability or similar socioeconomic status are quite a bit smaller than those between different ethnic groups overall. Whereas the overall difference in rates of four-year degree completion between white students and Hispanic and black students was about 23 percent (see table 2.15), it averaged about 12 percent between white and Hispanic students of similar ability and similar socioeconomic status, and about

Table 2.17   Six-Year Persistence Rates for Students Entering
Four-Year Colleges Full Time Immediately after High School,
by Ethnicity and Socioeconomic Status

	Completers	Persisters	Departers
Hispanic Students			
Lowest quartile	22.7	20.1	57.1
Second quartile	32.6	16.4*	51.1
Third quartile	34.4	11.7*	53.9
Highest quartile	22.5*	24.9*	52.6
Black Students			
Lowest quartile	22.8	8.3	68.9
Second quartile	21.9	12.3*	65.7
Third quartile	32.5	15.1*	52.4
Highest quartile	44.1	4.3*	51.6
White Students			
Lowest quartile	32.5	15.0	52.5
Second quartile	35.6	13.0	51.4
Third quartile	50.0	10.9	39.1
Highest quartile	56.6	10.9	32.6

Note: An asterisk (*) indicates unweighted N less than 30.
Source: Derived from Porter (1990, table 21).

10 percent between black and white students of similar attributes. In other words, roughly half, if not somewhat more, of the overall difference in rates of completion can easily be assigned to differences between those groups in their average test scores of ability and socioeconomic background. And for Hispanic students, at least, differences between them and white students of similar attributes are likely to diminish further over time.

Thus it may be argued that overall differences in rates of four-year degree completion between Hispanics, blacks, and whites are at least partially due to the differences between those groups in their average ability test scores and socioeconomic status backgrounds. At the same time, it may also be argued that differences in ability test scores may be somewhat more important than differences in socioeconomic status.[17] Presumably differences in the former are more likely to mirror differences in those groups' prior educational experiences, which favor the educational achievement of whites relative to blacks and Hispanics.

It might be observed that these data paint a picture of degree completion that is not very different from that observed by Eckland and Henderson (1981) and reported in the first edition of this book (Tinto 1987, tables 2.7–2.9). As observed among the 1980 cohort generally, differences between white and nonWhite groups in the 1972 cohort ranged from roughly 5 to 15 percent even after controlling for status and ability test score. Of course, both data sets reflect a period prior to the widespread adoption of programs for students with special needs. As a result, one cannot use these data to conclude that recent efforts to enhance persistence among the "disadvantaged," which we shall speak to in chapter 5, have been unsuccessful. That judgment must await more recent data.

Concluding Observations

In attempting to map out the attributes of student departure from higher education we have often been blocked by our inability to collect sufficiently detailed information on the variety of departing behaviors. Only recently have we begun to collect the sorts of system-wide longitudinal data needed to disentangle the complex interplay of individual and institutional forces which shape the extent and patterning of student departures from higher education. More importantly, we have only recently started to arrange those data in ways which enable us to distinguish between forms of departure from individual institutions of higher education and those which lead to withdrawal from the system as a whole.

Now that we have begun to do so, it has become evident that we must approach with great caution the question of how one explains student departure from institutions of higher education. The paths to degree-completion are many and often long-drawn-out. Individuals are more tenacious in their pursuit of college degrees and more varied in their patterns of departure than previously pictured. More importantly, their leaving appears to be more situational in character than patterned by broad attributes of either individuals or institutions. At this point in our inquiry, at least, there does not appear to be any easy or simple way of characterizing student departure from higher education or of explaining its patterning among different students and institutional settings.

—3—

Roots of Individual Departure from Institutions of Higher Education

We now turn our attention to the phenomenon of institutional departure and to those events largely internal to an institution that help shed light on its occurrence. Though we will endeavor to understand the impact of external forces upon institutional departure, *our central concern will be to understand how events within the institution come to shape the process of departure from that institution.* In effect, we will ask how an institution comes to influence the leaving of its own students. Our answers will, in turn, enable us to address the practical question of how institutions can alter their activities and policies to retain more of their students (chapter 5).

Since our primary interest is in explanation rather than description, we will avoid the simple cataloging of attributes, individual and institutional, which have been shown to be associated with departure (e.g., Pantages and Creedon 1978, Raimst 1981). Instead we will focus on the longitudinal process of student leaving and attempt to explain how it is that student experiences *within* the institution lead over time to different forms of withdrawal. In doing so, we intend to move toward a theory of student departure that seeks to explain how and why it is that particular individual and institutional attributes come to be associated with student departure from institutions of higher education. The development of that theory will occupy chapter 4.

In the present chapter, our synthesis of research will first be directed toward those events that can be said to influence the departure of students generally. That is, we will treat the question of departure as if the process of withdrawal were invariant across students and institutions. After having done so, we will then seek to ascertain to what degree and in what manner that process differs, if at all, for different groups of students and types of institutions. As to the former, we will examine the experiences of females, of minority and disadvantaged students, and of adult students and inquire whether there is any evidence to support the notion that their departure from institutions of higher education arises from sources other than those which affect the white male who enters college immediately after graduating from high school. As to the latter, we will ask if discernible differences among institutions as described, for the most part, by the attributes of size, level, and residential character, in any way affect the process of student departure. Is there any evidence to support the claim, for example, that student departures from two-year institutions arise from different sources than those from four-year institutions? In the course of addressing these and other questions, we also hope to shed light on the question of why it is that rates of departure do in fact vary among individuals and institutions of differing attributes.

Sorting through Past Research on Student Departure

Student departure has been a much studied phenomenon. Few problems in higher education have received as much attention (e.g., McNeely 1937, Iffert 1956, Summerskill 1962, Spady 1970, 1971, Skaling 1971, Tinto 1975, Cope and Hannah 1975, Pantages and Creedon 1978, Raimst 1981, Lang and Ford 1988, and Bean 1990). Yet there is still much we do not know. Though we have been able to map out the dimensions of the patterning of rates of departure among the student population generally and have come to associate certain individual attributes with differences in rates of departure, we have only recently begun to scratch the surface of the complex processes of interaction among people within institutions that give rise to those patterns. In addition, there is still some confusion concerning both the varied character of different forms of departure and the complex causes which lead different individuals to depart from varying institutions of higher education.

That this is the case, despite widespread research, reflects to a significant degree the failure of past research to distinguish adequately between quite different forms of leaving. Most commonly, researchers have failed to distinguish between involuntary departure resulting from academic dismissal and voluntary departures occurring despite the maintenance of adequate grades. It is not uncommon, for example, to find one set of studies claiming ability to be directly related to leaving, another arguing the reverse, and yet another asserting that no relationship exists between the two.[1] Unless the character of student departure is so variable as to permit such conflicting conclusions, those studies must, in fact, refer to quite different forms of leaving. The uncritical use of the term "dropout" to label all such forms of leaving has only made matters worse. It has led researchers to assume that all forms of leaving are essentially the same.

At the same time, little attention has been given to distinguishing the many differences between those who leave institutions (*institutional departures*) and those who withdraw from all forms of formal higher educational participation (*system departures*). Researchers often employ one definition of departure in attempting to study two different types of behavior (Astin 1975, Ethington 1990). In multi-institutional studies such as Astin's (1975) study of a national sample of college students, *dropout* is commonly defined as referring to those persons who fail to obtain college degrees within a specified period of time. Institutional departures who transfer and obtain their college degrees elsewhere are not counted as dropouts. Yet such studies, Astin's in particular, do not hesitate to speak to questions of institutional policy and therefore to what institutions can do to reduce institutional departure. Though their data and definitions do not focus on institutional departure, they argue, by implication, that analyses of aggregate patterns of system departure can illuminate the character of institutional departure.

Regrettably, this is not the case. Results from studies of system departure cannot be used to study institutional departure. While it is true that such multi-institutional studies can be quite revealing of the aggregate patterns of departure from the enterprise as a whole and of the manner in which individual and institutional attributes may be associated with those patterns, they are of little use to either researchers or policy planners concerned with the character and roots of student departure from specific institutions. Though it might be of some value for an institutional official to know that bright students are on the average more likely to earn college degrees than are persons of lower ability, that finding is of little direct value in the development of institution-specific policy. For any single institution it may well be that the reverse is true.

Even among those relatively few institutional studies that are clear in their definition of departure, there is a tendency for research to be descriptive rather than analytical and to take a cross-sectional view of the departure process rather than a truly longitudinal one.[2] Most typically, such studies yield information which indicates that a given type of student is more likely to depart from the institution than another type, and/or that departers as a group tend to share a given set of attributes which differ from those shared by persisters in that institution. What such studies do not reveal, however, are the processes leading to departure which give rise to those descriptive facts. To study those processes one needs longitudinal data which track each and every individual from the point of his/her entry into the institution to that of completion or departure. Such data shed light upon the important social and intellectual processes of interaction within institutions that lead individuals to leave prior to degree completion. Unfortunately, those sorts of data often go uncollected in institutional studies of departure.

The problem before us then is manifold. First, it is to sort out, from the great many studies of departure, those relatively few which yield useful information regarding the character and roots of individual rather than of aggregate departure from institutions of higher education. Second, we must do so in ways which distinguish between the various forms of departure which may arise on campus, especially between the voluntary and the involuntary. Third, we must be sensitive to the institution-specific character of the departure process. Our synthesis must distinguish between those studies which reveal something of the organizational character of the particular institution being studied and those which provide insight into the complex and variable character of departure which may occur in a variety of institutional settings. Fourth, we must come to distinguish those studies that are merely descriptive and/or associative in character from those which shed light on the longitudinal character of the processes of institutional departure. And we must do so in a manner which enables us to determine to what degree, if at all, those processes differ for different groups of students and in different types of institutional settings. Finally, our synthesis of research must yield information that is of more than academic interest. It must be policy relevant. We must be able to use that information as the basis for the development of effective institutional policy.

Individual Roots of Student Departure

In many respects departure is a highly idiosyncratic event, one that can be fully understood only by referring to the understandings and experiences of each and every person who departs. Nevertheless, there does emerge among the diversity of behaviors reported in research on this question a number of pertinent common themes. These pertain to the dispositions of individuals who enter higher education, to the character of their interactional experiences within the institution following entry, and to the external forces which sometimes influence their behavior within the institution.[3]

On the individual level, the two attributes that stand out as primary roots of departure are described by the terms "intention" and "commitment." Each refers to important personal dispositions with which individuals enter institutions of higher education. These not only help set the boundaries of individual attainment but also serve to color the character of individual experiences within the institution following entry. On the institutional level, for the four forms of individual experience which affect departure we use the terms "adjustment," "difficulty," "incongruence," and "isolation." Each describes an important interactional outcome arising from individual experiences within the institution. Though these are largely the result of events which take place within the institution following entry, they necessarily also mirror the attributes, skills, and dispositions of individuals prior to entry and the effect of external forces on individual participation in college. As to the external forces that shape persistence, two factors stand out. These can be described by the terms "obligations" and "finances." The former refers to the responsibilities individuals have in regard to associations with groups or communities external to the college (e.g., families, work), whereas the latter refers to the ability of the individual to finance college attendance.

Intentions: The Goals of Individual Action

Whether they are phrased in terms of educational or occupational goals, individual intentions regarding participation in higher education and attendance at a specific institution are important predictors of the likelihood of degree completion (Panos and Astin 1968, Rossmann and Kirk 1970, Astin 1975, Weingartner 1981, Bean 1982, Wilder and Kellams 1987, and Rodgers and Pratt 1989). Generally speaking, the higher the level of one's educational or occupational goals, the greater the likelihood of college completion. This is especially true when the completion of college is seen as part of a wider career goal (Hanson and Taylor 1970, Frank and Kirk 1975), and it is particularly evident for those occupations, such as medical doctor and natural scientist, which require the earning of a college degree as a prerequisite for occupational entry. In these instances, the goal of occupational attainment becomes the motivating force for the undertaking and completion of a particular academic degree program.

This is not to say that the attitude which considers college completion valuable for its extrinsic outcomes is preferable to that which values its intrinsic outcomes. That judgment is one for the individual to make. Rather it suggests that the stronger the links between the goal of college completion and other valued goals, the greater the likelihood that the former goal will be attained. Indeed it could be argued that persons who place greater emphasis on the intrinsic rewards of college might in fact be somewhat more inclined to leave. They are more likely to be sensitive to the character of the education they receive. As a consequence, they are also more likely to respond to perceived weaknesses in the education they receive not only by speaking out but also by transferring to other institutions where education is perceived to be superior.

SCOPE OF INDIVIDUAL INTENTIONS

Individual intentions, however, are not always framed in the form of degrees and specific occupations. Nor are they always clear at entry or unchanging during the course of the college career. To understand the role of intentions in institutional departure one has to determine the specificity, stability, and clarity of individual intentions.

It is important to recognize that individuals will sometimes choose to leave institutions of higher education prior to degree completion simply because they did not intend to stay until degree completion (Rossmann and Kirk 1970). Most common among these leavers are those individuals who enter college seeking to gain additional skills, learn a specific content area, and/or acquire an additional number of course credits. Not infrequently such limited forms of educational participation are associated with occupational needs or demands. Indeed, in some occupations such as teaching and medicine there are employer inducements or contractual agreements to accumulate additional higher educational credits. In some instances, pay scales themselves are geared to the number of credits one obtains beyond a given educational level. But, lest we forget, there are always a number of persons who partake of higher education for limited periods of time simply because they want to learn. Fortunately the joy of learning for learning's sake is not yet an extinct form of higher educational participation.

It is difficult to gauge the exact extent of such forms of educational investment in higher education. Institutions rarely collect the sorts of information from beginning students—namely, intentions—which would permit one to make that assessment.[4] Nevertheless we do know that limited participation is not uncommon, nor localized in any particular educational sector. Though forms of work-related educational investments are quite common in the two-year-college sector and within extension divisions of four-year colleges and universities, temporary participation is not new to the main campuses of the larger colleges and universities, either. Interestingly, recent evidence suggests that these persons are sometimes past college graduates who seek to retrain themselves for new types of work in a rapidly changing occupational market. Therefore it is not surprising to find that persons who typically enroll for more limited and very specific educational ends are somewhat older than the typical college entrant and more often enrolled on a part-time basis and/or holding a job while attending college.

It is also the case that some persons enter institutions of higher education with the explicit intention of departing prior to degree completion in order to transfer to another institution. Though this is most obviously the case among two-year-college entrants it also applies to students in the four-year sector who are unable to gain entry to the institution of their first choice (Voorhees 1987, Williamson and Creamer 1988). Indeed it appears to be at least as common among the latter institutions as among the former. As of the fall of 1990, 30.3 percent of freshmen in the two-year colleges indicated that their current college was not their first choice, while in the four-year colleges and in universities those figures were 29.8 and 26.7 percent respectively (Astin, Korn, and Berz 1990). For both groups, entry into a particular institution or sector may be seen as a short-term step in working toward a long-term goal calling for graduation from another institution or sector. Departure from their initial institution of registration reflects their efforts to achieve that goal, not a rejection of it.

CHANGE AND UNCERTAINTY OF INTENTIONS

But not all students enter colleges with clearly held educational and/or occupational intentions. Nor do original intentions necessarily remain unchanged during the course of the college career. A good many, if not a majority of, entering students are uncertain of their long-term educational or occupational goals. In a survey of 1982 entering college freshmen, for instance, only a little over one-third reported themselves as being very sure of their educational and occupational goals (Astin, Hemond, and Richardson 1982). The remainder were either unsure or only moderately clear about their future goals.

The 1982 situation did not appear significantly different from that of fifteen years before. Similar information dating back to 1967 indicates that college entrants were no more or less sure of their choices then. It would be surprising if this were not the case. We are quick to overlook the fact that most college students have had little opportunity to realistically confront the question of their adult futures.

But even among those who enter higher education with at least moderately well defined goals, many will change their goals during the course of the college career. At the same time that many undecided individuals come to solidify their future goals, many other previously decided persons will alter their goals. Thus it has been observed that nearly three of every four college students will experience some form of educational and/or occupational uncertainty during the course of their college careers and that uncertainty among new students will frequently increase rather than decrease during their first two years of college.[5]

This is neither surprising nor, in itself, an issue for concern. Among any population of young adults who are just beginning in earnest their search for adult identity, it would be surprising indeed if one found that most were very clear about their long-term goals. For many, if not most, young adults, the college years are an important growing period in which new social and intellectual experiences are sought as a means of coming to grips with the issue of adult careers. They enter college with the hope that they will be able to formulate for themselves, not for their parents, a meaningful answer to that important question. Lest we forget, the college experience is as much, if not more, one of discovery as one of confirmation.

These observations lead to the seemingly obvious conclusion that uncertainty about one's educational and occupational goals is a much more common feature of the student college career than we might care to admit. More importantly, it suggests that movements from varying degrees of certainty to uncertainty and back again may in fact be quite characteristic of the longitudinal process of goal clarification which occurs during the college years. Not only should we not be surprised by such movements, we should expect, indeed hope, that they occur. Presumably it is part of the educational mandate of institutions of higher education to assist maturing youth in coming to grips with the important question of adult careers. The regrettable fact is that some institutions do not see student uncertainty in this light. They prefer to treat it as a deficiency in student development rather than as an expected part of that complex process of personal growth. The implications of such views for policy, as we shall see in a later chapter, are not trivial.

Uncertainty, however, is not necessarily a cause of departure. As reported by Raimst (1981, 11), there is no indication that first-year indecision, for instance as related to area of study, is in any direct fashion related to subsequent early departure. But unresolved intentions over an extended period can lead to departure both from the institution and from the higher educational enterprise as a whole (Abel 1966, Elton and Rose 1971, Frank and Kirk 1975, Waterman and Waterman 1972, Bean 1982, and Janasiewicz 1987). Waterman and Waterman's (1972) study of occupational decision making found, for instance, that career indecision was a much more common theme among student leavers than it was among student persisters. Of those that left, nearly 80 percent were found not to have finalized their career plans at the time of their departure. Interestingly, though, Waterman and Waterman found no significant difference in grade-point average between those who had and those who had not crystalized their career plans.

Apparently the two processes, namely, college grade performance and career decision making, are not related to each other in any simple fashion. Rather, it is argued by some, persistence and departure should be seen as one component of the larger process of career and identity formation. When those careers and identities are crystalized, that is, when individuals are more certain as to their futures, they are more likely to finish college. When plans remain unformulated over extended periods of time, that is, when uncertainty persists for several years, students are more likely to depart without completing their degree programs. Many become discouraged and withdraw, expressing as they do so a sense of not having been successful in college (Janasiewicz 1987).

Commitments and Student Departure

Individual commitments, whether expressed as motivation, drive, or effort, also prove to be centrally related to departure from institutions of higher education. It is obvious, research findings aside, that a person's willingness to work toward the attainment of his/her goals is an important component of the process of persistence in higher education. Conversely, the lack of willingness or commitment proves to be a critical part of the departure process. The unavoidable fact is that college completion requires some effort. Even in nonselective colleges, it calls for a willingness to commit oneself to the investment of time, energy, and often scarce resources to meet the academic and social demands which institutions impose upon their students.

It is equally clear that not all entering students possess that commitment. There are among any cohort of entering students some who simply are unable or unwilling to commit themselves to the task of college completion and expend the level of effort required to complete a degree program. Their subsequent departure, whether in the form of academic dismissal or voluntary withdrawal, is less a reflection of the lack of ability or even of intention than it is of an inability or unwillingness to apply their talents to the attainment of desired goals.

In this regard, Pace's (1980) study of student effort is most revealing. His "Quality of Student Effort" scale measures the extent to which students engage in higher level activities frequently associated with the "serious" or highly motivated student. It is derived from student responses to questions which seek to determine the frequency with which they perform various activities in different domains of college work (e.g., classroom, library, and so forth) and their perceptions of the degree to which college has helped them progress in several areas of social and intellectual development. Pace found that the multiple correlations between background variables such as age, sex, race, and parental education and four composite outcome factors, namely, personal/interpersonal understanding, intellectual competencies, general education objectives, and understanding science, ranged from only 0.14 to 0.36. The multiple correlations between the quality of student effort scales and those outcomes were, however, considerably higher. They ranged from 0.62 to 0.68, sizable correlations by anyone's standards. Thus Pace concludes that quality of student effort is more closely related to academic outcomes than are the background factors which mark student entry into college. Though background attributes may be useful indicators of student potential to succeed, they do not tap the orientations and activities of students which transform potential into learning outcomes (Amos 1990).

But quality of student effort is not merely an attribute of the individual. As we shall see in chapter 4, quality of effort is at least somewhat reflective of social and academic context. It partially mirrors the actions of the institution, so that quality of student effort varies across institutions in a manner that is not strictly tied either to student ability or to selectivity of the institution (Amos 1990).

Roots of Individual Departure

GOAL AND INSTITUTIONAL COMMITMENT

Individual commitments take two major forms, goal and institutional. Goal commitment refers to a person's commitment to personal educational and occupational goals. It specifies the person's willingness to work toward the attainment of those goals. Institutional commitment refers to the person's commitment to the institution in which he/she is enrolled. It indicates the degree to which one is willing to work toward the attainment of one's goals within a given higher educational institution. In either case, but especially the latter, the greater one's commitments, the greater the likelihood of institutional persistence (Mallette and Cabrera 1991).

Cope and Hannah's (1975) review of research on this matter led them to conclude that of all personal attributes studied, "personal commitment to either an academic or occupational goal is the single most important determinant of persistence in college" (Cope and Hannah 1975, 19). Among other studies, they cite Abel's (1966) study of persistence to graduation of failing students (less than C average), which found that graduation rates were twice as high among students who were committed to specific career goals as they were among students who were uncertain of their futures.

The impact of goal commitment upon departure is, in part, contingent upon the intervening effects of student ability. By employing the combined effects of both academic competence and commitment to the goal of college completion, Hackman and Dysinger (1970) were able to distinguish between persistence, transfers, voluntary withdrawals, and academic dismissals. Students with high academic competence and moderate to high goal commitment were most likely to persist. Students with high competence but only moderate to low commitment tended to transfer to other colleges or depart and re-enroll at a later time. Individuals with low competence but with moderate to high commitment tended to persist in college unless forced to leave because of failing grades. Those persons with both low competence and moderate to low commitment were most likely to depart and not re-enroll in any other college at a later date.

Knowledge of students' institutional commitment enables one to further distinguish between those who stay and those who leave, especially those who transfer to other institutions (Pascarella and Terenzini 1980, Terenzini, Lorang, and Pascarella 1981, Mallette and Cabrera 1991). Other things being equal, individuals who are committed to graduating from a specific institution are more likely to graduate from that institution than are persons whose commitments have no specific institutional referent (Terenzini, Lorang, and Pascarella 1981).

Institutional commitment may arise in a number of different ways. It may arise before entry as a result of the impact of family traditions upon college choice (e.g., the father or mother having attended the same institution), from family and/or peer pressure, or from the perception that graduation from a specific institution enhances one's chances for a successful occupational career (e.g., graduating from one of the elite colleges). It may also mirror the manner in which graduation from a particular institution is seen as an integral part of one's occupational career (e.g., graduation from a military academy or from an institution with a specific professional mission or program).

Understandably, prior institutional commitments can have considerable influence on subsequent experiences and, together with goal commitment, help distinguish between different forms of leaving. Given sufficiently high goal commitment, individuals may decide to "stick it out" even in unsatisfactory circumstances because the perceived benefits of obtaining a college degree are so dependent upon obtaining that degree from a particular college. Conversely, the absence of prior commitment may lead individuals to withdraw at the first sign of difficulty. In those situations, high goal commitment may lead to transfer whereas low commitment may result in permanent withdrawal from all forms of higher education.

Personality and Student Departure

Though we have already alluded to the role of personality in student departure, it bears repeating here that there is little evidence to support the notion that, beyond the issues of commitment or motivation, early leavers have a *unique* personality profile. At one time or other virtually every attribute of personality has been cited as being related to the likelihood of departure. Some researchers, such as Suczek and Alfert (1966), argued that departing students valued sensations more than persisters did, were more imaginative, enjoyed fantasy more, and were motivated by rebelliousness. Others, like Astin (1964) using the California Psychological Inventory, found that leavers were more aloof, self-centered, impulsive, and assertive than stayers. Still other studies suggest that withdrawing students are more autonomous, mature, intellectually committed, and creative than persisters (Trent and Ruyle 1965, Keniston 1968), and yet others that persisters tend to be irresponsible, anxious, impulsive, rebellious, unstable, immature, and unimaginative plodders (Grace 1957, Brown 1960, Beahan 1966, Gurin et al. 1968, Vaughan 1968, Hannah 1971).

To add to the confusion, Sharp and Chason (1978) used the Minnesota Multiphasic Inventory to study the role of personality in departure among two groups of students of the same "personality type" from the same institution. Results obtained for the first group were not replicated among the second group. Sharp and Chason therefore concluded that many of the prior research studies which showed significant relationships between personality types and persistence were either incorrect or were sample specific in that they were referring to very different students in very different situations. This is not to say, however, that there may not be specific traits of personality which, *on the average*, tend to describe real differences between the patterns of response of persisters and leavers generally. Individual responses to situations of incongruence or isolation, for example, are necessarily dependent upon personalities. What may lead one isolated person to "stick it out" and another to depart without seeking out assistance must somehow be associated with differences in their personalities.

Unfortunately, our broadly defined studies of personality traits tend to blur many of these potentially important differences. More importantly, they tend to overlook the possibility that the impact of personality upon an individual's responses may be situational in character and therefore very much a function of the setting in which people find themselves. As a result, though we sense that personality must play a part in student departure, we are thus far unable to say just how different elements of personality affect student leaving in different institutional settings.

Interactional Roots of Institutional Departure

But commitments, like intentions, are subject to change over time. Over the course of the college career, they come to reflect the character of individual experiences within the institution. Though prior dispositions and attributes may influence the college career and may, in some cases, lead directly to departure, their impact is contingent on the quality of individual interactions with other members of the institution and on the individual's perception of the degree to which those experiences meet his/her needs and interests. It is for this reason that researchers generally agree that what happens following entry is, in most cases, more important to the process of student departure than what has previously occurred.

Of the great variety of events or situations which appear to influence student departure, four clusters stand out as leading to institutional departure. These are best described by the terms "adjustment," "difficulty," "incongruence," and "isolation."

Adjustment to College and Student Departure

At the very outset, persistence in college requires individuals to adjust, both socially and intellectually, to the new and sometimes quite strange world of the college. Most persons, even the most able and socially mature, experience some difficulty in making that adjustment. For many, the period of adjustment is brief, the difficulties they encounter relatively minor, but some find it so difficult that they quit.

Difficulty in making the transition to college arises from two distinct sources. On one hand, it may result from the inability of individuals to separate themselves from past forms of association typically characteristic of the local high school and its related peer groups (Benjamin 1990, Christie and Dinham 1991). In the case of residence away from home, it may also mirror the inability to manage the pains often associated with first-time separation from the family of upbringing. On the other hand, difficulty frequently arises from the individual's need to adjust to the new and often more challenging social and intellectual demands which college imposes upon students (Attinasi 1989, Christie and Dinham 1991, Thompson and Fretz 1991). Though past performance in high school may help prepare new students for college, the preparation is rarely perfect, the transition to college rarely without a period of sometimes quite difficult adjustment.

Roots of Adjustment and Early Withdrawal from College

The academic difficulties, social isolation, and sheer sense of bewilderment which often accompanies the transition may pose real problems for the individual (Attinasi 1989, Christie and Dinham 1991). Though most students adjust, others do not. Some are simply unable to clear the first hurdle to college completion and withdraw from further participation. Most of these depart very early in their college career, prior to the first grading period, that is, within the first six to eight weeks. (Blanc, DeBuhr, and Martin 1983). Frequently they leave without giving themselves a chance to adjust to the demands of college life.

In some cases, departure of this sort is temporary rather than permanent. Some persons need time to regain their confidence and stability. After a brief period of time, they may reenter their institution to continue their studies. Among large residential institutions, however, a number will withdraw in order to transfer to a college closer to home. By doing so, they are able to continue in higher education while returning to the known world of their local communities.

Understandably, differences in individual goals and commitments help shape individual responses to the stress of transition. Many students will stick it out even under the most trying conditions, while others will withdraw even under minimal stress. Presumably either lofty goals or strong commitments, or both, will lead individuals to persist in very difficult circumstances. Conversely, modest goals and/or weak commitments may lead persons to withdraw. The unavoidable fact is that some students are unwilling to put up with the stress of transition because they are not sufficiently committed either to the goal of higher education or to the institution into which entry is first made. Others, however, are so committed that they will do virtually anything to persist.[6]

But early withdrawal from college need not always imply a lack of commitment or the absence of intention. Though uncertainty of intentions may heighten the problems of adjustment, it is not always the primary cause of leaving. Rather, adjustments to new situations are often painful and sometimes so difficult as to cause young people, and sometimes older students, temporarily to give up on even strongly held goals. For some, it is a question of learning how to apply previously acquired intellectual skills to new situations. Others who are faced with the task of living away from home for the first time may have to learn an entirely new set of social skills appropriate to the life of the college. For those persons the adjustment to college may be particularly stressful, for it combines both intellectual and social forms of adjustment. Lest we forget, most new students are teenagers who have had precious little chance to live on their own and attend to the many challenging issues of adult life. For them, college is as much a social testing ground as an academic one.

Little wonder, then, that problems of separation and adjustment to college are frequently linked to differences in individual personality, coping skills, and the character of past educational and social experiences (Tinto 1975, Pantages and Creedon 1978). It is understandable, for instance, that persons who have acquired skills in coping with new situations or have had past experiences in making similar, though smaller, transitions (e.g., living away at summer camp, traveling) seem to have less difficulty in making the transition to college than do other students. Some students have not yet learned how to cope with such situations. They have not acquired the skills which enable them to direct their energies to solve the problems they face (Bandura 1977, Lazarus and Launier 1978). Without assistance, many flounder and withdraw without having made a serious attempt to adjust to the life of the college.

Past experience aside, however, some individuals find it more difficult to manage the pains of adjustment than do others. In these instances, personality rather than past experience shapes the person's response to the stress of transition. Some students seem to adjust more rapidly to changing situations and are better able to handle the stress those changes entail (Lazarus 1980, Thompson and Fretz 1991). They tend to be more mature, emotionally stable, more flexible, and adaptive to new circumstances. But whether that suggests, as some researchers have argued, that personality per se is an important cause of departure is, as we shall argue in a following section, uncertain.

Difficulty and Student Departure

Persistence in college requires more than mere adjustment. It also calls for the meeting of a number of minimum standards regarding academic performance. Regrettably, not all entering students are able to meet those standards. Though some students experiencing academic difficulty will withdraw voluntarily to avoid the stigma of failure, many will endure until forced to leave.

Not surprisingly, difficulty and departure in the form of academic dismissal are often found to be associated with measures of individual ability and past school performance (e.g., Blanchfield 1971, Morrisey 1971, Johansson and Rossmann 1973). Thus it is commonly observed that the "typical" academic failure is generally of lower ability and has inferior high school grades (Astin 1975). But the association between academic failures, on the one hand, and standard measures of ability and high school performance, on the other, is not very great. Irvine's (1966) five-year follow-up study of 659 men who entered the University of Georgia in 1959 found that high school grade average was the single best predictor of college persistence. In this case, high school grade-point average correlated 0.34 with five-year graduation from the institution. Correlation of this size, not uncommon to such research, translates into the observation that high school grades (and other related measures of ability) account for but 12 percent of the variance in staying or leaving behaviors. Approximately 88 percent of the variance is left unaccounted for.

That this is the case is partially explained by the failure, already noted, of most studies of departure to distinguish between varying forms of withdrawal from institutions of higher education, in this instance between academic dismissal and voluntary withdrawal. Since voluntary withdrawal generally has little to do with academic difficulties, failure to distinguish between the two forms of departure weakens the observed relationship between measures of ability and/or past performance and persistence generally.

But even when academic dismissals are studied separately, it still is the case that prior performance and measures of ability are not very highly correlated with departure (i.e., correlations of less than 0.50). In part this reflects the previously discussed effect of intentions and commitments upon departure, namely, that limited intentions and/or weak commitments may be manifested in poor academic performance. More importantly it also mirrors the fact that common measures of ability and past school performance are neither good predictors of the study skills and habits required for successful academic performance in college (Demitroff 1974, Astin 1975) nor useful proxies for the sorts of social skills that enable individuals to successful master the socially defined role of "college student."[7]

The finding that the development of poor study habits and inadequate study skills is frequently the reflection of poor high school preparation leads in turn to the observation that the quality and, sometimes, type of high school (i.e., public or private) are themselves associated with withdrawal from college. Astin (1975), for example, theorizes that this may in part be due to the fact that grading policies are usually more rigorous at private schools than at public ones and that, on the average, students from the former schools are better prepared for the academic demands of college. Other researchers, most notably Coleman, Hoffer, and Kilgore (1982), reach the same conclusion even after controlling for differences in the attributes of the individuals who attend those schools (e.g., ability and social status backgrounds).

Since it has been demonstrated that individuals from disadvantaged and/or minority origins are much more likely to be found in public schools generally and in the lower quality public schools in particular, it follows that they will be less well prepared for college. As a result, they will also be more likely to experience academic difficulty in college regardless of measured ability, and more likely, therefore, to leave because of academic failure. Of course, this is also partially explained by the differential social experiences of disadvantaged youth and thus the difficulty they encounter in attempting to successfully act out the largely middle-class role of "college student."

It would be misleading, however, to leave the impression that academically unprepared students are solely or even largely from lower-class origins. There is, in fact, an increasing array of students, young and old, from a diversity of backgrounds who enter higher education unprepared to meet the academic demands of college life (Moore and Carpenter 1985, Cross 1971, 1981). Indeed, it has been estimated that the incidence of academic unpreparedness has grown to the point where between 30 and 40 percent of entering freshmen are to some degree deficient in college-level reading and writing skills (Moore and Carpenter 1985) and where approximately one-quarter of all freshmen take remedial coursework in either mathematics, writing, or reading (U.S. Department of Education 1985). To the degree that this is the case, it also follows that the incidence of academic dismissal will also increase.[8]

Integration and Departure from Institutions of Higher Education

Though the issue of academic preparation for college is far from trivial, academic dismissal still represents a small proportion of the total leaving of students from institutions of higher education. Less than 25 percent of all institutional departures, nationally, take the form of academic dismissal. Most departures are voluntary in the sense that they occur without any formal compulsion on the part of the institution. Rather than mirroring academic

difficulties, they reflect the character of the individual's social and intellectual experiences within the institution. Specifically, they mirror the degree to
which those experiences serve to integrate individuals into the social and intellectual life of the institution. Generally, the more satisfying those experiences are felt to be, the more likely are individuals to persist until degree
completion. Conversely, the less integrative they are, the more likely are individuals to withdraw voluntarily prior to degree completion.

The absence of integration appears to arise from two sources referred to
here as incongruence and isolation. Incongruence, or what is sometimes referred to as lack of institutional fit, refers to that state where individuals perceive themselves as being substantially at odds with the institution. In this
case, the absence of integration results from the person's judgment of the
undesirability of integration. Isolation, however, refers to the absence of
sufficient interactions whereby integration may be achieved. It is that condition in which persons find themselves largely isolated from the daily life of
the institution. Though obviously related, in that one may lead to the other,
incongruence and isolation are distinct roots of student departure. While the
former arises from interactions and the person's evaluation of the character
of those interactions, the latter results from the absence of interactions. Incongruence is almost always an unavoidable phenomenon within institutions
of higher education. Isolation, though common, need not occur.

INCONGRUENCE AND VOLUNTARY WITHDRAWAL

Incongruence refers in general to the mismatch or lack of fit between the
needs, interests, and preferences of the individual and those of the institution. Reflecting the outcome of interactions with different members of the
institution, it springs from individual perceptions of not fitting into and/or of
being at odds with the social and intellectual fabric of institutional life. In
such situations, individuals leave not so much from the absence of integration as from the judgment of the undesirability of integration. Withdrawal
mirrors, in effect, the person's decision that further attendance would not be
in his/her own best interests. Thus, the tendency of some individuals to describe their withdrawal from college not in terms of leaving but in terms of a
conscious decision to stop going to college.

Individuals come to experience the character of institutional life through a
wide range of formal and informal interactions with other members of the
institution, faculty, staff, and students. The needs, interests, and preferences
of those persons may be expressed individually, in group form, or in sum as a
reflection of the general ethos or culture of the institution. They may be expressed formally in either the academic and social system of the college
through the rules and regulations which govern acceptable behaviors. For

example, they may be discerned through the regulations which govern the academic requirements for given degree programs, regulations which may be quite rigid or quite flexible in character. They may also be manifested informally, through the daily interactions which occur between various individuals both inside and outside the domains of institutional life as seen in the daily life of classrooms or in the meeting of faculty, staff, and students outside the classrooms and laboratories of the institution.

However discerned, what matters is the view of the student. Whether there are objective grounds for mismatch is not necessarily of direct importance to the issue of individual departure. In most situations what matters is whether the individuals perceive themselves as being incongruent with the life of the institutions, not whether other observers would agree with that assessment (Pervin and Rubin 1967).

THE SOURCES OF INCONGRUENCE WITHIN THE COLLEGE

Lack of congruence or mismatch between the individual and the institution may arise in a number of different ways both academic and social. It may arise from a mismatch between the abilities, skills, and interests of the student and the demands placed upon that person by the academic system of the institution. Academic and/or intellectual incongruence may be the result. In the formal academic realm of the college, incongruence may take the form of a quantitative mismatch, if you will, between the skills, interests, and needs of the individual and those which are characterized by the demands of academic life. Such demands may be seen as either too hard or too easy.

Excessive demands tend to result, as we have already noted, in departure in the form of academic dismissal. It can sometimes also lead to early voluntary withdrawal when the students decide that it would not be in their best interests to continue. They choose to withdraw prior to the likely event of academic failure, sometimes in order to transfer to other institutions where academic demands are seen as more reasonable.[9] The recent work of Getzlaf, Sedlacek, Kearney, and Blackwell (1984) is, in this regard, revealing. They found that students were more likely to withdraw when they perceived too great a decrease in academic performance. And this proved to be the case even after controlling for a variety of pre-entry characteristics which included measures of ability. In other words, the effect of a marked decline in performance upon persistence was similar for both able and less able students.

Though much public attention has focused on the plight of students who find college work too difficult, many students leave because the academic life of an institution is not challenging enough. In short, they leave because they are bored. Thus the finding noted earlier that one sometimes finds that those who voluntarily withdraw are somewhat more able and creative than the typical persister. Frequently they are among the more serious and committed members of the student body. Understandably, it is those sorts of students that are most likely to be sensitive to the character and shortcomings of the intellectual life of the institution. In those situations, it is not surprising that dissatisfaction with the quality of teaching and dissatisfaction with the level of intellectual inquiry prove to be the most frequently cited reasons for departure (Demitroff 1974, Steele 1978).

It should not be assumed, however, that such mismatches are entirely due to weaknesses or shortcomings in the academic system of the college. Though this is very often the case, it is also true that some students are unable or unwilling to partake of the full range of academic resources available to them.Individuals must also exhibit personal initiative. Even though it is, as we shall argue later, the responsibility of all institutions to provide all their students the opportunity to be so challenged, one cannot ask them to insure that all persons make use of those opportunities. While it is undeniably the case that many institutions are not sufficiently challenging to many of their students, it is also true that some students are not sufficiently committed to academic work to challenge the institution. Regrettably, some students who are otherwise intellectually able are also intellectually lazy. Thus the related finding that some, but by no means all, such departing students either lack the commitment to intellectual goals and/or possess personalities which hamper their search for intellectual challenge (e.g., intellectual rigidity).

But not all forms of incongruence reflect quantitative mismatches between the individual and the demands of the institution (e.g., being too hard or too easy). They may also arise from what might be described as qualitative differences between the individual and the institution that reflect differences between the intellectual and social values and preferences of the individual and those of other members of the institution. That is, they may arise from issues pertaining to personal fit.

Typically, incongruence is manifested in the individual's judgment that the institution's intellectual climate is unsuited or irrelevant, perhaps even contrary, to his/her own intellectual preferences. Such judgments often lead departing students to cite the irrelevance of academic life as a prime reason for their leaving. This leads institutional officials to describe many able voluntary withdrawals as intellectual deviants or misfits. Clearly the term "deviant" is best understood here as meaning different from the common orientation of the majority within the institution. It need not imply deviance in any other domain (e.g., behavior) or with regard to some wider pattern of intellectual orientations. One need not be a societal deviant to find oneself at odds with the intellectual climate of a given institution.[10]

However described, it is evident that student interaction with faculty appears to play a central role in individual judgments of intellectual congruence (Stoecker, Pascarella, and Wolfle 1988, Boyer 1987, Pascarella and Terenzini 1991). The faculty, more than any other group, represents the primary intellectual orientations of the institution. Their actions, within and without the classroom, provide the standards by which individuals come to judge the intellectual ethos of the institution. Issues of quality of intellectual work, commitment to student intellectual growth, and opportunities for student involvement in learning, especially in the classroom, are all deeply affected by the way the faculty interacts with students over matters of intellectual substance. The classrooms, the hallways, and the offices of the institution become testing grounds for student judgment as to the intellectual character and worth of the college experience.

Incongruence may also reflect a person's experiences within the social realm of the college, in particular with one's student peers. In this instance, it mirrors a perceived mismatch between the social values, preferences, and/or behavioral styles of the person and those which characterize other members of the institution, expressed individually or collectively. Though it may sometimes result from experiences within the formal domain of the social life of the institution (e.g., extracurricular activities), it more frequently mirrors the day-to-day informal, personal interaction among students, faculty, and staff. Among young adults, especially those in residential settings, interaction with one's student peers, especially one's roommate, proves to be a particularly important element in voluntary departure. For them, social identity is sometimes as important as intellectual identity, especially in the first year of college (Moffatt 1989). Among older students, however, this may not be the case, as their social orientations are generally less sensitive to the particular life of younger student peers. Their sense of fit may be more reflective of their experience with other adults, students, faculty, and staff.

That some degree of incongruence will be experienced by most students is not itself surprising. Few college settings are so homogeneous that virtually no disagreement occurs on campus as to the appropriate character of intellectual and social behavior. But when that perception leads the person to perceive him/herself as being substantially at odds with the dominant culture of the institution and/or with significant groups of faculty and student peers, then withdrawal may follow. Most often it results in transfer to other institutions, those seen as more concordant with one's likes and dislikes, rather than to permanent withdrawal from all forms of higher educational participation (Getzlaf et al. 1984). The character of that move depends of course on the nature of individual preferences, intentions, and commitments and the availability of other settings to which the person may transfer. In this regard, it is not surprising that black students often transfer to traditionally black colleges after leaving largely white institutions of higher education (Fleming 1985).

INCONGRUENCE, EXPECTATIONS, AND COLLEGE CHOICE

The phenomenon of incongruence as a source of departure leads to the practical question of how individuals go about choosing an institution of higher education. It might be reasonably argued that mismatches are largely the result of poor and/or uninformed choices on the part of the individual. It results, in other words, from the person's having picked an institution unsuited to his/her needs and interests. Though it is not our intention here to explore the process of college choice, it does bear pointing out that poor choices and the expectations upon which such choices are made can have immediate and lasting effects upon institutional participation (see Hossler, Bean, and Associates 1990). Cope and Hannah (1975), for instance, estimate that poor choice of college is the primary cause of at least 20 percent of transfers (p. 33). Our own guess is that the figure is considerably higher when all forms of departure are considered.

The process of choosing a college involves the formation of a set of expectations as to the character of the institutions among which a choice is to be made (Zemsky and Oedel 1983, Braxton 1990). Presumably, one's final choice depends in large part upon the nature of those expectations, especially those pertaining to the social and intellectual character of the college. The more accurate and realistic those expectations are, the more likely is it that the resulting choice will lead to an effective match between the individual and the institution. Pre-entry expectations generally become the standard against which individuals evaluate their early experiences within the institution. When expectations are either unrealistic and/or seriously mistaken, subsequent experiences can lead to major disappointments. Though some students come to modify their expectations to suit the situation, others feel betrayed. They may believe they were intentionally misled by the institution.

The regrettable but unavoidable fact is that for many students the process of selecting a college is quite haphazard. Often it is informed by the least accurate and reliable of information. Though all potential college students can avail themselves of a wide range of data on the attributes of differing colleges, many do not. But even when individuals do seek out information, it is frequently the case that those data are either inappropriate to the important issues of choice or misleading in character.

Most typically information is provided as to the formal attributes of college: its size, faculty, and students. Mission statements, descriptions of resources and programs abound. But infrequently can one obtain accurate information as to the informal social and intellectual climates which characterize student life on campus. Though some colleges attempt to provide that information, it is not always provided in a manner which depicts how the student is likely to experience the institution. More often than not, such information is either self-serving or misleading in character, reflecting the view of adults rather than that of other students. Yet it is precisely the latter sort of information which is most important for accurate expectations and appropriate choice. And it is precisely that sort of information which, short of visiting the campus for several days, is most difficult to obtain.

It is noteworthy, in this regard, that a majority of students apply to no more than two institutions. Recent data from the 1990 study of the national norms of first-year college students indicates that 31.9 percent of all freshmen applied to but one college, 15.7 percent to two colleges, 16.7 percent to three colleges, and the remainder, or 35.7 percent, to four or more colleges (Astin, Korn, and Berz 1990). In noting the reasons which were very important in their final choice of college, only 7.6 percent indicated the advice of a guidance counselor and but 4.1 percent that of a high school teacher. These figures were nearly matched and/or exceeded by the influence of relatives (6.6 percent), the suggestion of a friend (7.2 percent), and that of a friend who attended the college in question (14.9 percent). Clearly the influence of a professional is no more, if not less, important than that of "interested parties" whose ability to judge the needs of the student may be open to question.

Though there is little doubt that more accurate information about colleges would help, it does not follow that one could ever eliminate the occurrence of mistaken choices among entering students. For large numbers of students there is no easy way they could acquire, outside of extended site visits, the sort of detailed information about the day-to-day nature of institutional climates and patterns of interaction that would permit them to discern which institution is best suited to their needs. Even if students were able to make that determination, that is, if they clearly understood their own needs, there is little reason to suppose that they could do so without first experiencing the institution on a day-to-day basis. For some students, the experience of having made a "poor choice" may in fact be an important part of their coming to identify their own needs and interests.

ISOLATION, CONTACT, AND STUDENT WITHDRAWAL

Departure also arises from individual isolation, specifically from the absence of sufficient contact between the individual and other members of the social and academic communities of the college (e.g., Anderson 1988, Stoecker, Pascarella, and Wolfle 1988, Stage 1989a, 1989b, Benjamin 1990). Though isolation may be associated with incongruence, in that deviants are often isolates as well, it arises independently among persons who are not very different from other members of the college. Individuals who might otherwise find membership in college communities are unable to establish via continuing interaction with other individuals the personal bonds that are the basis for membership in the communities of the institution.

Husband's (1976) study of voluntary withdrawal from a small liberal arts college, for example, found that voluntary leavers were much less likely than were persisters to identify someone on campus with whom they had a significant relationship and/or who served as a significant definer of their actions. Though such leavers frequently maintained adequate grades, they reported little satisfaction from their limited daily personal interactions with other members of the institution. Typically, they noted feelings of social isolation, the absence of opportunities for contact, and the remoteness of faculty as instrumental in their decisions to leave (Bligh 1977). Yet in most other respects they were quite similar to those who stayed. Rather than being noticeably different from persisters, as one might expect to be the case for those who are labeled incongruent, isolated students differed only in their failure to have established a significant personal tie with someone on campus, faculty or student.

Similar conclusions can be drawn from other studies in the extensive body of research on the effects of student-student and student-faculty contacts on voluntary withdrawal from college (Tinto 1975, Terenzini and Pascarella 1977, Pascarella and Terenzini 1977, 1991, Pascarella 1980, Munro 1981, Pascarella and Terenzini 1983, Stoecker, Pascarella, and Wolfle 1988). That research demonstrates that the degree and quality of personal interaction with other members of the institution are critical elements in the process of student persistence. By contrast, the absence of sufficient contact with other members of the institution proves to be the single most important predictor of eventual departure even after taking account of the independent effects of background, personality, and academic performance (Pascarella and Terenzini 1979). To paraphrase the extensive work of Pascarella and Terenzini and their colleagues, voluntary withdrawal is much more a reflection of what occurs on campus after entry than it is of what has taken place before entry. And of that which occurs after entry, the absence of contact with others proves to matter most.

STUDENT-FACULTY CONTACT AND STUDENT WITHDRAWAL   Of the variety of forms of contact which occur on campus, frequent contact with the faculty appears to be a particularly important element in student persistence (e.g.,

Pascarella and Terenzini 1979, Terenzini and Pascarella 1980, Pascarella and Wolfle 1985, Terenzini and Wright 1987b, Stage 1989a). This is especially true when that contact extends beyond the formal boundaries of the classroom to the various informal settings which characterize college life (Stage 1989a). Those encounters which go beyond the mere formalities of academic work to broader intellectual and social issues and which are seen by students as warm and rewarding appear to be strongly associated with continued persistence. By contrast, the absence of faculty contacts and/or the perception that they are largely formalistic exchanges limited to the narrow confines of academic work prove to be tied to the occurrence of voluntary withdrawal (Pascarella and Terenzini 1977).

This does not mean, however, that what goes on inside the classroom is unimportant to decisions regarding departure. Quite the contrary, the actions of faculty inside the classroom prove to be important precursors to subsequent contact (e.g., Terenzini and Pascarella 1978, Pascarella and Terenzini 1991).[11] Faculty behavior within the classroom not only influences academic performance and perceptions of academic quality, it also sets the tone for further interactions outside the classroom. Classroom behaviors influence student perceptions as to the receptivity of faculty to further student contacts outside the classroom (Wilson, Wood, and Gaff 1974, Astin 1975). Behaviors seen as unreceptive may constrict further contacts even when the faculty member is in fact accessible.Classrooms often serve as gateways for further involvement in the intellectual life of the campus. In nonresidential settings generally and for commuting students in particular, they may be the primary if not the only place where students and faculty meet. If further contact is to occur, it is most likely to arise out of their interactions within the classroom.

In some instances, faculty may be initiators of contact. They may sometimes reach out and pick someone in the class to whom they give special attention. They become actively involved in nurturing individuals whom they see as having unusual potential for future growth (Valadez and Duran 1991). But not all faculty behave in this manner nor are all students equally likely to be chosen for tutelage. When queried, faculty describe selected individuals not only as being a "cut above other students" in initiative and drive, but also as reminding them of something in themselves as former students.

But faculty must be available and interested in such interactions for them to occur, and conditions must be such as to encourage those interactions when they are desired by students and faculty. Though classroom behaviors may be important precursors to further interactions, it is the occurrence of those interactions outside the classroom which help shape student decisions regarding departure (Terenzini and Wright 1988b). In this respect, the absence or presence of interactions between faculty and students also serves as a predictor of institutional rates of departure. That is, it may typify the experience of most students who go there. Rather than mirror only the experience and perhaps personality of any one person, it may reflect a wider ethos which influences interactions generally. Thus it is of little surprise to discover that institutions with low rates of student retention are those in which students generally report low rates of student-faculty contact. Conversely, institutions with high rates of retention are most frequently those which are marked by relatively high incidence of such interactions. They foster such interactions as a means of involving students in their intellectual life (Kuh, Schuh, Whitt, and Associates 1991).

ISOLATION AND THE TRANSITION TO COLLEGE   That social isolation is often a primary cause of voluntary withdrawal leads us to a deeper appreciation of the often cited fact that withdrawal from institutions of higher education is most frequent in the first semester of the freshman year.[12] It is, as we have noted previously, a period of transition in which the individual has to make a number of adjustments and endure at least temporary isolation. This is characteristically true in very large institutions where newcomers face the daunting task of trying to find their way around socially remote and organizationally complex landscapes with few recognizable guideposts. Though some students find a way of making the transition, others flounder.

For many the isolation is only temporary, the sense of normlessness only fleeting. Most establish new friendships and soon come to feel at home among the byways of the college. But some do not. Those who have difficulty meeting people and making new friends and/or who respond to ambiguous situations by withdrawing into themselves tend to have greater difficulties than do those whose typical response is to reach out to others. Their isolation frequently becomes a lasting and eventually debilitating experience. It can and indeed often does lead to early withdrawal from college.

But isolation is not merely the outcome of individual personality. It may mirror the character of the person's past social experiences and the absence of familiar social groups with which to make contact. It may therefore be particularly common for students for whom the college represents a very foreign social landscape (e.g., students of color in largely white residential institutions). For them, the process of "getting in" may be particularly challenging (Attinasi 1989). Of course the experience of transition to college may also reflect the characteristic interactional fabric of that institution into which entry is sought. That is, it may be an experience shared by many, if not most, of the students entering the institution. In this regard, some institutions may be "involving" while others may be quite remote. And some may take pains to help newcomers make their way about the campus during the first year of college, while others may do little. Finally, it should be observed that while transitions to college are often difficult, they may be a necessary, though bittersweet, first step on a longer path to adult attainment. The term "breaking away" used by first-generation college students to describe their first-year college experience in London's (1989) study speaks, in this regard, to the sense of upward mobility and discontinuity that many students typically experience.

Multiple College Communities: The Role of Student Subcultures in Student Persistence

Congruence and contact need not imply a perfect or even extensive match between the individual and the institution as a whole. Nor does it require wide-ranging contact with other members of the institution. But it does argue that the person must find some compatible academic and/or social group with whom to establish membership and make those contacts. Few institutions are so small or so homogeneous that they are unidimensional in character, either academically or socially. Most institutions, especially the large ones, are made up of a variety of academic and social communities which exhibit their own distinct patterns of intellectual and behavioral interaction. Among students, for instance, we commonly employ the term "student subcultures" to describe the diversity of student communities on campus, and we have been accustomed to the use by students of various labels which serve to highlight their salient characteristics (Clark and Trow 1966).

Congruence may occur within any one of these communities or subcultures without its necessarily occurring across the institution generally. It is quite possible for the person to be at odds intellectually and socially with a great number of persons or groups within the institution and still find sufficient social and intellectual contact and support for continued persistence. This is precisely what Simpson, Baker, and Mellinger (1980) find in their study of persistence and departure among students at the University of California at Berkeley. Students who might be considered deviant in other educational settings were no more likely to leave than were other students. In that setting, at least, those students were able to find sufficient support to continue. Thus the notion of finding one's niche within the institution as a requisite part of persistence in college.

The concept of subcultures also serves to highlight the particular experience of students of color in many institutions of higher education and the importance of critical mass (i.e, a sufficient number of persons of like backgrounds and interests from which viable communities can be formed) in the forming and sustaining of diverse student communities. Specifically, it points up the repeated observation that the persistence of students of color

often hinges upon there being a sufficiently large number of similar types of
students on campus with whom to form a viable community (Research Triangle Institute 1975). Though the existence of "minority" student subcultures does not, in itself, insure persistence, as race alone is not sufficient
grounds for congruence, the absence of compatible student groups does appear to undermine the likelihood of persistence. And it does so not only for
racial minorities but also for other students who might otherwise find themselves alone on campus.[13]

Marginality, Centrality, and Student Withdrawal

The social and intellectual life of most institutions has a center and a periphery.[14] The center or mainstream of institutional life is normally that
which establishes the prevailing climate or ethos of the institution, that is,
the characteristic and distinguishing attitudes, values, beliefs, and patterns
of behavior of the institution. It is in fact made up of one or more communities of individuals or dominant subcultures whose orientations come to define the standards of judgment for all members of the institution. The
periphery, in turn, comprises other communities or subordinate subcultures
whose particular values, beliefs, and patterns of behavior may differ substantially from those of the center. Though each such community may have a
life of its own, that life exists outside the mainstream and is typically marginal to the power relationships that define campus politics. Its particular
attributes tend to have little impact on the overall ethos of the institution and
the decisions that frame it.

The point of our noting the existence of dominant and subordinate subcultures is to argue that the effect of subculture membership upon persistence is
often dependent upon the degree to which that subculture is marginal to the
mainstream of institutional life. Other things being equal, the closer one is to
the mainstream of the academic and social life of the college, the more likely
is one to perceive oneself as being congruent with the institution generally.
That perception impacts in turn upon one's institutional commitment. Both
act to enhance the likelihood of persistence. Conversely, the more removed
one is from the center of institutional life, that is, the more marginal one's
group is to the life of the college, the more likely is one to perceive oneself as
being separate from the institution. Though one may develop a strong attachment to the immediate group, one's attachment to the institution is likely to
be considerably weaker.

It bears repeating that absence of membership in one of the communities
in the mainstream of institutional life is not of itself a necessary and sufficient
condition for withdrawal. As noted above, membership in at least one sup-

portive community, whatever its relationship to the center, may be sufficient to insure continued persistence. Nevertheless, it does seem to be the case that students who identify themselves as being marginal to the mainstream of institutional life are somewhat more likely to withdraw. Of course, they themselves are less likely to leave than are students who see themselves as incongruent with any of the available communities.

There are, however, institutions which do not have a dominant subculture. These institutions are characterized by a diversity of subcultures or communities each with its own particular social and intellectual lifestyle. In such a case, one's community membership may have little to do with one's sense of institutional incongruence. Like large material bodies, centers often have their own gravitational field which binds people to the institution. The absence of a center or dominant culture may, in turn, result in loosely coupled institutions which lack the force to bind individuals to them. Higher institutional rates of departure may be the result.

Some institutions, however, are culturally pluralistic and inclusive, rather than exclusive, in their view of what constitutes "normative" behaviors and beliefs. They are likely to view the absence of a dominant culture as a positive state of affairs. In such settings all community membership, regardless of its rootedness, is valuable. Lacking any pervasive pattern of inequality that distinguishes "good" and "bad," "central" and "marginal" subcultures, such institutions may foster persistence, especially among traditionally under-represented students, through multiple patterns of community membership.

The point of making this observation is to remind us that the meaning individuals attach to community membership is very much a reflection of the culturally laden definitions members of the institution attach to different subcultures or subcommunities within the institution. To repeat, though it is apparent that membership in some type of community is important to persistence, its particular impact upon persistence in that institution is dependent on the prevailing ethos of the institution that specifies the relationships between different subcultures on campus and gives meaning to group and community membership.

It might be noted in passing that the notion of centrality and marginality is particularly evident in studies of the effect of Special Service Programs upon the persistence of disadvantaged, largely minority youth in institutions of higher education (Research Triangle Institute 1975, Systems Development Corporation 1981). That research suggests that there is an important association between program success (i.e., having a high proportion of its students persist) and its location within the mainstream of institutional life. Those programs whose students and staff identified themselves as being integrated within the mainstream were also those which were more successful in helping students complete their degree programs. The success of programs, like that of students, may also hinge upon their centrality to institutional life.

External Communities and Withdrawal from College

No institution is an island unto itself. With the possible exception of students at the most strictly contained residential institutions (e.g., military academies and small, isolated private colleges), most students find themselves exposed to a range of individuals and communities external to the college campus. Though they seek to become members of the new academic and social communities of the college, they often participate as well, in varying degrees, in communities external to the college. For many persons, especially those living at home or off campus, membership in external communities may play a pivotal role in persistence (Weidman 1985, Bean and Vesper 1990, Christie and Dinham 1991, Padilla 1991). For persons whose initial goal and/or institutional commitments are weak the impact of those communities may make the difference between persistence and departure. But they may do so in either a positive or negative fashion. When the value orientations of external communities are such as to support the goals of college education, they may aid persistence (Roth 1985, Bean and Vesper 1990). When they oppose them, the reverse may apply. For that reason one would expect that persons from cultural backgrounds and/or home communities with low rates of higher educational participation (e.g., persons from disadvantaged backgrounds) may face particularly severe handicaps in attempting to complete higher educational degree programs. In trying to do so they may frequently be forced to at least partially reject membership in communities that have been part of their upbringing. Centrality of participation in the life of the college may be achieved only by becoming marginal to the life of those communities. Padilla's (1991) study of Chicano students is, in this regard, quite revealing in that it highlights "the sense of social isolation" and "the strong pressures (they feel) by peers and significant others to maintain their ethnic allegiances and heritage" as they attempt to succeed in college (pp. 7–10).

Individuals who seek to retain past friendships while attending college may find the transition to college especially problematic. Christie and Dinham's (1991) study of beginning commuting and residential students at a large public university is especially illuminating. Students who retained their high school friends, especially those living off campus, tended to have the greatest difficulty in becoming socially integrated. As one student told an interviewer, "Most (of my friends) are from my high school, yeah. Not here (at the university)." (Christie and Dinham 1991, p.423).

In the same sense that external peer groups may hinder social integration in the college, so too may family pressures influence college persistence. Again quoting from Christie and Dinham's (1991) study, a student told an interviewer that "my parents have been really bugging me about it (transfer closer to home)." For that student and several others, parental influence was a major factor in their decision to withdraw (Christie and Dinham 1991, 427). But parental influence may also prove to be a positive element to persistence (see Bean and Vesper's [1990] finding for first-generation college students). To quote Nora, Castaneda, and Cabrera (1992), "Family support . . . increases the chances of students to successfully engage in interactions with faculty and peers on both social and academic levels. As a result . . . it is more likely that the student will persist to graduation" (p. 20).[15]

Though the competing external pressures of families and peers for disadvantaged students are no different in kind than those for other students, they may well be more intense. The conflict between the expectations of external communities and those of the college may be greater for disadvantaged students. Little wonder then that several researchers have noted the importance of residential programs for the retention of disadvantaged students in higher education (e.g., Muehl and Muehl 1972, Chickering 1974, Crosson 1988, Giles-Gee 1988). Yet if external family, peer, and work communities do have an effect on persistence, that effect may sometimes be positive. Take the case of students of color on most predominantly white campuses. While several studies point out the difficulties they often encounter in trying to make the transition to college (e.g., Lichtman, Bass, and Ager 1989, Flores 1992), a study by Roth (1985) of persistence among ninety-one Dominican students who entered the City College of New York in the fall of 1982 points out the ways in which strong links with pro-college family and community members aids persistence. Particularly revealing was the finding that persisting students felt that other Dominicans shared their belief in the importance of being college educated. Persistence may be aided by the existence of a supportive subculture in one's home community as well as within the college.

External Obligations and Withdrawal from College

In some cases, however, participation in external communities does hinder persistence. It does so because of the ways in which external obligations limit one's ability to meet the demands of college. Such obligations serve, in effect, to "pull" one away from participation in the local communities of the college. The obligations entailed in employment are a most obvious case in point. When employment is not tangential to but part of a larger career plan, the effects of work upon contact and therefore upon retention may be partic-

ularly great. In those situations, the demands of the external workplace may
be such as to direct the individual away from college-related activities. Spare
time may have to be spent in furthering one's work career, not one's educational career. Generally speaking, employment not only limits the time one
has for academic studies, it also severely limits one's opportunities for interaction with other students and faculty. As a consequence, one's social integration as well as one's academic performance suffers.

Problems of making contact are further complicated for adult learners
and/or for those students whose family obligations draw them away from
campus activities. In residential institutions, for instance, commuting students may face especially difficult problems in attempting to make contact
with faculty and other students. Frequently they are temporary visitors to the
campus, attending classes between other responsibilities. As a result they
tend to be less likely than residential students to be involved in the intellectual and social life of the institution and interact with the institution's major
agents of socialization, faculty and students (Chickering 1974, Bean 1990).
The same conclusion was reached by Nora and Wedham (1991) in their study
of students at an urban commuter campus. They found that students who had
more family responsibilities (e.g., taking care of siblings and housework)
and a hard work schedule were less likely to interact with faculty and peers
and, therefore, less likely to be involved both socially and academically in
their college.

But here several important caveats are called for. The effect of employment upon persistence depends in part on how the employer views college
attendance. In some situations, employers may see it in their interest that
their employees spend time on campus and acquire skills and/or degrees associated with college attendance. Thus the notion of "cooperative education." At the same time, the impact of work upon persistence also depends
on the amount of employment and the degree to which it removes the individual from campus life. Though employment is generally associated with
lower rates of college persistence, full-time work is clearly more harmful
than part-time. Similarly, working off campus is more clearly related to leaving than is on-campus employment. Indeed some forms of work on campus,
for instance part-time work-study programs, appear to somewhat improve
one's chances of finishing a degree program (Astin 1975). In this instance,
on-campus employment seems to enhance one's interaction with other members of the institution and heighten one's integration into the life of the college.

The impact of work and family obligations may not, however, be the same
for all students. Studies of retention among married students, for example,
suggest that family responsibilities may sometimes hinder persistence but
may do so more for females than for males. Though being married is gener-

ally associated with higher rates of persistence among men, it is often related to lower rates of completion among women (Astin 1975). In the former case, the family may work to aid the student's progress. In the latter case, it may constrain progress by insisting that the female continue to be housewife and mother as well as college student. Among Chicana students, for example, women leavers typically report extensive family duties as a prime cause of their inability to complete a college degree program (Chacon, Cohen, and Strover 1983). Interestingly, this appears to be true also for single Chicanas, who are often required to perform family duties in their homes.

Finally, it should be noted that significant changes in family and/or work obligations may also lead to departure, but not necessarily to permanent departure. Thus the observation that the primary difference between many "stopouts" and permanent withdrawals is not that they experience any different external demands on their time but that the former's commitment to college and experience on campus is such as to draw them back into college when external situations change.

Finances and College Persistence

Although finances are very commonly cited by researchers and withdrawing students alike as important reasons for leaving, the evidence regarding the impact of finances upon persistence leads one to conclude that the issue is much more complex than commonly assumed. Though there is little doubt that personal finances can and do impact upon persistence, there is still some question about how and why they do so.

Generally, the effect of finances upon departure appears to be largely indirect and to be long-term as well as short-term in character. Apparently much of the impact of finances upon persistence occurs before or at the point of entry into higher education (Jackson and Weathersby 1975, Jackson 1978, Cabrera, Stampen, and Hansen 1990). Family finances affect persistence indirectly through their influence on educational goals (Baum 1987, Cabrera 1987, Cabrera, Stampen, and Hansen 1990). The question of finances will not only influence decisions on whether to attend college in the first place and how much education to seek, but also shape choices as to the specific college into which entry is sought (Tierney 1980). This in turn may influence subsequent persistence.

Financial considerations may also induce persons to enter institutions in ways which over the long run may increase the likelihood of departure prior to degree completion. For instance, they may lead persons to initially enter relatively low-cost public two-year institutions as a means of lowering the overall cost of completing a four-year program, or to choose a second-choice, less expensive public institution rather than the more expensive preferred private institution. Manski and Wise (1983) argue, for example, that the primary impact of Basic Education Opportunity Grants has been to enhance enrollments among lower-income students in the two-year college sector. The same grants among middle- and upper-income groups (nearly 40 percent of all BEOG monies go to those persons) appear not to have altered their patterns of college-going.

Financial considerations may also lead individuals to obtain part-time work while attending college. In this case, students modify their form of participation rather than their choice of institution. But in doing so they also constrain their ability to spend time on campus interacting with other members of the institution, both faculty and student peers (Cabrera, Nora, and Castaneda 1992). In either case, the net effect of altered choice may be to enhance the likelihood of permanent departure or bring about transfer to a less expensive institution.[16]

Beyond entry, finances may influence departure directly. Marked short-term changes may prevent the individual from meeting the minimum financial requirements of institutional participation. This is especially likely among those segments of the college population whose available financial resources are already quite limited, namely the disadvantaged and children from less affluent families (Manski and Wise 1983). It is also more likely to arise in the early stages of the college career when the goal of college completion is still quite remote. When the potential benefits of college graduation are still quite distant and subject to some uncertainty, the costs of obtaining that degree tend to weigh more heavily in decisions regarding persistence than they do much later after a sizable proportion of the costs have already been borne and the likelihood of obtaining the degree is considerably greater.

For most families, however, these effects occur at the margin of decision making regarding college attendance and are but one element in the broader weighing of the total costs and benefits of college attendance (Murdock 1987). Though there undoubtedly are many students, primarily the disadvantaged, for whom the question of finances is absolutely central to decisions regarding continuance, for most students the question of finances occurs within the broader context of costs generally and of the character of their educational experiences within a specific institution.

It might be noted, in this context, that institutional studies of departing students (e.g., exit surveys) that ask students to indicate reasons for their leaving often yield quite misleading findings. Though departing students very often cite financial problems as reasons for their leaving, such statements are frequently ex post facto forms of rationalization which mask primary reasons for their withdrawal. Students who see their college experiences as rewarding and/or as being directly tied to their adult futures will continue to bear great financial burdens and accept considerable short-term debt in order to complete a degree program. When college is seen as irrelevant and/or as unrewarding, however, even the slightest financial pressure will lead to withdrawal.

The point here is rather simple, namely that the citing of financial problems as reasons for departure is often merely an end product of decisions regarding departure. It reflects the weighing of benefits as well as of costs and as such mirrors the nature of the student's academic and social experiences on campus.

Fluctuation in Financial Resources

This does not mean, however, that widespread short-term fluctuations in the availability of financial support will not have a significant impact upon overall patterns of persistence. After choices have been made and college careers begun, short-term alterations in the amount of financial aid or family support can and often does lead students to alter their educational participation. Significant economic shifts, changes in student loan programs, unexpected changes in family and/or individual finances, and termination of part-time employment may all act to significantly reduce the available resources students have at their disposal for college attendance. For some students, especially those whose financial situations are already tentative, such changes over the short term may well spell the difference between college attendance and at least temporary withdrawal. Others may change their forms of participation. Some students, those unable to obtain supplementary aid, may shift their enrollment from full- to part-time. They and others may enter the job market either in part-time or full-time employment. Others still may leave their initial institution in order to transfer to less expensive colleges and universities.

Over the long term, one would expect such changes to lead individuals and families to readjust their collegiate plans so as to take account of the altered availability of financial aid. That is, one would expect economic shifts to alter patterns of college choice more than it would patterns of persistence. Families and individuals may, for instance, shift their choices to local colleges and/or to less costly public rather than private institutions. They may also alter their forms of participation in order to make time for employment. Increased part-time attendance may be the result, especially for those whose resources are already quite limited (Mortenson 1991). And of course some families may decide not to invest in any form of higher education whatsoever. For them, the question of persistence is a moot one.

The Impact of Financial Aid on Persistence

The apparent fact that personal or family finances do not, in themselves, play a major direct role in persistence *following entry* does not mean that financial aid given to needy students *upon entry* cannot enhance persistence. Quite the contrary. The evidence accumulated over the past decade, especially over the last five years, indicates that financial aid does impact upon student persistence (e.g., Olivas 1986, Stampen and Cabrera 1986, 1988, Murdock 1987, Stampen and Fenske 1988, Nora 1990, and St. John, Kirshstein, and Noell 1991). Among four-year colleges Stampen and Cabrera (1988) found that aided students of low- income origins had rates of persistence comparable to those of non-aided students. To quote Stampen and Cabrera, financial "aid effectively compensates for the disadvantage of low income by making low-income students as likely to persist in college as higher income students who do not receive aid." (p. 29). The same conclusion, for both two- and four-year colleges, was reached a decade earlier by Peng and Fetters (1977) in a longitudinal study of the high school graduating class of 1966. In effect, the overall impact of "student financial aid appears to eliminate financial reasons for dropping out of college" (Stampen and Cabrera 1986, 34). In part, its impact is that it provides students the freedom to engage in social and additional academic activities that further the likelihood of persistence (Cabrera, Nora, and Castaneda 1992).

The question might then be posed as to the type of financial-aid packaging that most enhances the likelihood of persistence. Here the research is less than clear. Studies of the impact of loans, grants, work-study, and other forms of aid packaging have yielded somewhat mixed results (Astin 1975, Terkla 1985, Carroll 1987, 1988, Leslie and Brinkman 1988, Stampen and Cabrera 1988, St.John, Kirshstein, and Noell 1991). Generally, the growing consensus among researchers is that grants and work-study are more effective in promoting persistence than are loans and other forms of aid. As noted earlier, the impact of work-study as a form of financial assistance upon persistence is twofold. On one hand it provides much needed financial aid. On the other, it leads students to make contact with other people on campus, in particular faculty and staff. As a result, work-study alters both the cost and benefit side of the economic equation.

This does not mean, however, that financial aid is, in and of itself, a major contributor to persistence *for most students*. Though it is significantly associated with persistence, a meta-analysis of over fifty studies of persistence found that it had a "less than small" effect (Murdock 1987, 91). The reasons for this finding are relatively clear, namely that financial aid is but one of a wider number of events that shape persistence (Stampen and Cabrera 1986). Financial impact is generally conditioned by the nature of student experiences on campus and the weighing of the costs and benefits of attendance.

Though financial aid does indeed alter the cost side of the equation, making college attendance as possible for low-income students as it does of more well-to-do students, it has, with the possible exception of work-study, little impact upon the benefit side of the equation. Nor does it appear to alter the skills students bring with them into the college setting. These, as noted earlier, also shape persistence. But of course the primary goal of financial aid is to remove finances as a cause of attrition. That it seems to do, at least in large measure.

It must be noted that while this conclusion, like those regarding other roots of attrition, holds for most students, it may not apply equally well for each and every subgroup of students. Nor need it apply equally well for every type of institution in which students find themselves. Though it is important to know of the broad forces that shape persistence in the aggregate, our knowledge of attrition must eventually be informed by the particular person and the particular setting with which we are dealing.

Involvement, Learning, and Leaving

Before we turn to a discussion of how the roots of leaving differ for different students and institutions of higher education, we must first review some very recent evidence regarding the impact of involvement upon student learning. This is the case not only because the issue of learning is important in its own right, but also because it has become evident that there is a critical and still unexplored link between student learning experiences and student leaving. Simply put, the same forces of contact and involvement that influence persistence also appear to shape student learning. Though the research is far from complete, it is apparent that the more students are involved in the social and intellectual life of a college, the more frequently they make contact with faculty and other students about learning issues, especially outside the class, the more students are likely to learn (Wilson, Gaff, Dienst, Wood and Bavry 1975, Terenzini and Wright 1987a, 1987b, Ory and Braskamp 1988, and Astin 1991). The same can be said of student affective development and critical thinking skills (Pascarella 1985b, Pascarella Ethington, and Smart 1988, Pascarella 1989, and Pascarella and Terenzini 1991) and of the development of humanitarian/civic values (Pascarella, Ethington, and Smart 1988). Students who become involved with faculty and other students are more likely to develop values stressing the importance of involvement with others. Involvement leads to the appreciation of the need for involvement and both lead, in turn, to an increased likelihood that students will continue to be involved in the future.

Even among those who persist, wide-ranging contact with faculty, especially outside the class, is associated with heightened intellectual and social development. And this is the case even after one takes account of differences in ability, prior levels of development, and prior educational experience (Endo and Harpel 1982). In other words, student contact with faculty, especially outside class, is an *independent* predictor of learning gain or growth.

In this context, one can refer to the body of research on faculty mentoring and its effects on student satisfaction and academic success (Cosgrove 1986, Pascarella, Terenzini, and Hibel 1978, Merriam, Thomas and Zeph 1987, Jacobi 1991, Valadez and Duran 1991). Cosgrove's study (1986) is especially helpful, because it sought to control for the inevitable self-selection that confounds studies of the effect of student-faculty contact; namely, it proceeded on the assumption that the occurrence of such contact may be largely the reflection of student attributes (e.g., commitment and ability). In this case, students who volunteered for the mentoring program were randomly assigned to treatment and control groups. Even after controlling for individual attributes such as ability, residence, and gender, Cosgrove found that students who participated in a mentoring program were more satisfied with the university and showed greater developmental gains than were students in the control group. Contact with faculty appears then to promote student development in ways that can be distinguished from other attributes of students that foster development.

Admittedly, contact with one's student peers may, for some students, somewhat compensate for insufficient contact with the faculty. Membership in the informal social system of the college may offset the absence of participation in the academic and intellectual life of the institution as constructed by faculty and staff (Stage 1989b). But it may do so at some expense to students'intellectual and social development (Theophilides and Terenzini 1981, Endo and Harpel 1982). Development is greatest when students interact with both faculty and student peers (Astin 1993).

Involvement and Student Effort

Another related strain of research regarding the linkage between involvement and learning is to be found in Robert Pace's (1980, 1984) work on the relationship between student effort and learning. A basic assumption of Pace's work is that what a student gets out of college depends not only on what the college does but also on the degree and quality of effort the student puts into college. In this view, it matters less where a student goes to college than what that student does once he or she gets there.

The "Quality of Effort" scales he developed to tap the extent and range of student usage of institution resources has now been used in both two- and four-year collegiate settings (e.g., Friedlander 1980, Amos 1990, and Kaufman and Creamer 1991). Though research is far from complete on this topic, it is evident that quality of student effort is significantly related not only to student growth and development (e.g., Kaufman and Creamer 1991) but also to student persistence (Ory and Braskamp 1988, Pascarella and Terenzini 1991, Tinto, Goodsell, and Russo 1993). Tinto, Goodsell, and Russo's (1993) study, like that of Ory and Braskamp's (1988) study is particularly revealing, because it demonstrates that the relationship between effort and gain is not simply a function of student ability, but a reflection of student involvement in the college setting.

Linking Learning and Leaving

The point of our referring to this body of work is not simply that learning and persistence are both shaped by contact and by quality of effort. Rather, there appears to be an important linkage between learning and persistence that arises from the interplay of involvement and the quality of student effort. Involvement with one's peers and with the faculty, both inside and outside the classroom, is itself positively related to the quality of student effort and in turn to both learning and persistence. And students who report having made learning gains while in college are more likely to persist, other things being equal (Tinto and Froh 1992, Tinto, Goodsell, Russo 1993). To paraphrase a comment by one student observer, students who learn are more likely to want to remain in college in order to continue learning.

The importance of this emerging line of research, as we shall argue in the next two chapters, is twofold. First it leads us to a more complex understanding of the importance of integration or involvement for student development and in turn persistence. It argues that such involvement, social and academic, with peers and faculty, impacts upon persistence directly and indirectly via its effect on the quality of effort student exhibit for their own learning. In this manner, it moves the argument about Pace's research one step beyond the notion that students are responsible for their own effort—that is, that it primarily mirrors the attributes of students—to the more complex notion that institutions also influence the quality of student effort via their capacity to involve students with other members of the institution, faculty, staff, and student peers. In other words, students will be more likely to invest in greater effort to learn where they become involved as members of the college community.

Second, this line of research enables us to frame the issue of student persistence in terms that are broader than the one typically used to describe attrition on most campuses, namely that it is largely a social matter for the staff of student affairs. If anything, the above evidence would lead one to argue that it is as much an academic matter, one that concerns the faculty as much as it might concern those in student affairs (Tinto 1989). It is for this reason that Neumann and Neumann's (1989) study of junior and senior persistence at a northeastern university is so revealing. Their study emphasizes what they refer to as a "Quality of Learning Experience" approach wherein persistence is conceptually linked to student perceptions of the quality of their learning environments and their interaction with faculty about learning issues. In this case, junior and senior persistence was significantly related to student involvement in learning activities, student views of the quality of teaching, advising, and coursework, and student contact with faculty. One of the points Neumann and Neumann make is the possibility that as students progress from freshman to senior years, their persistence is increasingly shaped by educational issues.

Individual and Institutional Variations in the Process of Student Departure

Though research on the departure of different types of students in different types of institutions has tended to reaffirm the overall character of departure, it has, in the last ten years in particular, also highlighted a number of significant differences both in the sources and the frequency of various forms of student leaving. The most noticeable are those which occur among students of different race, age, sex, and social class, and among institutions of different level (two- and four-year), residential character (commuting and non-commuting), and size.

In describing these differences, we must be careful, however, to avoid the tendency to attribute to each and every member of a group of individuals or institutions the characteristics which may serve to describe the group generally. It would be a serious mistake to assume that all group members are alike in their experience of higher education or that all institutions, however similar in structure, exhibit similar patterns of student leaving. This is particularly true in studies of "students of color" and "adult students." Nevertheless, to the extent that we can talk of *aggregate* differences in patterns of departure between groups of students and types of institutions, so too can we talk of the character of the forces which shape the experience of different individuals in varying institutional settings. In so doing, we can move toward both the formulation of a theory of institutional departure and the development of policies which are sensitive to individual and institutional differences. But as we do so, we must remind ourselves that policy is best founded on knowledge of the specific individuals and institutions for which that policy is intended.

Variation in Departure Among Differing Groups of Students

DEPARTURE AMONG STUDENTS OF DIFFERENT ETHNICITY AND SOCIAL CLASS

Studies of departure among students of different race and social class have focused almost entirely on black students (e.g., Tracey and Sedlacek 1987, Nettles 1988, Lichtman, Bass, and Ager 1989, Hood 1990, Thompson and Fretz 1991) and Hispanic students (e.g., Padilla and Pavel 1986, Nora 1987, 1990, Attinasi 1989, Flores 1992). For the most part, these studies support the contention that departure among black and Hispanic students, like that among white students, reflects both issues of social contact/congruence and academic performance.

But relative to white students, attrition among these groups tends to be more a reflection of academic difficulties than of social ones (Kendrick and Thomas 1970, Shaffer 1973, Sedlacek and Webster 1978, Allen et al. 1982, Eddins 1982, Gosman et al. 1983, Donovan 1984). Since under-represented students, as a group, are more likely to come from disadvantaged backgrounds and to have experienced inferior schooling prior to college, they are also more likely to enter college with serious academic deficiencies. It is therefore not surprising that Eddins's (1982) longitudinal study of attrition among specially admitted black students at the University of Pittsburgh, like Donovan's (1984) multi-institution study of low-income black students, finds that their departure is primarily determined by the nature of their on-campus academic behaviors, especially those pertaining to the meeting of the formal demands of the academic system.

Recent studies by Tracey and Sedlacek (1985, 1987) extend our view of the role of academic integration in the persistence of disadvantaged black students. Specifically, they note that the ability of students to meet academic standards is related not only to academic skills, as Eddins (1982) notes, but also to positive academic self-concept, realistic self-appraisal, and familiarity with the academic requirements and demands of the institution (also see Pascarella, Smart, Ethington, and Nettles 1987). In their view, noncognitive components of academic integration are more important to the persistence of black students than they are to that of white students (Tracey and Sedlacek 1987). Having the requisite skills for persistence is one thing. Being able to apply them in perhaps strange, unfriendly settings is another.

But academic performance in predominantly white institutions, as Fleming (1985) and Martin (1990) so aptly point out, is also a reflection of black student experiences within the classrooms, laboratories, and offices of the institution and the support they find in those places. As Fleming (1985) did earlier, Martin finds that black students are more likely to succeed academically and persist when they believe there is support for their efforts and equity in assessing their work. Minority retention mirrors, she argues, the academic climate in which minority students find themselves as much as it does their academic abilities (also see Crosson 1988). Academic climates that discourage and discriminate, however subtly, are also climates that give rise to student failure and departure.

This is not to say, however, that social issues outside the classroom do not matter. For black students, as much as for white students, social involvement also influences persistence (Suen 1983, Allen 1985, Martin 1990). But the types of involvement, activities, and interpersonal relationships which lead to effective social integration of minority students may not be the same as those for majority students. Pascarella's (1985a, 1985c) nine-year follow-up of persistence among black and white students in over 350 four-year colleges and universities, for instance, suggests that social integration among black students may be somewhat more influenced by formal forms of association (e.g., serving on a university or department committee) than is the case for white students generally. For the latter group of students, informal types of association (e.g., contact with one's peers) appear to matter most.

Students of color, specially admitted or not, face particularly severe problems in gaining access to the mainstream of social life in largely white institutions (Loo and Rolison 1986, Attinasi 1989). Beyond the existence of possible discrimination, students of color may find it especially difficult to find and become a member of a supportive community within the college. Besides the important question of there being on campus a critical mass of persons of like backgrounds and interests from which viable communities can be formed, there is the related question of the range of available supportive communities. Sharing a common racial origin—or any other single attribute for that matter—is no guarantee of the sharing of common interests and dispositions. Though differences in racial origins do not preclude commonality of interests and dispositions, it is the case that on all but the very largest campuses students of color have relatively fewer options as to the types of communities in which to establish membership than do white students. In such situation, they are more likely to experience a sense of isolation and/or of incongruence than are white students generally.

But even when a supportive social and intellectual community is found, questions remain as to the degree to which that membership will be central to the mainstream of institutional life. It bears repeating that national evaluations of Special Service Programs indicate that the success of a program and that of its students hinge upon the degree to which administrators and students alike perceive themselves as central to the daily life of the institution. Perhaps it is not surprising that perceptions of centrality are relatively uncommon among such programs and that students of color generally are less likely than white students to see themselves as being integrated within the mainstream of life in largely white colleges. A sense of marginality is regrettably more common. And where a sense of marginality exists, when students see themselves located in enclaves, departure is more likely (Murguia, Padilla, and Pavel 1991).

Finally, some evidence exists to suggest that finances and financial aid may be more important to disadvantaged students from traditionally underrepresented groups than it is for white students generally (Olivas 1986, Stampen and Fenske 1988, Nora 1990). Nora's (1990) very careful study of financial aid and retention among Chicano community college students argues that the interplay between financial aid (campus and noncampus based) and financial resources is paramount to their persistence. In the particular research in question, both factors were found to have a larger impact on retention than did students' high school grades and their accumulative grade-point average at the two-year institution (p. 326). Unfortunately, without disentangling the multiple effects of low-income and community-college attendance, we have no way of knowing whether this finding is specific to Chicano students or is a reflection of the economic conditions facing students attending two-year colleges.

For students of color then, especially for those from disadvantaged backgrounds, departure appears, in large measure, not to differ so much in kind as in degree. They tend to face greater problems in meeting the academic demands of college work, in finding a suitable niche in the social and intellectual life of the college, and perhaps in obtaining sufficient financial resources. Academic difficulties, incongruence, isolation, and perhaps finances seem to be more severe for them than for students generally.

But this conclusion should not be taken to suggest that the experience of students of color on campus can be understood by simply extrapolating the experiences of white students. As several authors have correctly pointed out, racism as a source of isolation on campus is not merely a matter of degree (Lowe 1989, Martin 1990, Johnson and Rodriquez 1991). It is a matter of qualitative differences in how individuals are valued and treated. Though the terms "isolation" and "marginality" refer to the same concepts as they do for white students, the way they are understood by students of color may be very different. Thus the use of the term "enclaves" to describe how Hispanic students understand their community on a predominantly white campus (Murguia, Padilla, and Pavel 1991).

At the same time, one should not be left with the impression that these issues are solely a reflection of black versus white or of poor versus rich. At least as the matter pertains to the questions of isolation and marginality, it is likely that somewhat similar conclusions would hold for any group of students who find themselves to be noticeably different from most students on campus. For rural Appalachian youth in the higher educational institutions of the South and Midwest, for foreign students in American universities, for students with disabilities, and quite possibly for older adults generally, there may be similar problems of social integration and therefore quite similar hurdles to be overcome in attempting to complete college.[17] Though it is undeniably the case that the position of minorities in America, especially that of blacks, Hispanic, and native American students, is unique in a number of very important ways, it is also the case that the issues of marginality and isolation on majority campuses are not unique to them alone.

VARIATION IN DEPARTURE AMONG STUDENTS OF DIFFERENT AGE AND SEX

Turning from the attributes of race and social class to those of age and sex, one quickly becomes aware of the limits of our understanding of the variations in the character of student departure. The fact is that even with the recent surge of interest in persistence we still know relatively little about the specific attributes of attrition among females and adults. Yet common experiences would tell us that the experience of older students and of females differ, at least in part, from that of the younger male college student.

In some respects, the experience of adult students is not unlike that of minority students. They too can feel marginal to the mainstream of institutional life. Besides having different values and different dispositions, older students are especially subject to external demands which may constrain their interaction with other members of the college (Boshier 1973, Cross 1981, Garrison 1985, Naretto 1991, Weidman 1985). They are more likely than the typical beginning college student to be married, to have children at home, to live off campus, and/or to be employed while attending college. Unlike the typical youthful high school graduate who goes to college *instead of doing something else,* the typical adult student goes to college *in addition to doing other things.* Adults are thus more likely to encounter greater problems in finding on-campus time to spend making contact with faculty and student peers and off-campus time to study enough to meet the minimum academic standards of the institution. For those whose commitment to the goal of college completion is weak, the difficulties they face appear to be instrumental in their failure to complete their degree programs.

Because of external obligations, adults students are more likely to be responsive to the employment outcomes of college than are most other students. For them going to college is more frequently a matter of economic needs than it is a youthful rite of passage. It is for that reason then that persistence among adults appears to be both a function of their commitment and the perceived utility of their education for future employment (Metzner and

Bean 1987). This does not mean that older students are less committed to college than younger students. Rather it is to say that their commitment to college is influenced by other commitments to family and work. Nevertheless, it remains the case that like students generally the persistence of adult students, however shaped by external obligations, is still influenced by the availability of supportive faculty and student groups on campus (Ashar and Skenes 1993, Naretto 1991).

In some measure, the same observations also apply to a discussion of differences in departure among male and female students. Despite significant gains for women in rates of both college entry and completion, evidence from a variety of sources continues to suggest that the experience of females in college is somewhat different from that of males (Astin 1975, Gosman et al. 1983, Magolda 1990). Females generally, and certainly those from specific ethnic groups, are more likely than males are to face external pressures which constrain their educational participation (Chacon, Cohen, and Strover 1983). This is particularly evident, as noted earlier, among married women. As Astin (1975) reports, while being married enhances the likelihood that men will complete college, it reduces the probability of women's doing so (pp. 44–45).

At the same time, the departure of females is, relative to that of males, more determined by social forces than by academic ones and therefore is influenced more by forms of social integration (Alexander and Eckland 1974, Pascarella and Terenzini 1983, Stage 1989a).

Female departure differs as well in the form that leaving takes. As a group, females are more likely to depart voluntarily than are males, whereas males are more likely to stay in college until forced to leave for academic reasons. Presumably the press for occupational attainment remains stronger among males. Not only are females less likely to be enrolled in occupation-specific programs of study, they are also less likely to plan to enter occupations after college (Astin, Hemond, and Richardson 1982, Astin, Korn, and Berz 1990).

The implication one draws from such findings is that women's departure, like that of minorities generally, differs from that of men's in a number of ways which extend beyond the boundaries of the college. It also seems to mirror the existence of wider social forces which continue, albeit in diminished fashion, to mold the expectations of people regarding the role women ought to play in society. Though there is ample evidence to suggest that this situation is changing, we have yet to observe those changes in studies of persistence among men and women.

Variation in Departure among Different Types of Institutions

DEPARTURE AMONG COMMUTING AND TWO-YEAR INSTITUTIONS

Compared to patterns of departure in largely residential institutions, departure from commuting colleges appears to be influenced less by social events than by strictly academic matters (Zaccaria and Creaser 1971, Pascarella et al. 1981, Pascarella and Chapman 1983, Pascarella, Duby, and Iverson 1983, Pascarella and Wolfle 1985, Williamson and Creamer 1988, Stage 1989a, Schwartz 1990, Staats and Partio 1990, and Webb 1990) and more influenced by external forces which shape the character of students' lives off campus than by events internal to the campus (Chacon, Cohen, and Strover 1983, Weidman 1985, and Schwartz 1990).

Presumably this points up the obvious fact that most commuting colleges do not possess significant on-campus student communities. Nor do they attract students who are likely or able to spend a great deal of time interacting socially on campus. Many students come to campus for very limited periods of time solely for the purpose of meeting their classes and attending to the formal requirements of degree completion. Their participation in the social life of the college is understandably quite limited. Conversely, their lives are much more shaped by the character of external forces—family, community, and work—which dominate their daily existence (Webb 1990). This is especially true in urban colleges that serve large numbers of working students. It is not surprising, therefore, that social congruency and social isolation appear not to be as important to the question of persistence and departure as they might be among residential institutions, and that prior intentions, commitments, academic performance, and external forces appear to be relatively more determinate of individual decisions to withdraw.

The same may also be said to apply to two-year colleges, especially to those in the public sector. Two-year-college students, like commuting students generally, are much more likely to be working while in college, attending part-time rather than full-time, and/or living at home while in college than are students in the four-year sector. They, too, are likely to experience a wide range of competing external pressures on their time and energies and to be unable to spend significant amounts of time on campus interacting with other students and members of the staff.

But it does not follow, as some researchers have claimed (Voorhees 1987), that informal contact with faculty, staff, and students on campus may not be important to persistence of students in two-year and nonresidential colleges. Though it is evident that those institutions typically do not have significant social communities on campus and that informal contact between faculty, staff, and students may not be as wide-ranging, there are reasons to believe that informal social and intellectual contact beyond the classroom may also be important to persistence in commuting colleges (Pascarella, Smart, and Ethington 1985). But it may apply less for the average student than for those who are marginal with regard to college completion.[18] A particularly revealing piece of research, in this regard, is a recent ethnographic study by Neumann (1985) of student persistence in a northeastern urban community college. Neumann selected for study a group of students who, by institutional standards, were deemed unlikely to complete their degree program (i.e., high-risk students). Specifically he focused on those individuals who did in fact complete their degree programs. The question was posed whether there were any differences in the pattern of their experiences which could be said to distinguish them from similar students who did not complete their degree programs. Contrary to the conclusions of past quantitative studies of departure in nonresidential institutions, he found that social contact was a consistently expressed theme in the students' accounts of their own success. Far from being unimportant, contact with other persons, especially a member of the faculty, was seen by individuals as being instrumental in their having completed their programs of study.

It is interesting that Pascarella, Smart, and Ethington (1985) came to the same conclusion in their long-term study of persistence among seventy-two two-year colleges. Contrary to earlier research on commuting institutions (e.g, Pascarella, Duby, and Iverson 1983), they found social contact to be important. In this instance, however, they followed students over a nine-year period rather than over the two-year period typical of earlier studies. Thus, it may be argued that prior studies of departure in two-year and possibly in commuting institutions may have underestimated the effects of social contact by focusing only on a very narrow range of student behaviors, namely those which led to completion in two years. In terms of social contact, the long-term process of student leaving from two-year colleges may not be substantially different from that which marks leaving from four-year institutions.

In other respects, however, there are important differences. These reflect both the particular character of two-year colleges and the sorts of students who typically attend them. Students in two-year colleges are less likely to hold lofty educational goals than are students in the four-year sector (Astin 1975, Astin, Korn, and Berz 1990) and are more likely to intend to depart prior to program completion even when holding lofty goals (Cross 1971). It is quite evident, for example, that a sizable number of two-year-college students leave their college prior to the completion of their degree program in order to transfer to a four-year college. For many, if not most, such departures are an intended, though often unstated, part of their educational plans. Their leaving is a reflection not of a lack of intention or weakness of commitment, but of the very character of those dispositions. At the same time, it also mirrors the continuing role two-year colleges play as lower-level entry points into the higher educational system. It is a role which enables them to attract a wide variety of students who might not otherwise go on to college, but who also might be inclined to transfer before completing their degree programs.

What is particularly interesting is the possibility raised by Nora (1987), Nora and Rendon (1990), and most recently by Russo and Tinto (1992) that the intent to transfer may itself be a reflection of positive academic and social experiences in a two-year college. That is to say that successful academic and social experiences may serve to heighten one's goals and thereby lead to transfer to a four-year institution when that was not one's initial intent (Nora and Rendon 1990). Of the many possible experiences that may have this effect, classroom experiences may be particularly important to empowering students and thereby broadening their vision of what is possible (Russo and Tinto 1992).

It should also be observed that departure from two-year college also reflects the fact that two-year-college students are, on the average, academically less able or less well prepared to meet the academic demands of college work. Even though two-year colleges are academically less demanding than are four-year colleges, academic dismissal appears somewhat more frequent among the former institutions than among the latter. Again, it is part of the mission of two-year colleges generally and public junior colleges in particular to provide an opportunity for higher education to those students whose prior academic work would not otherwise enable them to enter higher education. That a greater proportion of such students leave because of an inability to meet the academic demands of college is not surprising.[19]

SIZE, DIVERSITY, AND PATTERNS OF INSTITUTIONAL DEPARTURE

The effect of size and diversity upon patterns of student departure can be best described as being two-pronged. While increased size heightens the possibility that the institution will house a greater variety of social and intellectual communities, it lessens the likelihood that students will have extensive contacts with faculty and staff. The reverse appears to apply to small colleges. Though they tend to be more socially and intellectual homogeneous, they normally provide for greater contact with faculty and staff (Astin 1975, Pascarella and Wolfle 1985). Consequently, while departure from large institutions is somewhat more likely to mirror isolation than incongruence, departure from small colleges is more likely to reflect incongruence.

For some students, especially those who have difficulty in making new acquaintances, the distant, relatively impersonal world of very large institutions may limit their social and intellectual integration. Though congruent communities may be available, these students are unable to make the personal contacts which lead to community membership. They would find the world of the small college more suited to their needs. For students who are unlike other students, however, small size and closeness may not help. Indeed it may act to undermine persistence by magnifying individual differences from the norm. Too much closeness, for some students, may be an undesirable state of affairs. The problem then for small institutions is often one of stimulating diversity, while that of large ones is of encouraging personal contact among often quite disparate individuals and communities.

It is noteworthy, in this regard, that studies which highlight the importance of fit between the individual and the institution are also studies of generally quite small and/or very homogeneous institutional settings. Rootman's (1972) study of voluntary withdrawal from the Coast Guard Academy, for example, finds that the closer the perceived fit between the person's perception of himself and that of the so-called "ideal" graduate, the more likely is persistence. In the smaller, homogeneous setting of the Academy, the "ideal" graduate serves to describe the prevailing ethos of the institution as seen in its students. In larger, more heterogeneous institutions such descriptions may not be possible.[20]

It bears repeating that the effects of homogeneity and isolation may, in some circumstances, be overshadowed by other attributes of the institution which attract students in the first place. In the case of the military academies, for instance, prior commitment to a military career may more than offset the effects of isolation. Similarly, institutions of high prestige may be more likely to hold students until graduation because of the belief among students that graduation from those institutions is likely to yield important occupational and economic benefits (Kamens 1971). These situations, however, are in the minority. In most colleges and universities, experiences within the college after entry are primary sources of student departure.

Concluding Observations

Individual departure from institutions of higher education arises from several major causes or roots. These have been described here as intention, commitment, adjustment, difficulty, congruence, isolation, obligations, and finances. The first two pertain to dispositions with which individuals enter institutions of higher education, the next four to experiences they have after entry, and the latter two to external forces which impinge upon their experiences within the institution.

Roughly speaking, student departure takes two forms, academic dismissal and voluntary withdrawal. The latter is the more common. As far as we can tell, only 15 to 25 percent of all institutional departures arise because of academic failure. For the most part, those departures reflect the inability and/or unwillingness of the person to meet the minimum academic requirements of college work. Though they often reflect individual abilities, they also mirror poor study habits and deficiencies in study skills. It is one thing to have the intellectual capacity for college, it is another to be able to apply it to the daily tasks of college work.

But for most departures, leaving has little to do with the inability to meet formal academic requirements. Indeed in some instances individuals who leave voluntarily achieve higher grade-point averages and are found to be somewhat more committed and creative than the typical persister. In these cases, leaving appears to reflect, on one hand, significant differences in the intentions and commitments with which they enter college and, on the other, real differences in the character of individual integrative experiences in the formal and informal academic and social communities of the college. The latter experiences have been described here as relating to the problems of adjustment to college life, to the issue of congruence between the individual and the institution, and to that of isolation from the life of the college.

Voluntary departure appears to be the result more of what goes on after entry into the institution than of what may have occurred beforehand. Though it is obvious that pre-entry experiences, for instance as measured by intentions and commitments, do affect subsequent departure, research supports the notion argued here that the character of one's integrative experiences after entry is central to the process of voluntary withdrawal. Of particular importance are those experiences which arise from the daily interactions between students and faculty inside and outside the classroom. Other things being equal, the more frequent and the more rewarding those interactions are seen to be by the student, the more likely the student is to persist—indeed, the more likely he or she is to develop socially and intellectually.

But not all persons are identical, nor are all institutions alike in their structure and student bodies. Though it is obvious that all students must attend to the same general set of problems in seeking to persist until degree completion, not all enter with the same sets of skills and dispositions, nor experience higher education in the same manner. Similarly, though all institutions face the same general set of issues in seeking to insure the persistence of their students, different types of institutions are constrained by somewhat different forces which determine the nature of institutional life. Thus one can discern a number of significant differences between groups of individuals (identified here by race, social class, sex, and age) and between types of institutions (classified by level, size, and residential character) in both the patterning and roots of student departure. Though the research on these issues is still quite limited, it does appear, for instance, that the departure of students of color arises from a somewhat different mixture of events than that of majority students, and that patterns and roots of departure among commuting colleges are not identical to those observed among residential institutions.

There is much that still remains unclear. The question of the role of personality is still unresolved. Though it is obvious that individual personality must affect individual departure, we have yet to discern anything resembling a "personality of departure." To date, our constructs of personality have yet to capture in a reliable fashion specific attributes which underlie individual responses to experiences within different institutions of higher education.

Similarly, we have yet to find strong evidence to support the contention by some observers that finances are an important cause of student departure. Though it is undeniable that changes in financial support can sometimes lead to institutional departure, the evidence suggests that the effect of finances upon departure is frequently subsumed within decisions as to choice of college. It appears, for many but by no means all students, to operate at the margin rather than at the center of decision making regarding persistence. Financial considerations appear to be but one part of a much more complex decision-making process, one that depends in large measure upon the nature of one's social and intellectual experiences within the college.

But having said all this, we are still left with an important question. What we have described is a series of causes which have been shown to have an impact upon student departure from institutions of higher education. What we have yet to describe is the longitudinal process of interactions which gives rise to those causes and leads over time to departure. For that purpose we have to have a longitudinal model or theory of student departure, one which is explanatory, not merely descriptive in nature. It must make evident how it is that the factors of intention, commitment, adjustment, difficulty, congruence, isolation, obligations, finances, and learning all come to affect student departure from institutions of higher education. It is to the development of that model that we now turn.

—4—

A Theory of Individual Departure from Institutions of Higher Education

Past Theories of Student Departure

The study of student departure from higher education is not lacking for models which seek to explain why it is that students leave or "drop out" from college. Regrettably, most have been neither very effective in explaining departure nor particularly well suited to the needs of institutional officials who seek to retain more students on campus. On one hand, this has been the result of the already discussed tendency of researchers to ignore and sometimes confuse the varying forms which departure takes in higher education and to downplay if not entirely overlook the role the institution plays in the withdrawal process. On the other, it mirrors the fact that most so-called theories of departure are in actuality atheoretical in character. They have suggested relationships between events in the form of a model without specifying a consistent form of explanation which accounts for those relationships. Though they are often able to describe behaviors, they have been unable to explain their occurrence.

Until recently, most attempts to explain student departure have relied heavily upon psychological models of educational persistence. These have tended to emphasize the impact of individual abilities and dispositions upon student departure. Models such as those by Summerskill (1962) and Marks (1967) point to the importance of intellectual attributes in shaping the individual's ability to meet academic demands, while those by Heilbrun (1965),

Rose and Elton (1966), Rossmann and Kirk (1970), and Waterman and Waterman (1972) stress the roles personality, motivation, and disposition play in influencing the student's willingness to meet those demands.

Typically, research of the psychological type has sought to distinguish stayers and leavers in terms of attributes of personality that help account for their differing response to supposedly similar educational circumstances. Heilbrun (1965), for example, in comparing stayers and leavers, argued that dropouts were likely to be less mature, more likely to rebel against authority, and more likely to be less serious in their endeavors and less dependable than persisters. Rose and Elton (1966) went one step further to argue that student leaving is an immediate reflection of maladjustment and directed hostility. Students with high hostility who are unable to adjust to the college tend to direct their hostility for their problems toward the institution and either leave higher education altogether or transfer to another institution. A more recent variant of the psychological view of persistence is contained in the work of Ethington (1990). Drawn from Eccles's model of student achievement (Eccles et al. 1983), this view emphasizes the role of individual expectations regarding success and the value placed on college attendance. It is argued that these orientations, which are themselves reflective of other personality traits, will shape how individuals approach college tasks and will ultimately influence their persistence via subsequent achievement.

However framed, all these views of departure share a common theme, namely that retention and departure are primarily the reflection of individual actions and therefore are largely due to the ability or willingness of the individual to successfully complete the tasks associated with college attendance. More important, such models invariably see student departure as reflecting some shortcoming and/or weakness in the individual. Leaving is, in this view, assumed to be reflective of a personal failure of the individual to measure up to the demands of college life.

Though there is no doubt some truth to the psychological view of departure, it is only a partial truth. It runs counter to the evidence, noted in the preceding chapter, that there is no one "departure-prone" personality which is uniformly associated with student departure (Cope and Hannah 1975). And it ignores the facts that individual behavior is as much a function of the environment within which individuals find themselves and that the effect of personality traits upon departure is very much a function of the particular institution and student body being studied (Sharp and Chason 1978).

Psychological theories of departure focus on but one set within a broader matrix of forces which impinge upon the withdrawal process. They generally ignore those forces that represent the impact the institution has upon student behaviors. As a result, psychological theories of departure invariably see student departure as reflecting some shortcoming or weakness in the individual. Leaving is, in this view, a personal failure on the part of the individual to measure up to the many demands of college life. Though external forces may matter, the individual alone bears primary responsibility for departure. By extension, such theories argue that attrition among college students could be substantially reduced either by the improvement of student skills and/or by the selection of individuals who possess the personality traits deemed appropriate for college work. Unfortunately there is no widespread evidence to support such an argument. Though it is the case, as we have seen in chapter 2, that more selective colleges have, on the average, lower rates of attrition, it is also the case that there is a considerable range in attrition rates among even the most selective colleges. In any case, most institutions do not have the luxury of being able to select from their applicant pools. Over half of all institutions of higher education admit virtually everyone who applies.

The difficulty, then, with the psychological view of student leaving is that it is not truly explanatory nor well suited to the policy needs of most colleges. Because it has largely ignored the impact context may have on student behaviors, the psychological perspective does not provide a suitable model of departure for either institutional research or institutional policy. Though it does point up the necessary role of personality in individual responses to educational situations, this perspective has not yet been able to tell us why it is that some personality attributes appear to describe differences among stayers and leavers in some situations but not in others. As a result, it does not yet provide a suitable guide either for researchers who seek to better explain the departure of different types of students from different types of institutional settings or for institutional officials who seek to enhance student retention by altering institutional actions.

At the other end of the spectrum from psychological theories are environmental theories of student departure which emphasize the impact of wider social, economic, and organizational forces on the behavior of students within institutions of higher education. One variant of the environmental perspective, societal theories of departure, see educational attainment as only one part of the broader process of social attainment and the success or failure of students in higher education as being molded by the same forces that shape social success generally. Rather than focusing on individual dispositions, societal theories have concerned themselves with those attributes of individuals, institutions, and society, such as social status, race, institutional prestige, and opportunity structure, that describe the person's and the institution's place in the broader hierarchy of society.

But the manner in which they have done so has varied considerably. Societal theories of departure, like the social theories from which they derive, differ because their views of the underlying causes of social success also differ. Conflict theorists, such as Karabel (1972) and Pincus (1980), argue that educational institutions are structured to serve the interests of prevailing social and educational elites. In their view, student departures must be understood not as isolated individual events but as part of a larger process of social stratification which operates to preserve existing patterns of educational and social inequality. Thus, it is argued that high rates of departure among two-year colleges, especially those that serve persons of lower-class origins, reflect the intentional desire of educational organizations to restrict educational and social opportunity in society (Clark 1960, Pincus 1980).

Other theorists, who hold the structural-functional view of society, see the outcome of schooling as reflecting the largely meritocratic contest among individuals for social attainment (Duncan, Featherman, and Duncan 1972, Sewell and Hauser 1975, Featherman and Hauser 1978). In their view, differences in educational attainment, and therefore patterns of student departure, tend to mirror differences in individual skills and abilities rather than social status per se. Though social origins as defined by social status and race matter, they tend to be less important than those attributes of individuals and organizations which directly affect their ability to compete in the academic marketplace.

Whether derivatives of structural-functional or conflict theory, societal theories of departure stress the importance of external forces in the process of student persistence. But they often do so at the expense of institutional forces. As a result, they are frequently insensitive to the situational character of student departure and the important variations in student leaving that arise *within* institutions. Though useful in the aggregate, that is, in describing broad trends in retention in society, societal theories are much less useful in explaining the institution-specific forces that shape differing forms of institutional departure.

This is not as true for those societal theories of schooling which stress the importance of economic forces in student decisions to stay or leave. Derived from economic theories of educational attainment, the works of researchers such as Manski and Wise (1983), Iwai and Churchill (1982), Jensen (1981), and Voorhees (1984) all share the view that individual decisions about persistence are no different in substance than any other economic decision which weighs the costs and benefits of alternative ways of investing one's scarce economic resources. In this manner, retention and departure mirror economic forces, especially those which influence both the economic benefits accruing to college education and the financial resources which individuals can bring to bear on their investment in continued college attendance.

Understandably, all such theories emphasize the importance finances and financial aid play in student retention (e.g., Iwai and Churchill 1982, and

Stampen and Cabrera 1986, 1988). In this regard, however, they have been
unable to explain many of the forms of departure that arise within institutions
of higher education. Indeed, there is little evidence of any type to support the
contention that financial forces, specifically those in the form of financial
aid, are for most students paramount to retention decisions (Stampen and
Cabrera 1986, 1988, Oosterbeek 1989). Though there is little doubt that financial considerations are important to the continued persistence of some
students, most notably those from working-class and disadvantaged backgrounds (e.g., Nora and Horvath 1989), they tend to be of secondary importance to the decisions of most other students. The reasons are twofold: First,
the effect of finances upon persistence is most often taken up in decisions
regarding college entry, that is, whether to attend, where to attend, and in
what form (full-time or part-time) to attend (Manski and Wise 1983).
Second, though students frequently cite finances as reasons for withdrawing, their true reasons often reflect other forces not associated with finances,
such as dissatisfaction with the institution. Their citing of financial reasons
for leaving is simply another way of stating their view that the benefits of
continued attendance do not outweigh the costs of doing so. Conversely,
when students are satisfied with their institutional experience, they often are
willing to accept considerable economic hardships in order to continue. For
them, the benefits of attendance more than justify costs.

This is not to say, however, that short-term fluctuations in financial resources do not lead to departure among some students, especially those from
disadvantaged backgrounds. They do. But such events are most often short-
term in character and cannot explain the continuing long-term patterns of
student departure that we observe in higher education. A general theory of
student departure, if it is to be fully explanatory, must be able to account for
the latter as well as the former mode of student departure.

It might be observed that economic theories may be better suited to the
analysis of retention at the level of the system than they are at the level of the
institution. Over time, for instance, it is quite likely that the availability of
different types of financial aid (e.g., the shifting of aid from outright grants
to loans) together with changing economic conditions in the marketplace do
influence the *aggregate* rate at which cohorts of students are able to complete
their college degrees (Mortenson 1991). But even here the track records of
such analyses are spotty. As Oosterbeek (1989) observes, there is still much
to be done before such theories can be gainfully employed in the study of
student retention in higher education.[1]

An entirely different approach to the study of departure comes from the
work of organizational sociology. Organizational theories of student departure, like environmental theories generally, are also concerned with the impact of environmental forces on student behavior. But rather than focus on

broad social or economic forces, they center their attention on the effect of the organization of higher educational institutions. Like studies of role socialization and worker productivity and turnover, from which they are derived, organizational theories of departure, such as those of Kamens (1971) and Bean (1980, 1983), see the occurrence of student departure as reflecting the impact that the organization has on the socialization and satisfaction of students. Their central tenet has been that departure is as much, if not more, a reflection of institutional behavior as it is of the individuals within an institution.

Typically, researchers have looked at the effect of organizational dimensions such as bureaucratic structure, size, faculty-student ratios, and institutional resources and goals on the aggregate rates of student institutional departure. Though individual attributes are sometimes included, they are not of primary theoretical interest. Kamens's multi-institutional study (1971), for instance, focused on the impact of organizational size and complexity on student role socialization and retention. He argued that larger institutions with distinct college "charters" would have lower rates of attrition because of their superior capacity to allocate students to the more prestigious positions in society. Such "charters" are a reflection not only of institutional resources but also of the links that larger institutions maintain with different occupational and economic groups (Kamens 1971, 271–72). Bean's study (1983) takes a somewhat different view of departure. An offshoot of an industrial model of work turnover (Price 1977, Price and Mueller 1981), this study looks at the impact of organizational attributes (e.g., routinization, participation, and communication) and rewards (e.g., grades, practical value, and development) on retention through their impact on student satisfaction. As in work organizations, it is argued, institutional rates of retention would be heightened by policies that increase students' participation and enhance the rewards they obtain for their "work" in the institution.

The strength of the organizational view of student departure lies in its reminding us that the organization of educational institutions, their formal structures, resources, and patterns of association, does impact on student retention. Braxton and Brier's (1989) recent study of persistence gives a special weight to this truth. As in formal organizations generally, organizational decisions within higher education necessarily impact on the satisfaction of all members within the organization, students as well as faculty and staff. In this respect, organizational models are especially appealing to institutional planners concerned with the restructuring of organizations to achieve greater institutional effectiveness, for they focus on organizational attributes that are directly alterable by administrative action. These models should also be appealing to researchers interested in the comparative analysis of institutional retention, since they enable us to highlight how different organizational structures are related to different retention outcomes among relatively similar student bodies.

As a theory of *individual* student departure, however, organizational theories such as Bean's (1980, 1983) and to a lesser extent Kamens's (1971) lack explanatory power in that they do not enable us to understand how organizational attributes eventually impact on student decisions to stay or leave. That is the case, in part, because these theories normally do not point out the intervening factors, such as student subcultures and patterns of student-faculty interaction, that serve to transmit the effect of the organization to student behaviors. Nor do they enable us to understand why it is that different types of students may take on different types of leaving behaviors within the institution. In this regard, these theories implicitly assume that all departures arise from the same sources—an assumption we know not to be correct. Though organizational models may be especially suited to comparative studies of rates of retention—for which they have unfortunately been rarely used—they are much less useful in explaining variations in student leaving behaviors *within* institutions of higher education. For this purpose, one has to look elsewhere, specifically to interactional theories of student departure.

Studies of Departure in Other School Settings

That past theories of student departure should so underestimate, if not wholly ignore, the role the social setting of the institution plays in the withdrawal process is surprising. In other fields of educational research this has not been the case. Coleman's (1961) study of high schools, for example, demonstrated that differences in student behavior could only be understood within the context of the social environment established by other persons in the school. He argued that differences in performance of students in differing high schools were a direct reflection of the degree to which the student peer culture made academic performance an important determinant of student status. The greater the emphasis upon performance as a determinant of status, the greater the press for achievement among students generally and among the more ambitious, brighter students in particular. Conversely, the more student values were directed toward nonacademic pursuits, the lower the average performance of the school and its most able students.

The same theme is echoed again in Coleman, Hoffer, and Kilgore's (1982) most recent study of student achievement in public and private schools and Lightfoot's (1983) study of "good" schools. In these instances, it is argued that the differences in school performance are very much a function of the ethos which pervades the daily life of schools and which informs the actions of students and teachers alike. Ineffective schools are often those whose faculty and staff hold little expectation for the success of their students. Student failure, then, comes to mirror the activities of the school. Though some researchers, such as Bowles and Gintis (1976) and Karabel (1972), see this as reflecting the intentional actions of educational institutions to encourage failure, others, such as Rist (1970) and Rosenbaum (1976), view it as a largely unintended by-product of the manner in which educational institutions have been organized and run. Whatever the particular view, all agree that the institution, in its behavioral and normative manifestations, has as much to do with the failure of students as do the students themselves.

It is unfortunate that these and other such insights into the multiple effects of educational environments upon student behavior have not been fully incorporated into the study of the process of student withdrawal. Though some researchers have taken note of the role of institutional environments (e.g., Bean 1980, 1983, Lenning, Beal, and Sauer 1980, Anderson 1981), they have rarely explicated the mechanisms by which those environments affect student departure. The few exceptions, namely the work of Knop (1967), Spady (1970, 1971), and Rootman (1972), while suggesting a mechanism for those impacts, fail to adequately distinguish among varying forms of departure.

In referring to prior studies of leaving in other contexts we do not mean to imply that what may hold for the study of student persistence-generally and/or in high school settings need necessarily apply to the study of student departure from higher educational settings. It does not follow that what serves to explain patterns of persistence or performance either in high school or college serves equally well to explain student departure. There is little evidence to suggest that departure is simply the absence of persistence or that one can be understood solely as a mirror image of the other. Similarly, it is not a foregone conclusion that existing explanations of student departure from high school can also serve to explain the withdrawal of individuals from higher educational institutions (e.g., Varner 1967, Elliott and Voss 1974, Hill 1979, Weidman and Friedmann 1984). There are enough significant differences between the two situations to limit the usefulness of the analogies which might be drawn from studies in either setting.[2] While it is possible to gain some insight into the phenomena of educational departure from a study of educational persistence and of high school dropout, one has to look elsewhere, as well, for a guide in thinking about departure from institutions of higher education. In the present case that "elsewhere" is the study of suicide and of the rites of passage to membership in tribal societies.

Stages in the Process of Departure from
Institutions of Higher Education

Van Gennep and The Rites of Passage

We begin our development of a theory of student departure by turning to the field of social anthropology and studies of the process of establishing membership in traditional societies. Specifically, we turn to the work of Arnold Van Gennep and his study of the rites of passage in tribal societies.[3] Van Gennep, a Dutch anthropologist, was concerned with the movement of individuals and societies through time and with the mechanisms which promote social stability in times of change. On one level, he was interested in the "life crises" that individuals and groups face during the course of their lifetime. He saw life as being comprised of a series of passages leading individuals from birth to death and from membership in one group or status to another. In studying those passages and life crises, he gave detailed attention to the ceremonies and rituals, including those revolving around birth, marriage, death, and entrance into adulthood, that help individuals and groups through those times of disturbance. On a broader level, he was concerned with the question of societal revitalization over time and with the general problem of social stability in times of change. Thus his interests in ceremonies and rituals also reflected a broader interest in the sorts of mechanisms traditional societies employ in providing for the orderly transmission of its social relationships over time. The two concerns are linked in that the recurring question of the orderly movement of individuals through their lives necessarily becomes that of the stability of communities and societies across generations.

Of his numerous concerns, that which is most directly related to the process of student departure focuses on the movement of individuals from membership in one group to that in another, especially as it occurs in the ascent of individuals from youth to adult status in society. In his now classic study entitled *The Rites of Passage,* Van Gennep (1960) argued that the process of transmission of relationships between succeeding groups was marked by three distinct phases or stages, each with its own specialized ceremonies and rituals. These so-called rites of passage were referred to as the stages of separation, transition, and incorporation. Each served to move individuals from youthful participation to full adult membership in society. They provided, through the use of ceremony and ritual, for the orderly transmission of the beliefs and norms of the society to the next generation of adults and/or new members. In that fashion, such rites served to insure the stability of society over time while also enabling younger generations to take over responsibility from older ones.

According to Van Gennep, each stage in the rites of passage to adulthood consists of a change in patterns of interaction between the individual and other members of society. The first, separation, involves the separation of the individual from past associations. It is characterized by a marked decline in interactions with members of the group from which the person has come and by the use of ceremonies whose purpose it is to mark as outmoded the views and norms which characterized that group. The second, transition, is a period during which the person begins to interact in new ways with members of the new group into which membership is sought. Isolation, training, and sometimes ordeals are employed as mechanisms to insure the separation of the individual from past associations and the adoption of behaviors and norms appropriate to membership in the new group. It is during this transitional stage that individuals come to learn the knowledge and skills required for the performance of their specific role in the new group. The third and last phase, incorporation, involves the taking on of new patterns of interaction with members of the new group and the establishing of competent membership in that group as a participant member. Full membership or incorporation in the new group is marked by special ceremonies which announce and certify not only the rewards of membership but also the responsibilities associated with it. Though the persons may begin to interact once again with past group members, they will now do so as members of the new group. They have completed their movement from the past and are now fully integrated into the culture of the new group.

Van Gennep believed that the concept of rites of passage could be applied to a variety of situations, especially those involving the movement of a person or group from one place to another.[4] In that movement, the individual or group leaves an old territory or community (separation), in some fashion crosses a border, whether it be physical or ceremonial, to a new setting (transition), and takes up residence in the new location or community (incorporation). For the individual, such movements necessarily entail moving from a position as a known member in one group to that of a stranger in the new setting. As a result, they are often associated with feelings of weakness and isolation. Having given up the norms and beliefs of past associations and not yet having adopted those appropriate to membership in a new community, the individual is left in a state of at least temporary normlessness. This absence of guiding norms and beliefs heightens the likelihood of departure from the community prior to incorporation. It is precisely for this reason that Van Gennep stressed the importance of the rituals and ceremonies of the rites of passage. They not only served to publicly announce the movement of the stranger to membership in the community but also provided a visible structure to assist the stranger in coping with the difficulties that movement en-

tailed. In that manner, rituals and ceremonies served both social and therapeutic functions.

Stages of Passage in Student College Careers

The point of our referring to the work of Van Gennep is not that the college
student career is always clearly marked by ceremonies and symbolic rites of
passage. Though this may be the case in a number of highly structured educational settings (e.g., military academies and institutions geared to the
training of very specific occupational groups such as medical doctors), such
ceremonial rites are no longer commonplace in higher education. Rather our
interest in the concept of rites of passage is that it provides us with a way of
thinking about the longitudinal process of student persistence in college and,
by extension, about the time-dependent process of student departure.[5] Specifically, it argues that it is possible to envision the process of student persistence as functionally similar to that of becoming incorporated into the life
of human communities generally and that this process, especially in the first
year of college, is also marked by stages of passage, through which individuals must typically pass in order to persist in college. By extension, it further
suggests that the process of student departure in part reflects the difficulties
individuals face in seeking to successfully navigate those early passages to
membership in the communities of the college.

Many college students are, after all, moving from one community or set of
communities, most typically those of the family and local high school, to
another, that of the college. They too must separate themselves, to some degree, from past associations in order to make the transition to eventual incorporation in the life of the college. In seeking to make such transitions, they
too are likely to encounter problems of adjustment whose resolution may
well spell the difference between continued persistence and early departure.
Those difficulties are not, however, solely the reflection of individual attributes. They are as much a reflection of the problems inherent in shifts of
community membership as they are either of the personality of the individual
or of the character of the institution in which membership is sought. They are
rooted in the character of college persistence and in the passages successful
persistence entails. For most high school graduates, the passage to college is
a movement from youthful associations to more mature ones, and for many
adults returning to college it frequently entails a shift from one pattern of
association with family, employers, and friends to another.

We must be careful, however, not to oversimplify what is a very complex,
quite fluid situation that need not be experienced in the same fashion by every student. In speaking of the stages of separation, transition, and incorporation as we have, it should not be assumed that these stages are always as

distinct and clearly sequenced as we have made them. There is no doubt, for instance, that some students are hardly aware of the transition required in becoming integrated into the life of the college. Others may not experience separation, transition, and incorporation in the same sequence or at the same time. For some, each stage may occur only partially and then be repeated as they move further along their college careers. For many, the stages may not be separate but may significantly overlap. Various elements of the process of incorporation may occur at the same time that other elements of separation and transition are being experienced. Moreover, the differing forms of adjustment they entail are often intertwined in such a way that experiences in one stage affect adjustments in another stage.

At the same time, the ways individuals experience these presumed stages can vary considerably. A white child of a college-educated family may look forward to and be rewarded for making the transition to college whereas a native American child from a poor family may find that he/she is seen as rebelling against the family and local community in going to college. For many adults, the passage to college may be quite different in another way. Unlike their youthful colleagues who leave home to attend college, they typically retain their membership in their communities, families, and places of work. Their transition is not a physical one, but a phenomenological movement that calls for altered patterns of relationships, both social and intellectual, with those communities. Though not physical, their separation may be just as "real."

Despite its limits, the work of Van Gennep allows us to begin our search for a theory of student departure by isolating for us the interactional roots of the *early stages of withdrawal from institutions of higher education*. It does so by providing us with a conceptual framework identifying three distinct stages or phases of association of the individual with the other members of the institution—stages which we will refer to here, as did Van Gennep, as the stages of separation, transition, and incorporation.

SEPARATION FROM COMMUNITIES OF THE PAST

The first stage of the college career, separation, requires individuals to disassociate themselves, in varying degrees, from membership in the communities of the past, most typically those associated with the family, the local high school, and local areas of residence. Such communities differ from college not only in composition but also in the values, norms, and behavioral and intellectual styles that characterize their everyday life. As a result, the process leading to the adoption of behaviors and norms appropriate to the life of the college necessarily requires some degree of transformation and perhaps rejection of the norms of past communities. In this regard, London's

(1989) study of first-generation college students reveals a sense of "breaking away" that many students experience in making the transition to college.

For virtually all students, separation from the past is at least somewhat isolating and stressful, the pains of parting at least temporarily disorienting. For some it may be so difficult as to significantly interfere with persistence in college. This may be especially true for those persons who move away from their local high school communities and families to live at a distant college. In order to become fully incorporated into the life of the college, they have to physically as well as socially disassociate themselves from the communities of the past.

This is not so true of persons who attend a local, nonresidential college. They need not disassociate themselves from past affiliations in order to establish membership in the newly met communities of the college. It is the case, however, that the social and intellectual communities of nonresidential institutions are often substantially weaker, that is, less extensive and cohesive, than those at residential institutions. While persons in such institutions may avoid some of the stresses of separation, they may not be able to reap the full rewards that membership in college communities brings. The same disadvantage may apply to those individuals who elect to live at home while attending largely residential institutions. Though such persons may find movement into the world of the college less stressful, they may also find it less rewarding. Thus the ironic situation that, though they may find the task of persistence initially easier, it may be measurably more difficult over the long run. In a very real sense, a person's ability to leave one setting, whether physical, social, or intellectual, may be a necessary condition for subsequent persistence in another setting.

In either case, students who stay at home expose themselves to a number of potential risks, not the least of which are external forces which may pull a person away from incorporation into the life of the college. If the orientation of the family or local peer group does not support, indeed opposes, participation in higher education, early separation and transition may be measurably more difficult. It may require the person to visibly reject the values of the family or local peers in order to adopt those appropriate to the college (London 1989). In some cases, however, families may aid persistence. As Bean and Vesper (1992) demonstrate, persistence for some students (e.g., young students fresh from high school) is positively influenced by parental encouragement and support.

In this and other ways, the experience of separation depends in part on the social and intellectual character of past communities of affiliation, especially their views regarding the worth of college attendance. Individuals from disadvantaged backgrounds and/or from families whose members have not attended college may, therefore, find separation more painful than would persons whose parents are themselves college educated. Similarly, foreign students, students from very small rural communities, and students from distinct social, ethnic, or religious communities may also find separation particularly difficult. For them, separation may represent a major shift in the way they construct their daily lives. But for many individuals from college-educated families, the transition to college may be an accepted, indeed encouraged, movement that most persons are expected to make in the course of their adult lives.

The Transition between High School and College

The second stage of passage, transition, comes during and after that of separation. It is a period of passage between the old and the new, before the full adoption of new norms and patterns of behavior and after the onset of separation from old ones. Having begun the process of separating themselves from the past, new students have yet to acquire the norms and patterns of behavior appropriate to incorporation into the new communities of the college. Many may find themselves in a highly anomic situation in which they are neither strongly bound to the past nor yet firmly tied to the future.

The scope of the transition stage, that is, the degree of change it entails, depends on a number of factors, among them the degree of difference between the norms and patterns of behavior associated with membership in past communities and those required for integration into the life of the college. Individuals who come from families, communities, and schools whose norms and behaviors are very different from those of the communities of the college into which entry is made face especially difficult problems in seeking to achieve competent membership in the new communities. Though they may have been successful in meeting the demands of past situations, they may not have acquired the social and intellectual skills needed for successful participation in the new communities of the college. Their past has not adequately prepared them to deal with the future. In the "typical" institution, this means that disadvantaged students, persons of minority origins, older students, and the physically handicapped are more likely to experience such problems than are other students. In very large residential institutions, persons from very small rural communities may face similar problems.

It should be noted that the scope of the transition also hinges upon the degree to which individuals have already begun the process of transition prior to formal entry (Attinasi 1989). Especially in those situations when the choice of institution is seen as central to the achievement of valued career goals, individuals will sometimes anticipate their socialization by moving toward perceived institutional goals prior to actual admission. Their desire to "fit in" moves them to emulate the life of the institution by "getting ready" well in advance of entry. But "anticipatory socialization" is unlikely to be widespread. It is most prevalent among those institutions which are either very distinct in character (e.g., small, elite private colleges) or directly tied to a specific career (e.g., military academies). In any case, it is doubtful that individuals' prior understanding of the life of colleges is so accurate as to correctly anticipate the character of transition they will have to make. Though anticipatory socialization may lessen the strain of transition to college, it is unlikely to eliminate it.

Virtually all students experience some difficulty in making the transition to college. For some, the stress and sense of isolation, if not desolation, which sometimes accompanies such circumstances can pose serious problems (Cutrona 1982). Though most students are able to cope with the problems of transition, many voluntarily withdraw from college very early in their first academic year, less from an inability to become incorporated in the social and academic communities of the college than from an inability to withstand the stresses that such transitions commonly induce.

It bears repeating that differences in individual goals and intentions have much to do with a person's response to the stress of transition. The problems associated with separation and transition to college are conditions that, though stressful, need not in themselves lead to departure. It is the individual's response to those conditions that finally determines staying or leaving. Though external assistance may make a difference, it cannot do so without the individual's willingness to see the adjustments through. This is not to say that assistance cannot help. It can. As we shall see in chapter 5, institutions have recently turned to a range of freshman-year programs (e.g., freshman seminars, "University 101") explicitly designed to assist new students in successfully navigating the transition to the new communities of the college. Their success is itself a recognition of the difficulties many students encounter in trying to navigate that academic and social passage.

INCORPORATION INTO THE SOCIETY OF THE COLLEGE

After passing through the stages of separation and transition, both of which tend to occur very early in the student career, the individual is faced with the task of becoming integrated, or, to use Van Gennep's terminology, incorporated into the communities of the college. Having moved away from the norms and behavioral patterns of past associations, the person now faces the problem of finding and adopting new ones appropriate to the college setting. Though the person has passed the first hurdle, persistence is still not insured. Incorporation into the life of the college must follow.

But unlike those being incorporated into the traditional societies which were of interest to Van Gennep, individuals in college are rarely provided with formal rituals and ceremonies whereby such connectedness is ratified. Of course, some institutions, especially residential ones, do provide a variety of formal and informal mechanisms for that purpose. Fraternities, sororities, student dormitory associations, student unions, frequent faculty and visiting-scholar lectures, extracurricular programs, and intramural sports, for example, may all serve to provide individuals with opportunities to establish repetitive contact with one another in circumstances which lead to the possibility of incorporation into the life of the college.

Though some institutions have established freshman-year programs, it is still the case that most new students are left to make their own way through the maze of institutional life. They, like the many generations of students before them, have to learn the ropes of college life largely on their own. For them, daily personal contacts with other members of the college, in both the formal and informal domains of institutional life, are the only vehicles by which incorporation occurs. Not all individuals, especially those recently removed from the familiar confines of the family and local high school communities, are either able or willing to make the needed personal contacts on their own. As a result, not all new students come to be incorporated into the life of the institution. Without external assistance, many will eventually leave the institution because they have been unable to establish satisfying intellectual and social membership.

But how that incorporation comes about is not yet clear. Though the work of Van Gennep has led us this far in the development of a theory of student departure, it does not give us a way of thinking about the largely informal processes of interaction among individuals on campus which lead to incorporation. For that purpose we now turn to the work of Emile Durkheim and the study of community and suicide.

Suicide and the Study of Departure from Higher Education

In using the study of suicide as a guide for our thinking, we do not mean to imply that institutional departure necessarily leads to suicide or that it represents a form of suicidal behavior. But there are enough intriguing analogies between the two situations to warrant our attention. The most obvious of these is that both forms of behavior can be understood, in most circumstances, to represent a form of voluntary withdrawal from local communities that is as much a reflection of the community as it is of the individual who withdraws.[6] Moreover, each can be seen to signal somewhat similar forms of rejection of conventional norms regarding the value of persisting in those communities.

Durkheim's Theory of Suicide

There are numerous theories of suicide. That which is most appropriate for our needs and our concern with the role of college communities in student leaving is derived from the early work of Emile Durkheim and that of Spady (1970), who first applied Durkheim's work to the study of persistence. An eminent French academician and intellectual, Durkheim was considered by many to be the founding father of the discipline of sociology. He held the first chair of education and sociology at the University of Paris and was a strong proponent of sociology's utility both as a tool of social science research and as a guide for the reconstruction of modern society. His interest in suicide sprang from a belief that its study would reveal much about the character and problems of the society within which it occurs.

In what is now considered to be a classic study of early sociology, *Suicide*, Durkheim sought to show how the principles of sociology could help explain why rates of suicide differed between countries and within countries over time (Durkheim 1951). Specifically, he sought to demonstrate how an understanding of the character of the social environment, its social and intellectual or normative attributes, could be used to account for those variations in ways which other disciplines (e.g., psychology or economics) could not.

Durkheim distinguished four types of suicide: altruistic, anomic, fatalistic, and egotistical. Altruistic suicide is that form of taking one's life which a society may hold to be morally desirable in given situations. In some societies high rates of suicide may be explained by referring either to culturally specific norms regarding the taking of one's life or to the occurrence of those situations which may evoke such norms. Thus, for example, one may account for differences in rates of suicide between nineteenth-century Japan, where hara-kiri was esteemed as a morally justifiable response to particular social situations, and a society like our own, which generally deplores as immoral the taking of one's own life. Similarly, one may understand the surge in apparent suicides in Japan during World War II, specifically the use of kamikaze warfare, as a situationally specific application of norms during times of national crisis.

A second form of suicide Durkheim described is anomic suicide. In this case, suicide is seen as reflecting the temporary disruption of the normal conditions of society and therefore the breakdown of the normal social and intellectual bonds which tie individuals to each other in the human fabric that we call society. Under the stress of plague, war, or religious or economic upheaval, the normal bonds may be sufficiently disrupted to produce for large numbers of people a situation of anomie, that is, normlessness. In this situation people are left without adequate guidelines for the conduct of their personal daily lives. The rise of looting, rioting, and family dissolutions are but some of the symptoms characteristic of such normless periods.

Durkheim argued that in such periods individuals are more likely to commit suicide. The normal bonds and normative constraints which limit self-annihilation are loosened. Individuals are increasingly isolated and left on their own to make difficult moral choices. Normlessness and isolation run hand in hand. But unlike altruistic suicide, which may be seen as a permanent feature characteristic of a particular society, anomic suicide is generally situational and temporary in character. It may arise for short periods of time in any society regardless of that society's particular normative structure. Thus it is possible to discern across time the rise of suicide rates during periods of significant social, economic, political, and religious upheaval. The Great Depression of 1929 is only one of many such temporary social upheavals associated with marked increases in rates of suicide.

A third form of suicide, fatalistic suicide, stands in stark contrast to anomic suicide. Rather than arising from the absence of norms, fatalistic suicide is the result of excessive normative control. It is, in Durkheim's words, that "suicide deriving from excessive regulation, that of persons with futures pitilessly blocked and passions violently choked by oppressive discipline" (Durkheim 1951, 276, n. 25). In these instances, suicide is seen by individuals as the only viable way out of hopelessly blocked situations in which any other response would be seen as a serious violation of existing norms. Societies which are highly regulated or which experience periods of excessive regulation will, therefore, exhibit higher rates of suicide and other forms of suicidal behavior (e.g., alcoholism) than will other societies.

Durkheim argued, however, that these three forms of suicide—altruistic, anomic, and fatalistic—though useful in explaining suicide rates within particular societies or their variation during specific time periods, were insufficient to account for the continuing characteristic differences in suicide rates which mark most societies. For those latter differences one had to concern oneself with the character of egotistical suicide in society, and therefore with the social conditions in society which give rise to its occurrence.

Egotistical suicide is that form of suicide which arises when individuals are unable to become integrated and establish membership within the communities of society. Durkheim referred to two forms of integration—social and intellectual—through which membership may be brought about. The former refers to that form of integration which results from personal affiliations and from the day-to-day interactions among different members of society. The latter comes from the sharing of values which are held in common by other members of society.

Insufficient integration and the absence of community membership may arise from the holding of values which deviate from those of other members of society (i.e., intellectual isolation or deviancy) and/or from insufficient personal affiliation between the individual and other persons in society (i.e., social isolation). Though distinct, the two are intimately interrelated. The holding of deviant values may lead to a person's social isolation. Conversely, insufficient personal affiliation may lead a person to adopt and/or continue to hold values which deviate from those of the wider community. Day-to-day interactions serve both as a gauge by which one measures one's values and as a social mechanism which constrains the development of highly deviant values.

Though each form of malintegration may produce a social press toward suicide, each alone is insufficient to explain high rates of suicide in society. Both conditions are needed to account for the occurrence of egotistical suicide. This is so because of the availability in most societies of deviant subcultures. These often quite localized communities can provide deviating individuals with an intellectual and/or social community within which membership can be established. A person holding deviant values who might otherwise become a social isolate may be able to find sufficient social affiliation and therefore social integration in a community of persons holding similar deviant values. Conversely, a social isolate might find intellectual integration via the sharing of ideas expressed in the media.

Durkheim further argued that, to understand the occurrence of egotistical suicide, one had to refer to the conditions in society which provide the context for individual integration. Specifically, one had to refer to the social and intellectual structure of society and to the integrative mechanisms which enable individuals to establish social and intellectual membership within the varying communities. In Durkheim's view, individual integration into the social and intellectual life of society and the social and intellectual membership which that integration promotes are essential elements of social existence in human society. Societies with high rates of suicide are those whose social conditions are such as to constrain such membership. They are malintegrated societies where the incidence of social and intellectual isolation and deviancy is relatively high.

In his concern for social reformation, Durkheim sought to discern the structural attributes of societies which give rise to conditions of malintegration. He argued that it was possible through the use of the tools of sociological analysis to work toward a social and intellectual restructuring of society for the benefit of all members. It was Durkheim's personal belief that the traditional vehicles of integration, namely, the family and the church, were no longer effective in providing membership in an increasingly divided industrial state, one in which modern division of labor served to separate people from one another. An alternative mechanism was required to restore the health and stability of modern society. However, the fact that he argued that the state and its modern educational system was indeed that mechanism is not central to our present concerns. Rather, what is important is the fact that he argued that one could reduce rates of egotistical suicide and restore social stability by the restructuring of society and by the provision of more effective means for the integration of individuals into the social and intellectual fabric of society. His belief in the power of communities to influence peoples' lives continues to echo today in discussions of college (Astin 1985, Boyer 1987).

Modes of Suicide and Rates of Institutional Departure: Some Observations

Though we are not yet to a theory of individual suicide, since Durkheim was concerned with aggregate rates of suicide, it might be observed that his analysis may be usefully employed in comparative study of the variation in rates of departure among different institutions of higher education. The most obvious application is that one could analyze differences in institutional rates of departure, both between institutions and within institutions over time, in very much the same fashion as Durkheim examined differences in rates of suicide between societies. One could apply the same distinctions between types of leavings to the study of the roots of variation of departure among institutions.

In seeking an analogue for altruistic suicide, for example, we would inquire into the development of periodic and/or institution-specific ideologies or subcultures which promote departure from higher education. Ideologies which extol the virtues of leaving higher education can have substantial, though temporary, impact on institutional and system rates of withdrawal. The call of the 1960s and 1970s to "drop out and drop in" did not go unheeded among the youth of the period. Though temporary. it did induce many students to suspend, if not permanently terminate, their higher education.

In a similar fashion, the concept of anomic suicide would turn our attention to the existence of disruptive forces on campus which undermine the daily operation of the institution and undercut the normal bonds which tie individuals to it. Not surprisingly, many institutions which experienced the disruption of student riots in the 1970s also experienced heightened rates of departure from their campuses. Indeed, many also witnessed a decline, albeit temporary, in rates of application. Widespread system disruptions can have similar effects upon departure. Though such disruptions are uncommon in the United States, other countries have virtually closed down their higher educational systems during periods of turmoil. By contrast, institutions which are highly structured and vigorous in their enforcement of intellectual and behavioral norms may find themselves losing numbers of students who leave in search of less restrictive environments. The same situation may arise during those periods when institutions move to raise standards or reinforce standards which may have been loosely applied in the past.

These analogies speak, however, only to temporary or extraordinary situations which may occur in institutions over a limited period of time or to broad differences in overall rates of departure between certain types of institutions. To understand the occurrence of continuing differences in patterns of departure, one has to refer, as did Durkheim in the study of suicide, to the structural conditions of institutions and to an educational parallel to egotistical suicide. Specifically, one has to inquire as to the social and intellectual character of an institution and the student and faculty communities that comprise it and the mechanisms which enable individuals to become integrated as competent members of those communities. As in the case of societies, one would expect institutions with low rates of departure to be those which are able to more fully integrate their students into their social and intellectual life.

By extension, it also follows from this analogy that one approach to the question of institutional policy on retention is that which looks toward a restructuring and/or modification of the social and intellectual conditions of the institution and the creation of alternative mechanisms for the integration of individuals into its ongoing social and intellectual life. This, in part, is the message of Kuh, Schuh, Whitt, and Associates'(1991) study of fourteen "involving" colleges that have found ways of integrating students by way of unusually rich out-of-class learning opportunities.

Toward a Theory of Institutional Departure from Higher Education

Egotistical suicide provides the analogue for our thinking about institutional departure from higher education. It does so not so much because voluntary leaving may be thought of as a form of educational suicide, but because it *highlights the ways in which the social and intellectual communities that make up a college come to influence the willingness of students to stay at that college.* In this manner, Durkheim's work, like that of Van Gennep, provides us a way of understanding how colleges, comprised as they are of differing social and intellectual communities, come to influence the leaving of their students.

But Durkheim's theory does not, of itself, yield a theory of departure that helps explain how various individuals come to leave institutions of higher education. Rather, it is a descriptive model which specifies the conditions in society under which varying types of suicide occur. It is concerned with accounting for differences in aggregate rates of suicide, not its individual occurrence. To adapt Durkheim's work to the question of individual departure from institutions of higher education we must move to a theory of individual behavior. Equally important, we must recognize that colleges are in structure and functioning different from the broader human societies which encompass them. The events which may explain suicide in the broader society need not explain equally well, or in the same fashion, departure from the more narrowly defined setting of the college.

Though institutions of higher education may often be thought of as small societies unto themselves, they are more bipolar in structure than society in general, being made up of distinct academic and social components. Moreover, college communities are less extensive in scope than those in the larger society. Unlike the settings with which Van Gennep and Durkheim were concerned, colleges are not places in which students take up permanent residence. For some, their communities are temporary places of residence during a person's life which do not have the same degree of holding power as do human communities generally. For others, especially commuting students, the term college residence has little meaning. For them, events external to the college play an important role in community membership.

It is also the case that Durkheim's use of the term "integration" contained the implicit assumption that individual membership was dependent on the adoption of the values and norms of the community's defining group. As pointed out by Tierney (1992), integration in this sense is not very different from conformity. In the same fashion that Attinasi's (1989) study critiques the implication that the use of Durkheim's theory implies that "moral consensus is . . . an independent cause of one's persisting in life or college" (p. 267), Tierney argues that Durkheim's vision of conformity contains a tacit recognition of the appropriateness of prevailing patterns of inequality in colleges that place one set of values above others.

But colleges, unlike the communities Durkheim and Van Gennep had in mind, are rarely so homogeneous or monolithic in character. Rather than being made up of a single dominant community, the great majority of colleges are made up of several, if not many, communities or "subcultures," each with its own characteristic set of values and norms. Though it is true that many colleges are marked by a dominant culture, one that sets the tone for the college generally, it is not always the case that students have to conform to that culture in order to persist. But it is true that they have to locate at least one community in which to find membership and the support membership provides (e.g., Nora 1987 and Attinasi 1989). Similarly, though conformity in Durkheim and Van Gennep's sense may occur for some students, it does not follow that membership *requires* a full sharing of values. Rather, it suggests that some degree of consensus or sharing of values is a requisite condition for persistence and by extension the absence of the sharing of values of any kind a precondition for departure. Though some degree of integration in the collegiate setting is seen as necessary for persistence, it need not imply the sort of conformity or consensus that Durkheim and Van Gennep may have envisioned in their work. It is for this reason, among others, that the concept of "membership" is, in this context, more useful than that of "integration." Though the former implies some measure of the latter, "membership" allows for greater diversity of participation.

At the same time, whereas Durkheim's and Van Gennep's analysis of membership spoke only to the process of individual adoption of norms, we must recognize that the process of integration in college is an *interactive* one in which individuals also act to reshape their environment. Rather than being passive, individuals are, in varying degrees, active participants in that process. Their behaviors, reflecting as they do personality and preferences, also play a part in their eventually "finding a niche" in college (Brower 1992).

As noted above, college student communities are rarely as permanent as those Van Gennep and Durkheim had in mind. The communities of the college are, by comparison, less extensive and weaker than those found in the broader society and may be but one group of a number of communities in which the student has membership. And unlike that of tenured faculty, student membership in college communities is almost always temporary. Though many students may hold that membership in high regard and may remain attached to the college through alumni organizations, their entry into the institution is always a passage aimed at eventual departure.

The point here is simple. Though the analogy of integration and community membership is still of value, we must, in applying Van Gennep's and Durkheim's work to the study of departure from college, be sensitive to the differences which mark the particular quality of the college communities and the situations in which many students find themselves. We can adapt the notions of integration and community membership to the world of the college without adopting wholesale the cultural judgments that underlie their particular application of those concepts.

The Academic and Social Systems of College

Colleges are made up of both academic and social systems, each with its own characteristic formal and informal structure and set of student, staff, and faculty communities. The former, the academic, concerns itself almost entirely with the formal education of students. Its activities center about the classrooms and laboratories of the institution and involve various faculty and staff whose primary responsibility is the education of students. The latter, the social system of the college, centers about the daily life and personal needs of the various members of the institution, especially the students. It is made up of those recurring sets of interactions among students, faculty, and staff that take place largely outside the formal academic domain of the college. For students, at least, it goes on in large measure in the residence halls, cafeteria, hallways, and other meeting places of the college. Its activities focus on the social as well as the intellectual needs of its members.

The important point here is not merely that such distinct systems exist within the college. Rather it is that experiences in each may lead in a somewhat different fashion to varying modes of departure from the institution. Thus, unlike the study of suicide, it is important in studying departure from higher education to distinguish not only between the differing types of individual departure (e.g., forced and voluntary) but also between the varying forms of intellectual and social integration (membership) which may occur in the academic and the social systems of the institution. As we have seen in the preceding chapter, the experiences of persons in each may have quite separate effects upon their departure from the institution.

It also follows that integration or membership in either system need not imply comparable integration in the other. A person can conceivably establish membership in the social system of the college, largely comprised of one's peers, and still depart because of an inability to establish competent membership in the academic domain of the college (e.g., failure to maintain adequate grades). Conversely a person may perform more than adequately in the academic domain of the college and still come to leave because of insufficient integration into its social life.

The impacts of the two systems are, however, not entirely symmetrical, and the degree of asymmetry appears to vary from institution to institution. In some colleges the academic system and its stress upon intellectual matters may dominate the wider social life of the institution. In others, the opposite may apply. Nevertheless, maintenance of adequate levels of grade performance in the academic system is, for most colleges, a minimum formal condition for persistence. Integration or membership in the social system is not. Failure to attain a minimum grade level leads to academic dismissal. But failure to meet the "minimum standards" of the social system need not lead to departure. Though departure often results, it does not arise out of any formal dictate or requirement.

The distinction between the academic and social domains of institutional life may also be applied to a comparative analysis of departure among different types of institutions. Differences in institutional rates of departure may arise out of discernible differences in the structure and strength of institutional academic and social systems. This is particularly apparent in those higher educational settings where the two systems are highly segregated and/or unequal in size, as is the case among nonresidential institutions, where local social systems are often quite weak. In the latter instances, the absence of strong, enduring social systems comprised of interacting students may pose, as we have previously noted, serious problems for institutions which seek to more fully integrate their students into the life of the institution.

In applying Durkheim's and Van Gennep's theories to a theory of student departure one must also distinguish between the formal and informal manifestations of each system and the manner in which experiences in either may impinge upon social and intellectual integration within the life of the college. At the same time, one must recognize that as the formal and informal worlds of the college are necessarily joined, as they involve some of the same people, experiences in one may influence what goes on in the other.

One must discern, for example, how forms of integration or membership which occur in the formal academic structure (e.g., classrooms and laboratories) may lead to similar integration in the informal academic milieu of the institution. Consider contact with the faculty in informal settings outside the classroom. It is, as we have noted in chapter 3, a critical component in student persistence generally and student intellectual development in particular. But its occurrence may be as much a reflection of what has taken place within the formal domain of the classroom (e.g., patterns of faculty teaching) as it may be of what occurs informally out of class.

The same applies to experiences within the social system of the college. Though one must separate those experiences which take place in the formal social system of the college (e.g., extracurricular activities) from those which are largely informal (e.g., arising out of the day-to-day activities among differing members of the institution over matters not formally addressed in the rules and regulations of the institution), experiences in each are necessarily linked. It is for this reason that student participation in extracurricular activities (e.g., theater groups, student government) often leads to friendships that extend well beyond those formal social activities.

In the same way that the formal and informal worlds of the academic and social systems are linked, so too is there an important interplay between the academic and social life of the college. Though experiences in each may have distinct impacts upon integration and therefore upon persistence, the two are necessarily interrelated (Stage 1989b). Colleges, like other human communities, are highly interdependent, interactive systems in which events in any one part may be felt in other parts of the system. Experiences in the formal social system, for instance via the well-documented effect of work-study, may have important effects upon one's success in the academic system of the college. At the same time, social isolation may undermine one's academic performance. In some instances, academic failure may arise not from the absence of skills but from the debilitating impact of social isolation upon a person's ability to carry out academic work. In the academic world of the institution, experiences in classrooms, especially those that are collaborative in nature, may come to enhance social relations among students outside the classroom (Tinto, Goodsell, and Russo 1993).

The point here is really quite simple. Though our theory of student departure must take account of the distinct academic and social systems of a college, it must be recognized that these systems are invariably interwoven. Events in one may directly or indirectly influence, over time, events in the other.

External Forces and External Choices

Events which occur elsewhere in the student's life may also play an important role in determining what transpires within the college. The actions of one's family, of members of one's community, as well as those of external actors in state and national organizations, can all play an important part in the decisions of individuals to depart from college.

This may be particularly important, as noted above, in those higher educational situations such as exist in nonresidential colleges, especially in urban settings, and among working students, where full-time participation in the social and intellectual activities of the institution is not a normal (or even possible) facet of college life. For many such students, going to college is but one of a number of obligations they have to meet during the course of a day. In these situations, the demands of external communities and the obligations or commitments they entail may work counter to the demands of institutional life. When the academic and social systems of the institution are weak, the countervailing external demands may seriously undermine the individual's ability to persist until degree completion. In a very real sense, students may be "pulled away" from college attendance.

In attempting, therefore, to adapt Durkheim's primarily societal view of suicide to departure from the more limited and bipolar society of the college, we must take seriously the possibility that social forces external to the formal confines of the institution may impinge upon decisions regarding behavior in that setting. That is, our model of departure must be able to discern when a voluntary departure, as we have defined it here, may in fact be involuntary in the sense that it arises as a result of external events which force or oblige the individual to withdraw, at least temporarily, despite the maintenance of adequate levels of academic performance.

Individual Dispositions and Individual Suicide

We are not yet to a point where we can move to a theory of individual departure from institutions of higher education. This is so because our reference, Durkheim's theory of suicide, is largely a descriptive model which specifies the conditions under which varying types of suicide occur. His largely structural argument does not, nor did it seek to, explain how different *individuals* come to attempt suicide. To move to a theory of individual suicide, and therefore to a theory of individual departure, one has to take account of the personal attributes of individuals which predispose them to respond to given situations or conditions with particular forms of behavior. In the jargon of the psychologist studying suicide, one has to include measures of the individual's suicidal tendency or proneness. It is that disposition, among others, which helps to explain why it is that in stressful (malintegrative) situations certain individuals are more likely than others to adopt a suicidal response. In order to produce a viable theory of individual suicide one must therefore combine notions of individual dispositions, specifically those which incline persons toward suicidal behavior, with those elements of Durkheim's structural view of egotistical suicide which specify the social conditions, namely the absence of social and intellectual integration, under which those behavioral responses are likely to occur.

The educational analogue of suicidal tendency are those–dispositions which incline individuals toward departure rather than persistence within the communities of the college. These fall into two categories involving dispositions, normally referred to as expectations and motivations. In the case of student departure these prove, as we have seen in chapter 3, to be best measured by intentions or goals and commitments. The former specify the valued goals, educational and occupational, toward which activities are directed; the latter the person's willingness to work toward the attainment of those goals both in the educational enterprise generally and within the context of a specific institution in particular.

Intentions, whether educational or occupational, reflect both aspirations and expectations. Most often stated in terms of goals, they mirror both the person's hopes for the future and his/her assessment, based upon past experience, of the likelihood of attaining that future. As such, they serve as a barometer of the character of individual experiences and their sum effect upon individual judgments of future attainment. Though commitments, too, reflect past experience, they mirror as well important aspects of personality which predispose a person toward the completion of tasks once begun and/or the attainment of goals once established. Highly motivated or committed persons presumably are those who are willing to commit themselves fully to the attainment of valued goals and expend the energies and resources required to do so. Persons lacking such motivation, however, may hold lofty goals for themselves but may be unable or unwilling to commit themselves to their attainment. And the more committed the person is to the attainment of those goals within a specific institutional context (institutional commitment), the more likely will he/she be to complete that degree within that institution.

Stated in this manner, our discussion of intentions and commitments parallels that regarding the effect of weakly and strongly held norms of behavior. Weakly held norms are those which are externally held and which will be followed when other observers are present and/or when a threat of punishment is present. Strongly held norms are those which are internally held. They are likely to be followed even in the absence of external observers or threat of punishment because those norms have been internalized by individuals as their own. Thus it may be said that normally law-abiding citizens who loot stores during major disasters have only weakly held the norm regarding theft of property. The absence of threat of capture and punishment leads them to act counter to the norm, when otherwise they might not. They may comply with the norm, but have not internalized it.

In this fashion it can also be argued that persons who only weakly hold the norm of college may give up on its achievement when the costs of doing so have been greatly increased or when significant others (e.g., parents) are no longer present to enforce it. Conversely, individuals who strongly hold the norm of college completion will see its attainment as in their own best interests. Motivation for goal attainment arises then from the natural tendency of individuals to maximize their interests, not from the often counterproductive fear of punishment.

As in the case of individual suicide, goals (intentions) and motivations (commitments) can be seen as helping to explain why it is that certain individuals, when experiencing the conditions of social and intellectual malintegration within the college, will choose to depart the institution. Sufficiently lofty intentions and/or strong commitments, for example, may lead the person to persist until degree completion despite unrewarding interactions within the college. This may be especially true when educational goals are clearly linked to one's occupational goals. Thus, other things being equal, one might expect rates of departure to be lower in professional preparatory programs than they might be, for instance, in general study programs, where such linkages are less distinct.

Two caveats should be made here. First, it does not follow that participation in general liberal-arts programs in and of itself necessarily increases the likelihood of departure. Many individuals place great emphasis on the intrinsic rewards of educational participation. For them the potential economic and occupational outcomes are less important than the immediate intellectual and social rewards accruing from participation in college life. Second, for those individuals who place great stress on the extrinsic rewards of college, the linkage between goals and commitments becomes a two-edged sword. Presumably the more committed the individual is to valued economic and occupational goals, the more sensitive he/she will be to the institution's perceived impact upon the attainment of those goals. Thus, while such persons are more likely to persist until degree completion than other individuals, they may be more likely to transfer to other institutions to do so. Interestingly, a parallel situation may also apply to those who place great import upon the intrinsic rewards of college. As such persons place greater value on the immediate rewards of participation they may also be more sensitive to the ability of the institution to meet their social and intellectual expectations regardless of its potential impact upon future activities.

A Longitudinal Model of Departure from Institutions of Higher Education

Until now we have focused our attention on the environmental conditions under which departure is likely to occur, namely inadequate intellectual and social integration into the systems of the institution, and on the delineation of the individual dispositions (intentions and commitments) which help explain why certain persons experiencing those conditions will in fact depart the institution. We now turn to the specification of an interactive model of student departure which describes and explains the longitudinal process by which individuals come to leave institutions of higher education. In so doing we will review how adjustment, difficulty, incongruence, isolation, finances, learning, and external obligations or commitments come to influence differing forms of student departure from campus.

Before we describe that model, a few comments are called for as to its specific aims—what it is designed to do and what it is not designed to do. First and foremost the model is intended to speak to the longitudinal process of departure as it occurs *within an institution* of higher education. It focuses primarily, though not exclusively, on the events which occur within the institution following entry and/or which immediately precede entrance to it. It is not a systems model of departure. Nor is it intended to account for individual behavior after departure. Whether the person transfers to another institution is not an issue of immediate concern. Though we will eventually look at such movements, the immediate focus of the model will be on explaining why and how it is that some individuals come to depart their institution prior to completing their degree programs. Second, the model pays special attention to the longitudinal process by which individuals come to *voluntarily* withdraw from institutions of higher education. Though the occurrence of academic dismissal will not be ignored, it will not be central to our discussions. Third, the model is *longitudinal and interactional* in character. It emphasizes the longitudinal process of interactions which arises among individuals within the institution and which can be seen over time to account for the longitudinal process of withdrawal or disassociation which marks individual departure. In this sense it is not merely a descriptive model of departure but an explanatory one. Its primary goal is not simply to describe the degree to which different individual and institutional attributes are associated with departure. Though that description may follow from the model, it is not its primary goal. Rather the model seeks to explain how interactions among different individuals within the academic and social systems of the institution and the communities which comprise them lead individuals of different characteristics to withdraw from that institution prior to degree completion.

In focusing on the multiple interactions which occur among members of the institution, the model is also primarily sociological in character. That is, it looks to the social and intellectual context of the institution, its formal and informal interactional environment, as playing a central role in the longitudinal process of individual departure. Though it accepts as a given the fact that individuals have much to do with their own leaving, it argues that the impact of individual attributes cannot be understood without reference to the social and intellectual context within which individuals find themselves. At the same time, it recognizes that much of the effect of context may be transmitted through its impact upon subsequent student intentions (Bean 1982, Cabrera, Castaneda, Nora, and Hengstler 1992). By extension, it further argues that the effect of the formal organization upon departure is largely indirect, occurring through the role the organization has in shaping the social and intellectual communities of the institution (Braxton and Brier 1989). In this fashion, the communities of the college mediate if not transform the effect of the formal organization upon student behavior.

The model also aims at being policy relevant in the sense that it can be employed by institutional officials as a guide for institutional actions to retain more students until degree completion. It is structured to allow institutional planners to identify those elements of the institutional environment, academic and social, which may interfere with degree completion. In permitting such identification the model is intended to enable institutional officials to ask and answer the question, How can the institution be altered to enhance retention on campus?

That model is depicted in figure 4.1. Broadly understood, it argues that individual departure from institutions can be viewed as arising out of a longitudinal process of interactions between an individual with given attributes, skills, financial resources, prior educational experiences, and dispositions (intentions and commitments) and other members of the academic and social systems of the institution. The individual's experience in those systems, as

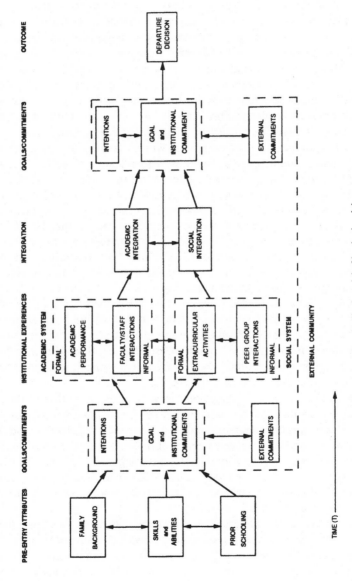

Fig. 4.1. A longitudinal model of institutional departure.

indicated by his/her intellectual (academic) and social (personal) integration, continually modifies his or her intentions and commitments. Positive experiences—that is, integrative ones—reinforce persistence through their impact upon heightened intentions and commitments both to the goal of college completion and to the institution in which the person finds him/herself (Cabrera, Castaneda, Nora, and Hengstler 1992). Negative or malintegrative experiences serve to weaken intentions and commitments, especially commitment to the institution, and thereby enhance the likelihood of leaving.

At the same time, the model sees the institution, and the social and academic communities which comprise it, as being nested in an external environment comprised of external communities with their own set of values and behavioral requirements. As such it recognizes the very obvious fact that for many students going to college is but one of a number of commitments they have to balance over the course of the college career. In this instance, external commitments are seen as altering the person's intentions (plans) and goal and institutional commitments at entry and throughout the college career. And they do so in a manner that is largely (but not entirely) independent of the internal world of the institution.

Individuals enter institutions of higher education with a range of differing family and community backgrounds (e.g., as measured by social-status, parental education, and size of community), a variety of personal attributes (e.g., sex, race, and physical handicaps), skills (e.g., intellectual and social), financial resources, dispositions (e.g., motivations; intellectual, social, and political preferences), and varying types of precollege educational experiences and achievements (e.g., high school grade-point average). Each attribute is posited as having a direct impact upon departure from college as suggested, for instance, by its well-documented effect upon levels of academic performance in college. More importantly, each affects departure indirectly through its effect upon the continuing formulation of individual intentions and commitments regarding future educational activities. Intentions or goals specify both the level and type of education and occupation desired by the individual. Commitments indicate the degree to which individuals are committed both to the attainment of those goals (goal commitment) and to the institution into which they gain entry (institutional commitment). These, together with skills and dispositions, describe the financial, social, and intellectual resources and orientations regarding educational continuance which individuals bring with them into the college environment. Along with external commitments, they help establish the initial conditions for subsequent interactions between the individual and other members of the institution.

Given individual attributes and dispositions at entry, the model further argues that subsequent experiences within the institution, primarily those arising out of interactions between the individual and other members of the college, student, staff, and faculty, are centrally related to further continuance in that institution. Interactive experiences which further one's social and intellectual integration are seen to enhance the likelihood that the individual will persist within the institution until degree completion, because of the impact integrative experiences have upon the continued reformulation of individual goals and commitments. Positive integration serves to raise one's goals and strengthen one's commitments both to those goals and to the institution within which they may be attained. Conversely, the model posits that, other things being equal, the lower the degree of one's social and intellectual integration into the academic and social communities of the college, the greater the likelihood of departure.

To the degree that the individual also participates in communities external to the college (e.g., family, work, and community), the model argues, events in those communities may also shape persistence in college. When those external communities are strong, as they are for commuting students, their actions may serve to condition, if not counter, events within the college. It posits that external events may influence departure indirectly via their impact upon student social and academic integration and/or directly via their effect on commitments—being "pulled away." As such, the model leaves open the possibility that individuals may withdraw from college even when experiences within the college are largely positive. At the same time, it also allows for the fact that external communities, for instance the family, may reinforce persistence (Bean and Vesper 1992).

Since financial resources are viewed as part of the broader set of individual attributes, the model argues that the primary impact of financial resources (as distinct from financial aid) upon persistence will be indirect. Their influence will be felt via their impact upon the character of college entry (i.e., where and in what form attendance occurs) and upon the nature of students' intentions and commitments (Cabrera, Stampen, and Hansen 1990, Cabrera, Nora, and Castaneda 1992).

Academic Dismissal and Voluntary Withdrawal from College

It is further postulated that experiences in the formal and informal components of the academic and social systems of the institution may have distinct, though necessarily interrelated, impacts upon institutional departure. Integration into the academic system of the college, especially in its formal components, is seen as directly linked to those forms of departure which arise from a substantial incongruence or mismatch between the skills and abilities of the individual and the level of demand placed on that person by the aca demic system of the college. Academic difficulty (and therefore academic dismissal) typically reflects a situation in which the demands of the academic system prove too great. Academic boredom and voluntary withdrawal, on the other hand, often result when the demands of the formal academic system are not challenging enough. Students fail to become involved in the intellectual life of the college in part because they find that life insufficiently rewarding. It must be noted, however, that some academic dismissals are in fact voluntary in the sense that they mirror a decision made by an individual not to invest the time and energy needed to maintain minimum academic standards. Though the individual may possess the needed skills, he/she may be insufficiently committed either to the institution or to the goal of education to meet the academic demands of the institution.

Incongruence may also result from a substantial mismatch between the intellectual orientation of the student and that of the institution. This does not have to do with formal academic activities alone; it also reflects the outcome of the day-to-day interactions between faculty, staff, and students which occur both inside and outside the classrooms and laboratories of the institution. Beyond the importance of those contacts for the social and intellectual development of students, they are central to the process by which students come to judge the degree of congruence between their own intellectual orientation and that which characterizes the life of the institution. Thus, contact with faculty and staff does not, in itself, insure congruence. Nevertheless, wide-ranging contact may increase the likelihood of its occurrence because of the impact extensive personal contact has upon value change among maturing adults.

Contact with faculty and staff may affect departure in quite another way. They may influence individuals' judgments about the degree to which the institution, as reflected in the actions of its representatives, is committed to student welfare. These influence, in turn, the development of individual commitment to the institution and therefore decisions as to continued persistence. Wide-ranging contact generally leads to heightened commitment and therefore serves, in this manner, to enhance the likelihood of persistence. The absence of interaction, however, results not only in lessened commitments and possibly lowered individual goals, but also in the person's isolation from the intellectual life of the institution. It may also reinforce, or at least leave unchecked, the development of deviant intellectual orientations that may further serve to disassociate the individual from other members of the academic system. Though the presence of interaction does not by itself guarantee persistence, the absence of interaction almost always enhances the likelihood of departure.

Experiences in the formal and informal social systems of the institution are also seen as leading to voluntary withdrawal. They may do so either in the form of social incongruence or social isolation. Interactions among students in that system are viewed as central to the development of the important social bonds that serve to integrate the individual into the social communities of the college. The social (personal) integration and resulting social rewards which arise from it lead to heightened institutional commitment. They also serve as guideposts for the development of social and intellectual identities so important to the life of young adults. In this sense, social isolation and/or intellectual and social deviancy with the social system of the college is, as in the case of suicide, an important element in the process of voluntary departure from institutions of higher education. Other things being equal, the greater the contact among students, the more likely individuals are to establish social and intellectual membership in the social communities of the college and therefore the more likely they are to remain in college.

The College as an Interactive System

Inherent in the model of institutional departure is the important notion that colleges are systematic enterprises comprised of a variety of linking interactive, reciprocal parts, formal and informal, academic and social. Events in one segment of the college necessarily and unavoidably influence events in other parts of the institution. This applies both within systems, between their formal and informal components, and between systems, in a variety of ways. The model argues that, to fully comprehend the longitudinal process of departure, one must take note of the full range of individual experiences which occur in the formal and informal domains of both the social and academic systems of the institution.

Experiences, for example, in the informal academic system may influence one's experiences in the formal domain of that system. This may happen in two ways. Rewarding interactions between faculty, staff, and students outside the classrooms and offices of the institution may lead directly to enhanced intellectual development and therefore to greater intellectual integration in the academic system of the college. They may also result in greater exposure of students to the multiple dimensions of academic work and therefore indirectly lead to heightened levels of formal performance. By the same token, the absence of student-faculty interactions and/or unrewarding interactions outside the classroom may lead to academic boredom and thus to voluntary withdrawal or to lower levels of academic performance which may in turn lead to dismissal.

Of course, the same effects may and do arise in the opposite fashion, that is to say when classroom experiences influence student-faculty contact beyond the classroom. Experiences in the formal academic domain spill over to the informal domain of the college. In some cases, classes which do not engage students in learning—as is frequently the case in the large lecture classes that dot the first year of college—tend to stifle subsequent contact with faculty. Students who find themselves alienated from learning in the classroom are unlikely to seek out contact with faculty beyond the classroom. By contrast, in those cases where classrooms actively involve students in learning, additional contact with faculty outside of class arises in part because engaged students will seek out that contact. This, as we shall see in the next chapter, is precisely one of the assumptions underlying the use of collaborative and cooperative learning in college classrooms.

The same interplay of formal and informal interactions may also occur within the social system of the college. It may arise, for instance, when individuals are able to gain a position in the formal social structure of the system. Working for the student newspaper, holding work-study jobs at the institution, or serving as an officer in the student government may serve to enhance individual integration into the informal world of student life. In the same fashion, membership in the informal social system may greatly assist the student in gaining access to those formal positions in the social world of the institution.

It should be clear by now that though integration or membership in the academic and social systems of the college are argued to be conceptually distinct processes, they are mutually interdependent and reciprocal (Tinto 1975, Stage 1989b). Since these systems necessarily involve many of the same actors, faculty, staff, and students, events in one system necessarily impact upon activities in the other. And this may be the case in both positive and negative ways. When the cultures of the academic and social systems are supportive of each other, then the two systems may work in consonance to reinforce integration in both the academic and social systems of the institution. In this sense, their interaction may further the institutional goal of retention (Kuh, Schuh, Whitt, and Associates 1991). When this is not the case, that is, when the demands of these systems are to some degree in competition if not conflict (i.e., they ask the student to allocate scarce time and energies among alternative forms of activities), it is entirely possible that integration in one system of the college may constrain, or at least make more difficult, integration in the other (Stage 1989b). Among institutions with particularly demanding academic requirements, for instance, this may lead to some degree of social isolation among students. Conversely, when social pressures for social interaction among student peers are great, individuals may find keeping up with even the minimum demands of the academic system quite trying. When institutional subcultures are varied in character, as they frequently are, then their interactive impact upon departure depends very much on how individuals come to choose between participation in those subcultures.

It might be noted, with some irony, that some forms of isolation may sometimes result less from the demands of the academic and social systems of the college than from how students choose to differentially allocate their time to those systems. Just as often as one hears of the academically gifted students whose involvement in academic work effectively precludes social contact with other members of the college, one learns of students whose active social lives greatly reduce their contact with members of the academic realm of the college, especially the faculty. Thus the not very surprising finding reported by Astin (1975) that departure is sometimes associated with high frequency of dating in college. In the interactive life of the college, actions in one domain almost always have ramifications in other domains of activity.

This point having been made, it is necessary to note that the model does not argue that full integration in both systems of the college is necessary for persistence. Nor does it claim that failure to be integrated in either system necessarily leads to departure. Rather it argues that some degree of social and intellectual integration and therefore membership in academic and social communities must exist as a condition for continued persistence.

Within the framework of the model it is entirely possible, for instance, for individuals to achieve integration in the academic system of the college without doing so in the social domain. Persistence may follow if the individual's goals and commitments are such as to bear the costs of isolation in the social system of the college. Though the converse may apply, the formal demands of the academic system are such as to require the individual to meet at least the minimum requirements of academic performance. In this instance, the social rewards accruing from integration in the social system of the college may not offset the inability and/or failure of the person to become integrated in the academic system of the college.

The interactive character of the model serves then to highlight the important dynamic interplay between the social and intellectual components of student life. To ignore one for the other or to suggest that each occurs independently of the other, even on nonresidential campuses, is to distort the integrative character of individual experiences in college. Both play a role, albeit different, in the process of student persistence. In this manner, the interactive model described above posits that individual integrative experiences in the formal and informal academic and social communities of the college and the interplay between them, as conditioned by external events, are central to the process of departure, especially that which takes place voluntarily. Such experiences continually act upon individuals' evaluation of their educational and occupational goals and their commitments both to the attainment of those goals and to the institution into which initial entry has been gained.

Departure and Membership in College Communities

In a very important sense the model described above takes as a given the notion that colleges, albeit more bipolar and less permanent, are very much like the broader human communities which surround them. Colleges are seen as being made up of a cluster of social and academic communities, comprised of students, faculty, and staff, each having distinct forms of association tying its members to one another. The process of persistence in college is, by extension, viewed as a process of social and intellectual integration leading to the establishment of competent membership in those communities. Conversely, departure from college is taken to reflect the unwillingness and/or inability of the individual to become integrated and therefore establish membership in the communities of the college.

Competent membership in college communities is at least partially determined by the formal demands of the academic system of the college and prevailing intellectual and/or academic culture of the institution. That culture helps define for the formal structure what is competent membership and what is not. For the broader collegiate setting it serves to establish the intellectual and social coordinates by which institutional interactions are gauged. The prevailing academic culture acts to define, in effect, what is appropriate and what is deviant. But as in the broader arena of society, full or total integration is not seen here as a necessary condition for college persistence. Individuals may persist without becoming so fully integrated. Rather the model argues that some form of integration—that is, some type of social and/or intellectual membership in at least one college community—is a minimum condition for continued persistence.

To return to a point made earlier, colleges, like most other organizations, are typically composed of a variety of communities or subcultures, each with its own distinct view of the world. One or more will be centrally located in the mainstream of institutional life. Sometimes referred to as dominant communities, these will often establish and/or be guardians of the prevailing institutional ethos, that distinctive signature which marks the institution as having a discernible character. Other communities often exist at the periphery of institutional life. Though viable on their own, they are normally subordinate to the dominant communities on campus in the sense that they do not form or shape the prevailing social and intellectual character of the institution.

Individuals may find membership in any one of these communities. It is entirely possible, for instance, for an individual to be isolated from a majority of local college communities and from the dominant communities and still persist if competent membership can be established in at least one locally supportive social or intellectual community. Insofar as individuals are able to find some communal niche on campus, then it is possible for a person to be seen as deviant from the broader college environment and still persist to degree completion.

At the same time, the model leaves open the very real possibility that individuals may find membership in several different communities, each with its own particular culture. In addition to the increased range of support that individuals may experience while in college, membership in multiple communities allows individuals to play out a multiplicity of roles and satisfy a range of needs that no one community may be able to fulfill. Presumably, the greater the number of memberships, the greater the likelihood of persistence and the greater the benefits accruing from persistence.

In some respects this notion of supportive communities is similar to social-support theory. This body of theory focuses on the role of supportive relationships in preventing and reducing the harmful effects of stress and enhancing individuals' ability to cope effectively with stress in specific social settings (House 1981, McCarthy, Pretty, and Catano 1990, Pearson 1990, and Jacobi 1991). In the collegiate setting, research has tended to support the conclusion that the establishment of supportive personal relationships—with faculty, peers, and other significant persons—enables students to better cope with the demands of the college environment (Ostrow, Paul, Dark, and Berhman 1986). This, in turn, has positive impacts upon student academic success. Fleming's (1985) finding that the existence of supportive relationships is essential for the persistence and intellectual development of black students can, in this regard, be applied to any student.

What is intriguing about this line of research is that it enables us to establish a link between the social psychological view of college success, as exemplified by Fleming (1985), and the more sociological view that is argued here. While the former tends to emphasize the role of social support in the development of personality and its associated performance outcomes, the present view of college places greater stress on the actions of the various actors in the collegiate environment (students, faculty, and staff) and how those actions shape the nature of the social and academic communities in which students find themselves. Though both views necessarily focus on the same individual outcomes (i.e., learning and persistence) and the importance of student initiative (i.e., commitments and intentions), the latter view places greater emphasis on the actions of others and on the formal and informal settings they help create. As we shall argue in the following chapter on policy, this latter view of student persistence leads to a policy orientation that stresses the collaborative effort of a variety of actors, faculty and staff alike, across the campus.

Colleges as Multiple Community Systems

One way to think about deviance (or marginality) in the multi-community world of the college is to refer to a model astronomers use to describe solar systems in which there may be one or more suns at or near the center of the system. In several important respects colleges are like solar systems in that they consist of a number of communities (or subcultures) which, like planets, revolve about the center of institutional life and which have their own satellite system of affiliated groups and individuals. Some colleges may have a single dominant center and a relatively uniform pattern of relationships to the center of institutional life. Others, with more than one dominant group, may have no one simple nucleus and therefore like multi-sun solar systems have quite complex, yet analyzable, patterns of association with the core or epicenter of the institutional system. In this case there is not single dominant group, but a cluster of groups which together form the nucleus or mainstream of institutional life.

When we speak of marginality and centrality of individual participation we can, to continue this analogy, refer to the degree to which a person is affiliated to any one community which provides the local center or planet in the system of the college. By ascertaining the distance of that community from the center or epicenter of the college, we can speak of the degree to which membership in that community ties the person to the dominant forces within the college, that is, to its social and intellectual center. Two forms of affiliation bind the individual to the life of the college, one which is localized in a particular community, like the bond of a moon to a planet, another which ties the individual via the networks of affiliations inherent in the community to the center of college life as a planet is tied to the center (sun) of the solar system.

The net outcome of these two forms of affiliation on institutional persistence depends both on the degree of centrality of the individual's membership in the local community and on that community's location relative to the institutional center. Though membership in a local community is a necessary minimum condition for persistence, it is not a sufficient one. Persistence also depends on the centrality of that community in the system of the college. Generally speaking, the closer one's community is to the center of the system, the stronger the forces which bind the individual to the institution generally. As in the case of a satellite about a planet close to the sun, the gravitational forces of both "planet" and "sun" are such as to keep the individual close or central to the mainstream of the life of the college. A person strongly tied to a marginal community, like a satellite about a distant planet, though affiliated locally, may have only weak, tangential bonds to the center of institutional life. A significant external force may pull that person away from the system generally. Nevertheless, in the absence of disturbing forces, that local affiliation may be sufficient to keep the individual within the broader system of the college.

The concept of multiple communities leads to several intriguing notions. First, it leads to the implied hypothesis that the greater the variety of locally available subcultures or communities on campus, the greater the likelihood that a greater range and number of persons will be able, if they so desire, to become integrated and establish competent intellectual and social membership while in college. More diverse institutions, in this regard, provide a greater array of niches into which a wider range of persons may find their place. Second, it suggests the much-referenced notion of critical mass and the attendant need for institutions to insure that sufficient numbers of individuals of varying types and/or dispositions are found on campus. Those numbers need be large enough for supportive communities to form and become self-perpetuating. Third, the notion of dominant and subordinate communities directs our attention to the hypothesis described above, that the more central one's membership is to the mainstream of institutional life the more likely, other things being equal, is one to persist. Conversely the more marginal one's membership, the more likely is departure. Presumably more central membership results in a greater array of benefits, social and intellectual, not the least of which may be the sense of being part of an important ethos or tradition which marks the continuing life of the institution.

In this very important sense, the term "integration" may be understood to apply both to the individual and to the particular subcommunity of which he or she is a member. It is entirely possible for persons to perceive themselves to be socially integrated into a local subcommunity, that is to see themselves as members of a community, without sensing the same degree of membership in other communities on campus or of being part of the dominant social mainstream on that campus.

Three final observations. First, on most racially and ethnically diverse campuses, local ethnic/race communities may provide much needed havens or safe places that, for some students, may be essential for continued persistence. In this way, ethnic communities on campus can provide a stabilizing anchor in what might otherwise be a large, foreign campus environment (Murguia, Padilla, and Pavel 1991). The fact that minority students sometimes refer to such local ethnic communities as "enclaves" suggests a pattern of segregation on campus where some communities see themselves in some way threatened by other, more powerful communities. Second, in any campus, especially the very large campuses that dot the public sector, the existence of many smaller local communities, such as those found in and around fraternities, sororities, clubs, and organizations, serve the important function of enabling new students to break down the university into smaller knowable parts where social integration is more readily possible. Such small communities may serve to cut the large university down to size and thereby make eventual integration more likely (Attinasi 1986, 1989). Third, insofar as colleges are made up of a multiplicity of academic and social communities comprised of faculty, staff, and students that are differentially located in the academic and social geography of a campus, it follows that individual persistence is framed by the interplay among the various communities, internal and external to the college, in which the person participates.

College Communities and the Temporal Process of Becoming a Student

This notion of cutting a large, unknown place down to knowable smaller parts returns us to the temporal character of persistence and to the concept of the stages of persistence that may characterize the early part of the student career, specifically the first year of college. It also leads us, as we shall see in chapter 5, to a view of the freshman year that speaks to a very particular way of thinking about policy in that year.

In seeking to make the transition between membership in past communities and membership in the new communities of the college, new students face the frequently daunting task of navigating their way around an unknown, remote campus geography. That geography, as described by Attinasi (1989), is comprised of at least three elements, the physical, the social, and the academic/cognitive. The strategies they employ in order to fix or locate themselves in these geographies involve "getting to know" and "scaling down." In the former case, new students seek out knowledgeable peers or mentors on campus who provide insight into the campus and advice on how to navigate it. In the latter case, they seek to cut the larger campus down to knowable smaller parts or niches that help anchor them. In some cases, that niche may be a club or organization. In other cases, it may be a small, like-minded and/or familiar community on campus that shares similar views or attributes with the new student (e.g., ethnic communities). And in still other cases, it may be found in the major area of study and therefore in a department or academic program.

The point here is that the notion of multiple communities, academic and social, provides us a way of understanding the possible ways in which differing students may be able to make the transition to college and become incorporated or integrated into the life of the college. More specifically, it suggests that smaller campus communities, formal and informal, may play an important role in enabling newcomers to find an early physical, social, and academic anchorage during the transition to college life. In doing so, they may provide, for many students and certainly for many students of color on predominantly white campuses, an early point of stability in the otherwise unsettling first year of college. In very large campuses, they may be essential in enabling students to successfully navigate and cut down to size the otherwise cold, remote landscape of college.

But early membership does not, in itself, guarantee persistence to degree completion. As argued above, the impact of that membership upon persistence is partially a reflection not only of where that community is located on the social/academic map of the institution, but also of the person's ability to establish membership in other communities and make meaningful contact with faculty both inside and outside the formal domains of the institution. Student interactions with multiple communities on campus may be quite fluid over the full course of the college career. What may describe student integration, that is community membership, in the first year of college may not equally well describe patterns of integration in the later years. Though we can still talk of social and academic integration as a necessary condition for persistence, it must be recognized that those are only umbrella terms under which fall many differing types of membership in very specific communities in the college that may vary over time.

Taken one step further, the notion of changing community membership across time opens up the intriguing possibility that student persistence, and quite possibly social and intellectual growth, involves, perhaps requires, a changing mix of social and academic memberships over time. For the moment, suffice it to point out that Attinasi's study (1989) opens up the possibility that for some students early social membership may be a necessary precondition for subsequent academic membership in college.

External Impacts upon Institutional Departure

All this is not to say, however, that individual decisions regarding staying at or leaving institutions of higher education are unaffected by events external to the college. We know that this is not the case (Christie and Dinham 1991, Bean and Vesper 1992, and Cabrera, Castaneda, Nora, and Hengstler 1992). Indeed we know that across the nation as a whole most students either attend nonresidential colleges or commute to colleges that have residential facilities. Much of their day is spent away from campus. And many have to attend to a range of completing demands on their time and energies. For those persons, especially returning adults, the issue of going to college is not a matter of "doing" college *instead* of something else, but of "doing" college *in addition* to a host of other things.

Though our model intentionally emphasizes the role of intra-institutional experiences, it does not exclude the possible impacts of external events upon persistence. By nesting the college within the larger external community, the model leaves open the possibility that events in communities external to the college may shape what occurs within the narrower confines of the college.

For commuting institutions generally and for commuting students in particular, especially those who have numerous other obligations such as work and family, the model provides a mechanism for the analysis of the possibly conflicting demands of college, work, and family. Conversely, it also enables us to understand how external support from families, friends, and employers may assist, rather than detract, from persistence in college (Pollard 1990, Bean and Vesper 1992).

In this regard it might be useful to think of the problem of external forces in terms of internal and external communities. External communities (families, neighborhoods, peer groups, work settings, etc.), like those internal to the college, have their own social and normative structure and patterns of interaction leading to membership. For any person, participation in external communities may entail accepting a range of external commitments that may counter, rather than support, participation in college communities. This is so not only because the demands of the former may take away time from participation in the latter, but also because the requirements of membership in one may work counter to those for membership in the other.

The normative requirements of membership in one's local peer group external to the college may, for instance, be such as to downplay the appropriateness of membership in the intellectual communities of the college. Membership in the latter may be seen as being a deviant form of activity within the former. Individuals in such situations may be forced to choose between membership in possibly long-standing external communities and that in the relatively new, still tenuous communities of the college. When those latter communities are either weak, as they may be in nonresidential, commuting institutions, or when one's experiences in them are largely unsatisfactory, the effect of external communities upon decisions to persist may be quite substantial. The direction of their impact may spell the difference between staying or leaving. For persons who are only weakly affiliated with any college community and/or whose local community may be marginal to the life of the institution, the effect of such external forces may be great enough to alter one's goals and commitments so as to induce one to leave the college for other pursuits.

This is not to say, however, that all external influences are negative in character. In some cases, external communities may aid student persistence (Pollard 1990, Christie and Dinham 1991, and Bean and Vesper 1992). For married students and older adults with families, for instance, external support may be instrumental in enabling individuals to withstand the difficulties typically faced in adjusting to the academic and social demands of college life. For some younger students, parental support/encouragement may be important to continued persistence (Bean and Vesper 1992). For others who are unable to find local communities of support (e.g., minority students in predominantly majority campuses) or whose time on campus is limited (e.g., working part-time students), external support, whether found in the family, on the job, or in one's local peer group, may be critical to continued persistence (Pollard 1990).

External events may also be seen as influencing departure by altering the mix of competing opportunities for the investment of individual resources. Like all decisions, individual judgments concerning continued participation in college may be viewed as weighing the costs and benefits of college persistence relative to alternative forms of investment of one's time, energies, and scarce resources. When the external mix of opportunities or the relative benefits of attending college change significantly, students may give more weight to the pursuit of noncollege activities. For instance, a reduction in the supply of available jobs for college graduates may lead individuals to leave college (or shift majors, if not colleges) because it means a decreased likelihood that energies invested in college activities will yield acceptable benefits in the future. In this case, individuals may decide to depart college voluntarily in order to invest their time and energies in alternative forms of activity even though their experience in college has been satisfactory. Similarly, a decline in jobs for persons without college degrees may lead individuals to stay in college. Persons may opt, however, to stay in college because of restrictions which limit their movement elsewhere (e.g., the effect in earlier years of the Selective Service draft). By the same token, removal of such restrictions may lead to departure (and in some cases to transfer) if only because it makes available to individuals desirable options that were largely unavailable before (e.g., the effect of the opening up of white colleges to black students upon transfer of able black students from largely black institutions of higher education).

Of course, some leaving arises because of the opportunity to transfer to another institution. In some cases such leaving is a part of an intended course of action. People enter colleges with the intent of transferring to another institution prior to program completion. In other cases, leaving occurs only after the individual discovers that transfer is indeed possible or even desirable. Not surprisingly, some of these instances reflect very positive, rather than negative, experiences. Some students "raise their sights" as a result of their college experiences.

Departure may also come about, however, because of a change in the individual's evaluation of the relative benefits of college activities. This may result not only from a change in the external benefits accruing to college graduates but also from alteration in the intrinsic rewards of college attendance. As argued here, these latter rewards are largely the consequence of one's social and intellectual integration into the communities of the college. The absence of such integration may then alter the person's judgment of the relative costs and benefits of continued persistence regardless of changes in the world external to the college. In such situations investment in an alternative form of college attendance—that is, transfer to another institution—may follow.

The point here is quite simple. Though external events may be very important for some students, especially those that have to negotiate constantly the competing demands of family, work, and college, for most students the impact of external events upon institutional departure is secondary to those within the college. While external forces may influence one's decisions to go to college and greatly constrain choices as to which college to attend, once entry has been gained, their impact for most students tends to be dependent upon the character of one's integrative experiences within that college. In other words, the model posits that view that experiences on campus are, for most students, paramount to the process of persistence. External experiences, though critical for a number of students, condition but do not determine the character of experience on campus.

For many students the impact of external events is largely subsumed in the process of college entry. Only when external situations change dramatically from those present at time of entry are they likely to play an important role in the process of institutional departure. In such situations, changes in family or financial circumstances may be sufficiently great to force the individual to depart at least until those circumstances are resolved. The term "voluntary departure" is hardly an adequate description of the character of individual leaving where individuals are literally "pulled away" from college participation. Not surprisingly, such departures typically result in temporary leaving or stopout rather than permanent withdrawal. In large measure this is the case because the forces that lead a person to be pulled away from college are not the same as those that determine whether the leaving is permanent or temporary. As is the case of the impact of finances upon persistence, decisions about returning to college are primarily a function of the sorts of academic and social experiences the person has had on campus prior to departure.

All this is not to downplay the significance of a student's life away from college. Nor is it to say that that life does not invade and condition academic and social life on the campus. It is quite evident that the external world of work and family are central to the experience of many students, especially those who commute, who work while in college and/or attend part-time. Rather it is to say that most voluntary departures from college reflect more what goes on within college following entry than it does either what has gone on before entry or what takes place outside college.

The Interplay of Goals and Commitments and Different
Forms of Institutional Departure

In the final analysis, the model argues that the interplay between individual goals and commitments (internal and external) influences not only whether a person leaves but also the form that leaving takes. Either reduced goals or weakened goal and/or institutional commitment can lead to institutional departure. Low goal commitment, for example, may result in total withdrawal from all forms of higher educational participation. Conversely, sufficiently high commitment to the goal of college completion may lead a person to "stick it out" until degree completion or to transfer to another institution. When goals have been diminished by one's experiences, downward transfer may follow either to a less selective college of the same level or to one of lower level. When goals have been enhanced, upward transfer may result.

It must also be noted that the notion of individual goals and commitments contains the related notion of multiple goals and commitments that arise from the individual's participation in multiple communities internal and external to the college. As noted earlier, it is the interplay between these differentially located communities and the goals and commitment membership entails that eventually shape the person's educational goals and commitments to the institution. Their impact upon persistence is mediated through their effect upon those goals and commitments (Cabrera, Castaneda, Nora, and Hengstler 1992).

Linking Learning and Leaving: The Educational
Character of Student Leaving

Before turning to a discussion of policy, we must first extend our discussion of student persistence to the issue of student learning and the manner in which college communities shape student learning and both influence student persistence. We do so not only because student learning matters in its own right, but also because its inclusion in our discussion deepens our understanding of the educational character of student experience and the way it shapes student leaving.

Colleges as Learning Communities

As noted in chapter 3, a range of recent evidence points to the conclusion that student involvement or integration is a key determinant for a variety of educational outcomes (Astin 1984, 1991, Friedlander 1980, Parker and Schmidt 1982, Ory and Braskamp 1988, and Pascarella and Terenzini 1991). Generally speaking, the greater students' involvement in the life of the college, especially its academic life, the greater their acquisition of knowledge and development of skills. This is particularly true with regard to student contact with faculty. That engagement, both inside and outside the classroom, appears to be especially important to student development (Endo and Harpel 1982, Astin 1991, 1993). We also know that there is a direct relationship between students' quality of effort and their learning (e.g., Pace 1984, Ory and Braskamp 1988, and Kaufman and Creamer 1991). Quite simply, the more students invest in learning activities, the more they learn.

The critical association for us is the apparent relationship on one hand between involvement and quality of student effort and on the other between learning and persistence. Regarding the former, it is increasingly clear that student involvement in the life of the college, especially its academic life, is an important mechanism through which student effort is engaged. The more students are involved academically and socially, the more likely are they to become more involved in their own learning and invest time and energy to learn (Tinto, Goodsell, and Russo 1993). Involvement, especially academic involvement, seems to generate heightened student effort. That effort, in turn, leads to enhanced learning. As to the latter, we also know that student learning is linked to persistence (Endo and Harpel 1982, Tinto and Froh 1992). Other things being equal, the more students learn, the more likely are they to persist, even after controlling for student attributes. And, in those cases when students are required to leave college, the more likely are they to eventually return to college to complete their program of study.

But in noting these relationships, it does not follow that the linkage between involvement and learning, on one hand, and between learning and persistence, on the other, is simple or symmetrical. Regarding the impact of involvement upon learning, one has to ask about the specific nature of student involvement. Not all involvements lead to learning in the same fashion. Much depends on the degree to which student involvement is a meaningful and valued part of the classroom experience. Having a voice without being heard is often worse than having no voice at all. As to the linkage between learning and persistence, though learning is in general positively associated with persistence, it is not the case that learning guarantees persistence or that failure to learn, beyond the obvious case of academic failure, insures departure. While it is the case for most, if not all, institutions that academic involvement matters more than social involvement, it is also true that both social and academic involvement influence persistence. For some students, even high levels of academic involvement and its consequent learning may not be enough to offset the effect of social isolation. For others, sufficient social integration or involvement may counterbalance the absence of academic involvement. They stay because of friendships they have developed. Of course, the absence of any academic involvement typically leads to academic failure and therefore forced departure.

The importance of these linkages for our inquiry is twofold. First it leads us to a more complex understanding of the importance of integration or involvement for student development and in turn persistence. It argues that academic and social involvement with peers and faculty impacts upon persistence directly and indirectly via its impact on the quality of effort students exhibit for their own learning. In this manner, the argument about student learning moves beyond the simplistic notion that students are alone responsible for their own effort to the more complex notion that institutions also influence the quality of student effort via their capacity to involve students with other members of the institution in the learning process.

It also makes it possible for us to extend our conversation regarding the nature of college communities and their role in student persistence to speak of colleges as consisting of many communities of learning, academic and social, comprised of faculty, staff, and students. It allows us to argue that involvement in those communities, especially those that are directed toward student learning, is the vehicle through which student learning and development occur and persistence arises. More importantly, it leads us to argue that our model of persistence is, at its core, *a model of educational communities that highlights the critical importance of student engagement or involvement in the learning communities of the college.*

Classrooms as Learning Communities

Nowhere is the importance of student involvement more evident than in and around the classrooms of the college. Though some institutions have successfully utilized purposeful out-of-class activities to unleash student effort (Kuh, Schuh, Whitt and Associates 1991), student engagement is, for most institutions, centered in and around the classroom. This is the case if only because a majority of institutions are nonresidential and most students commute to college. Their time on campus is primarily spent in class.

It is for that reason that we can speak of classrooms as smaller communities of learning comprised of faculty and students. By their very nature, classrooms are located at the very heart of the academic community of the college. They serve as smaller academic meeting places that intersect the diverse faculty and student communities of the college. If involvement is to occur, if student effort is to be enhanced, in most colleges it must begin in the classroom. For new students in particular, engagement in the community of the classroom becomes a gateway for subsequent student involvement in the larger academic and social communities of the college (Tinto, Goodsell, and Russo 1993). Involvement in the classroom leads students to seek out contact with faculty and their classmates after class.

In this fashion, colleges can be seen as consisting not merely of multiple communities, but of overlapping and sometimes nested academic and social communities, each influencing the other in important ways. Classrooms, in turn, can be understood as smaller educational communities that serve as both gateways to and intersections for the broader academic and social communities of the college. By extension, the broader process of academic and social integration (involvement) described in the preceding pages can be understood as frequently emerging from student involvement with faculty and student peers in the communities of the classrooms. It is a process which, over time, links classroom engagement with faculty and student peers to subsequent involvement in the larger academic and social communities of the college.

This view of the central role of classrooms leads us in turn to reiterate the importance of the faculty to student development and persistence. This is the case not only because contact with the faculty, both inside and outside the classroom, serves to directly shape learning and persistence, but also because their actions shape the nature of classroom communities and influence the degree and manner in which students become involved in learning in those settings.

Parenthetically, this line of reasoning enables us to shed new light on the extensive body of research on the impact of teaching, curriculum, and instructional strategy upon student development (see Pascarella and Terenzini 1991). Specifically, it allows us to highlight the role the faculty plays in the shaping of the nature of the classroom community and therefore in influencing student involvement in the learning communities of the college.[7] It must also be noted, however, that this view of college communities and their impact upon learning and persistence has yet to be adequately explored. Our conversation here is one of informed impression. It is not yet one documented by extensive empirical evidence. Though we have begun to carry out some research in this area, it is quite clear that much remains to be known about the processes of involvement in the nested and overlapping communities of the college and their multiple impacts upon student effort, learning, and persistence.

Finally, in thinking ahead to the issue of policy, it should be observed that this argument enables us to frame the issue of student persistence in terms that are broader than those typically used to describe attrition on most campuses, namely that it is largely a matter for those who work in student affairs. If anything, the above line of reasoning would lead one to argue, as we will in the next chapter, that it is as much an academic matter, one that concerns the faculty as much as it might concern those in student affairs (Tinto 1989).

At the same time, this line of speculation leads us to consider the notion, also to be more fully discussed in the next chapter, that it may be possible to think of beginning-year classrooms as serving a somewhat different function than do classes in subsequent years. To continue the analogy of classrooms as gateways, freshmen classes may be seen as serving as academic and social gateways to involvement in the broader academic, as well as social, communities of the college. As a result, they, more than other classes, must emphasize and encourage active student involvement in the intellectual and social life of the classroom. If student involvement is to occur, it must begin from the very first encounter students have with the academic life of the institution.

The Temporal Process of Learning and Persistence

If we take seriously the notion argued above of the dynamic interplay between involvement, effort, learning, and persistence, we are led to postulate a more complex view of the longitudinal process of student persistence as it occurs over the course of the student career than we have thus far described. Specifically, our preceding conversation suggests that the manner in which social and academic involvements (integration) shape learning and persistence may vary over the course of the college career and may do so in differing ways for different students.

During the first several weeks of the first year of college, the work of Attinasi (1989) and very recently that of Goodsell, Maher, and Tinto (1992) suggest, issues of social membership may be somewhat more important than those of academic membership, at least for younger students who leave home after high school to attend residential four-year institutions. Attinasi (1989) notes that new students—in this case Mexican American students entering a large public university—talk about the need to attach themselves to relevant social groups as a means of coping with the difficulties of "getting in" to college. More importantly, he argues that that attachment may be a necessary precondition for subsequent involvements. The same observation is made by Goodsell and Tinto (1992) in their study of the first-year experiences of students attending a large public university on the West Coast. At first, their attention is focused on the need to make social connections with their student peers. Though classes matter, their concern regarding academic involvement appears to be played out against a broader backdrop of social issues and concerns they have over social membership.

As students progress toward their degree, however, their concerns appear to shift toward a greater emphasis on academic issues. Once social membership has been achieved or at least once concerns over it have been addressed, student attention appears to increasingly center on academic involvements. Neumann and Neumann's (1989) study of junior and senior persistence at a northeastern university is, in this regard, quite revealing. It emphasizes what they refer to as a "Quality of Learning Experience" approach wherein persistence is conceptually linked to student perceptions of the quality of their learning environments and their interaction with faculty about learning issues. The significant predictors of junior and senior persistence proved to be student involvement in learning activities, students' views of the quality of teaching, advising, and coursework, and their contact with faculty. In this case, contact with faculty was a composite measure reflecting a broader range of educational issues, specifically accessibility and contact with faculty outside class, helpfulness of faculty, and the concern they show for students. One of the points, then, that Neumann and Neumann make is the possibility that as students progress from freshman to senior years, their persistence is increasingly shaped by educational concerns and by their educational experiences in the academic life of the institution.[8]

The likelihood that persistence is marked by a changing balance of academic and social involvements leads us to consider some intriguing possibilities about the parallels between the longitudinal process of persistence and those processes that describe other domains of human activity. Not the least of these comes from theories of human development and growth. Could it be that the process of persistence in being linked to that of learning is, like Chickering's (1969) or Perry's (1970) model of student development, also shaped by a shifting need in students for differing forms of social and intellectual engagements? Might it be that fulfilling one need, the social, is, for many students, a developmental precondition for addressing the need for intellectual engagement?

We should be very cautious, however, about pushing these parallels too far. By noting the possible parallel between our view of the temporal process of persistence and that of student development, we are forced to ask whether our impressions are merely a reflection of the types of students who have thus far been studied, namely youthful students attending four-year institutions. Would the same results apply equally well to older students or to students in two-year institutions who are immersed in external communities of work, family, and friends? For older students who commute to school, for instance, early academic involvements may be more important, especially as they shape the person's sense of his or her own ability to cope with the academic demands of college. Unfortunately, given the absence of research, these are questions that cannot yet be answered.

A Model of Institutional Departure: Some Observations

In its full form our model of student institutional departure sees the process of persistence as being marked over time by different stages in the passage of students from past forms of association to new forms of membership in the social and intellectual communities of the college. Eventual persistence requires that individuals make the transition to college and become incorporated into its ongoing social and intellectual life. A sizable proportion of very early institutional departures mirrors the inability of new students to make the adjustment to the new world of the college.

Beyond the transition to college, persistence entails the incorporation, that is integration, of the individual as a competent member in the social and intellectual (academic) communities of the college. In this regard, colleges are viewed as being made up of a range of academic and social communities whose interactional attributes have much to do with the eventual leaving of many of their students. Student institutional departure is as much a reflection of the attributes of those communities, and therefore of the institution, as it is of the attributes of the students who enter that institution. Though the intentions and commitments with which individuals enter college matter, what goes on after entry matters more. It is the daily interaction of the person with other members of the college in both the formal and informal academic and social domains of the college and the person's perception or evaluation of the character of those interactions, and of those that involve the student outside the college, that in large measure determine decisions as to staying or leaving. It is in this sense that most departures are voluntary. Though some departures reflect the person's inability or unwillingness to meet the minimum academic standards of the college, most mirror the individual's own decision to leave. Patterns of incongruence and isolation, more than that of academic incompetence, appear to be central to the process of individual departure.

Several observations about the model should be made before we proceed to its application to the question of institutional policy. Perhaps the most important is the implied notion that departure hinges upon the individual's perception of his/her experiences within an institution of higher education. The model takes seriously the ethnomethodological proposition that what one thinks is real, has real consequences. As regards integration, the mere occurrence of interactions between the individual and others within the institution will not insure that integration occurs—that depends on the character of those interactions and the manner in which the individual comes to perceive them as rewarding or unrewarding. Thus the term "membership" may be taken as connoting the perception on the part of the individual of having become a competent member of an academic or social community within the college. Therefore, no study of the roots of student departure is complete without reference to student perceptions and the cultural contexts that shape them (Tierney 1992). Similarly, no institution should initiate an attempt to deal with departure without first ascertaining student perceptions of the problem being addressed. Though this is by no means a simple task, it is not an impossible one.

Second, the model is an interactional system model of individual leaving.

It recognizes the fact that the individual and the institution as represented by other members of its communities are, over time, continually in interaction with one another in a variety of formal and informal situations. Both play an important part in the process of departure. The institution, in acting to foster the development of locally available social and academic communities, helps establish the conditions under which individual social and intellectual integration may take place. The individual, in bringing to that setting a variety of skills, goals, and commitments, behaves both as an actor and as an interpreter of interactions which occur within that setting.

Third, the model takes seriously the notion that both forms of integration, social and intellectual, are essential to student persistence. Though it is conceivable that persistence can occur when only one is present, evidence suggests that persistence is greatly enhanced when both forms of personal integration occur. By extension, the model also argues that both social and intellectual experiences are essential to the education of maturing individuals.

Finally, it should be observed that our model of institutional departure is also a model of educational communities. It is a view of the educational process which emphasizes the role of social and intellectual communities, especially those that may emerge from involvement in classroom communities, in the shaping of student life and the importance of involvement in those communities to student development. In particular, it is a view of college communities that allows for the necessary linking of learning and leaving and the very important role classroom experience plays in the process of student persistence. In this way, it is a model of educational communities that places the classroom at its very center. It argues, in effect, that persistence is, at its core, an educational phenomena.

Equally important, the model specifies both the conditions which foster involvement and the social mechanisms through which involvement occurs. In so doing, it moves beyond the noting of the obvious importance of student involvement in the educational process to the development of a view which suggests ways in which diverse forms of social and intellectual involvement may be generated on campus for different types of students. And it suggests the many important ways in which involvement in classrooms and beyond classrooms with faculty may spill over to a broader set of involvements in the campus generally.

—5—

The Dimensions of Institutional Action

We now turn to the important question of policy, specifically to the sorts of actions institutions can take to enhance student retention on campus. But we will not simply list or catalog programs. In the sections that follow, we will first turn our intention to the important question of defining dropout. We will do so because an answer to that question is a necessary beginning point to the development of any policy on student retention. Having done so, we will then focus on the principles of action and thought that mark successful retention programs. However different in structure or appearance, successful retention programs are similar in a number of fundamental ways. Understanding these commonalities of action and thought provides insight into the "secret" to the development of successful retention programs. Following upon that discussion, we will turn to the issue of program implementation and to the strategies successful institutions have followed in the course of developing successful retention programs. We will do so because it is important to distinguish between what institutions do to retain students—that is, the programs they adopt—and the strategies they employ to successfully develop those programs over time. Lest we forget, it is one thing to ask what programs institutions use to retain students. It is entirely another to ask how successful institutions have come, over time, to develop their retention programs. Finally, we will attempt to highlight, against the preceding background, some of the more successful types of programs colleges and universities have employed to retain more of their students.

It must be noted, however, that while we will attempt to identify institutions that have successfully employed different types of retention programs, it is beyond the scope of the present work to name all such institutions. The fact is that there are many noteworthy programs in a great variety of institutions across the country. To identify and catalog them all is simply not possible here. Instead we have sought, in the aggregate, to indicate how a wide range of institutions, two- and four-year, public and private, have successfully employed different types of programs to enhance student retention. Citing specific institutions is simply one way of helping readers begin the search for programs that might be adapted for their own particular institution.[1]

Defining "Dropout" from Higher Education

In order to address the practical question of what institutions can do to increase student retention, we must first consider the prior question of how student dropout ought to be defined. The resolution of that question is essential to the development of effective retention programs. As a necessary part of the development of such programs, institutions must come to decide which forms of departure are to be defined as "dropout" and should therefore be the object of institutional action and which, for the lack of a better term, should be considered the regrettable, but perhaps unavoidable, outcome of institutional functioning.

To do so, institutions must also take seriously the task of assessing the character of student retention. Institutions have to know not only who leaves but also why. To that end, institutions need to devise student retention assessment systems that assess the character of student experiences within the institution in such a way as to lead to the determination of how those experiences are linked to different forms of student progression and departure. More importantly, institutions must be able to reliably discern how their own actions impact upon the forms of student departure they seek to remedy. Though we will not deal with the assessment of student retention here, we will devote an appendix to a discussion of the character of effective student assessment and its use in institutional policies for student retention.

The Mislabeling of Student Dropout

From the perspective of the institution it can be reasonably argued that all students who withdraw can be classified as dropouts regardless of their reasons for doing so. Each leaving creates a vacancy in the student body that might otherwise have been filled by someone who would have persisted until degree completion. As such, each and every departure can be seen by the institution as representing the loss of not only a potential graduate (and alumnus), but also of much-needed tuition revenue. Continued high rates of student departure may be a serious strain on the financial stability of the institution. When additional entrants are not "waiting in line" to fill those vacancies, the strain may be serious enough to threaten the very existence of the institution. Since it is estimated that nearly half of all institutions of higher education admit virtually everyone who applies, it is little wonder that the concern over student retention is so widespread and the tendency to view all departures as dropouts so common.

To do so, however, is a mistake, for several reasons. First, as we have already noted, the labeling of all departures as dropout serves to gloss over important differences among forms of leaving. As a result, institutions often make the unwarranted and quite mistaken judgment that all student departures can be equally well treated by a single policy action. This is clearly not the case. Since the roots of differing forms of departure are distinct in nature, the preventive actions institutions take to treat those behaviors must also be distinct.

Second, the indiscriminate use of the label "dropout" to describe all forms of departure may lead institutions to believe that all departures can in fact be treated by institutional action. Yet there is little reason to suppose that this is possible even if institutions had unlimited resources. Indeed evidence already presented suggests that some forms of withdrawal, for instance those associated with goals and commitments, may be relatively immune to institutional intervention regardless of the resources invested. By spreading their actions among all forms of leaving, institutions may weaken their ability to address any one form. It may even be the case that such mistargeting of services and diffusion of action will prove counterproductive in the long run.

Last and perhaps most importantly, the term "dropout" has come to connote a form of individual failure, a failure of the person to measure up to the demands of college life regardless of their content and character. In effect the common usage of the label "dropout" leads one to believe that all student departures are primarily the result of the failure of the individual to meet the social and academic demands of college life, and therefore reflect individual rather than institutional failure. Again this is not the case. Though some forms of departure, for instance those which arise from insufficient individual commitment, may be so understood, others are much less clearly a reflection of individual failure.

The generalized application of the term "dropout" to all leavers may, in effect, blind institutions to the manner in which they themselves are at least partially responsible for the leaving of their students. Thus the unrestricted use of "dropout" may hinder the necessary process of social and intellectual change that must mark the continued development of institutions of higher education and may serve as a barrier to institutional change and revitalization.

Toward an Institutional Definition of Student Dropout

Defining dropout appropriately, however, is no simple matter. There are a variety of different types of leaving behaviors which arise from a range of different sources and which involve a range of differing students. Some forms of student leaving may be amenable to forms of institutional action. Others may not. Some may involve specific segments of the student population while others may include a diversity of student types. And some leavings may result in permanent withdrawal from all forms of higher educational participation while others lead to immediate transfer to other institutions or to only temporary withdrawal or stopout from studies. The problem facing institutions is deciding which of these varying forms of leaving warrant institutional action.

The process of making such decisions is never easy. It entails making some very difficult choices between several courses of action. No general discussion, such as our own, could possibly deal with all the specific issues which institutions will have to face in the course of their deliberations. Obviously each institution's situation calls for specific forms of decision making appropriate to its own circumstances. Nevertheless there are some principles which may help institutions establish guidelines for their own deliberations. These principles concern two separate issues: the correspondence between the needs, interests, and goals of the students and those of the institution, and the educational mission of institutions of higher education.

DROPOUT AS INDIVIDUAL AND INSTITUTIONAL FAILURE

The first of these principles of definition can be roughly phrased in the following manner:

> *Institutions should not define dropout in ways which contradict the students' own understanding of their leaving. If the leaver does not define his/her own behavior as representing a form of failure, neither should the institution.*

For every action, there are at least two different perspectives, that of the actor and that of an external observer who witnesses that action and experiences its effects. Since the interests and needs of each are likely to differ, so too will their perceptions and therefore interpretations of the meaning of that action differ. As regards the forms of leaving we have commonly labeled as dropout, it is very likely that though an external observer may categorize all those leavings as dropout and impute to each a form of educational failure, the departing actor may not do so. Individuals may define their leaving in

ways which have little to do with the notion of educational and personal failure as it is implied in the common usage of the term. Rather they may understand their departure as representing quite positive steps toward goal
attainment.

In order to discern to what degree individuals see their own leaving as a
form of educational failure, one must at the very minimum make reference to
the intentions and commitments with which individuals begin their collegiate careers. Within any population of entering students these will vary
greatly. Not all goals are either coterminous with degree completion or necessarily compatible with those of the initial institution. Furthermore, many
individuals enter college without a clear goal in mind and others change their
goals during their college career. Similarly, students do not enter the higher
educational enterprise with comparable levels of goal or institutional commitment. Whereas many enter higher education committed to the completion of
their degrees, others begin their careers with only modest commitments to
the enterprise.

The point here is really quite simple, namely that a potentially large number of individuals will choose to depart from an institution of higher education because they have come to see that further participation in that
institution no longer serves their best interests. In some cases this may reflect
differences in goals. In others it may mirror the absence of sufficient commitment to pursue those goals. In either case it is quite likely that many such
persons will not understand their leaving as representing a form of educational or personal failure. Indeed, a good many may view their leaving as
quite positive forms of behavior. This is very likely to be the case, for example, for those students whose educational goals do not call for degree completion or whose goals call for transfer to another institution prior to degree
completion. It is also very likely to be the case for those persons who come to
find the social and intellectual communities of the college unsuited to their
own personal preferences, as well as for those whose goals are substantially
different from those which characterize the institution. Not surprisingly
many such persons transfer to another institution after departure. It is revealing, in this context, that many students describe their behavior not as leaving
college but as ceasing to come or as moving to somewhere else.

For the institution to categorize those behaviors as dropout is to make a
serious error in interpretation. It is an error which may lead institutions to
believe they can remedy forms of leaving which they are unlikely to effect
and which would entail inducing individuals to work counter to their own
definition of the situation.

It is when individuals also view their leaving as failure that the term "dropout" is best applied. For it is in this sense that there is a commonality of inter-

ests between the individual who enters the institution and the officials who seek to enhance retention within the institution. Insofar as dropout is defined as a failure on the part of the individual to attain a desired and reasonable educational goal, so too does that leaving represent a failure on the part of the institution to assist the person achieve what he/she initially set out to do in first entering the institution. Here the interests of both parties overlap.

Several conclusions follow from this view of dropout. First, it follows that it is in the institution's own best interest to assess the intentions (educational and career goals) of entering students. Beyond issues of advising and counseling, such information allows the institution to better gauge its "true" attrition rate, namely that rate which reflects the failure of the institution to help students attain reasonably held educational goals. By the same token, it enables the institution to counter claims that it must be judged by the completion of all its entering students as if they all had the same intentions. For two-year colleges and four-year state colleges that typically serve as jumping-off points to other institutions, such claims can never be taken lightly, especially when state funding is geared to measures of institutional productivity.

Second, the viewpoint stated above also argues that it may be in the best interests of both students and the institution that the latter act to assist the leaving of some students to other settings which may be more suited to their needs and interests. By extension, it also argues that it may be of little value to either party for the institution to commit its scarce resources to persons who are not sufficiently committed to the goal of college completion to put forward the effort required to attain that goal. In diffusing scarce resources, the institution weakens its ability to assist those who remain.

Clearly this is not the case for those persons whose goals are compatible with those of the institution and whose commitments and capacities are sufficient to achieve those goals. For those persons, especially those who are having difficulty adjusting to the academic demands of the institution and those who are having difficulty making contact and establishing competent membership within the communities of the college, institutional intervention may prove beneficial. Their inability to complete a reasonable college program represents both a personal failure and an institutional failure.

THE QUESTION OF EDUCATIONAL MISSION

The question of how one defines dropout is not yet resolved, for it remains unclear how one would determine whether or not a given student's goals and commitments are "compatible" with the setting of the institution. To attend to this question, we address the second of the two principles noted above, namely that of educational mission.

This second principle can be stated as follows:

In the course of establishing a retention policy, institutions must not only ascertain the goals and commitments of entering students, they must also discern their own goals and commitments.

Ultimately the question of institutional choice in the matter of the definition and treatment of student dropout is one concerning the purposes of institutional existence. It is, in effect, a question of educational mission. To put it in a slightly different form, the first step in the course of institutional action for retention is for the institution to ask itself the question, For what educational problem(s) is the institution the proposed solution? The answer to that question provides the necessary guidelines or standards by which the institution can then proceed to address subsequent questions regarding student departure, namely, what forms of educational departure are to be defined as dropout and, of those, which are to be the object of institutional action?

Within the limits imposed by scarcity of resources; the specification of action priorities will reflect the priorities established in the specification of educational mission. If the institution deems, for instance, that its central mission calls for the retention of its most able students, then it will or should focus its actions on that segment of the student body. If, however, it sees itself as providing guidance for maturing adults to further their education, it may be concerned with that form of leaving which does not lead to further education. In this fashion, some institutions, especially two-year colleges, may come to see as part of their mission the aiding of student departure. The answer to the critical question of educational mission may—and, in fact, will—often lead to the recognition that in seeking to retain some students, an institution may have to act so as to encourage the leaving of others. Whatever the character of that difficult decision, the point here is that prior decision regarding educational mission is the only sound educational procedure for institutions to follow in attempting to establish policies for student retention.

The view has spread that it is the duty of higher educational institutions to attempt to educate all those who enter, regardless of their goals, commitments, and capacities. In this view, higher education becomes a right of all individuals. However, though it is in a very important sense true that institutions owe each admitted student an equal degree of attention, it does not follow that institutions should be held accountable for the equal education of all admitted students. To absolve, in effect, individuals of at least partial responsibility for their own education is to make a serious error. To do so denies both the right of the individual to refuse education and the right of the institution to be selective in its judgments as to who should be further educated. More importantly, it runs counter to the essential notion that effective education requires that individuals take responsibility for their own learning.

Lest we forget, the point of retention efforts is not merely that individuals be kept in college. Education, the social and intellectual development of individuals, rather than just their continued presence on campus, should be the goal of retention efforts. Insofar as the very notion of education entails a commitment on the part of individuals to their own education, then too our policies for retention for educational goals must also take account of that commitment to the same degree that it takes account of the institution's commitment to its students. The consideration of educational mission involves, then, a decision not only of what the institution should be expected to do, but also of what its students should be expected to do on their own behalf.[2]

Few, if any, institutions have at their disposal unlimited resources for retention programs. Institutions are always faced with tough decisions as to where and how to best allocate their scarce resources to achieve desired goals which themselves may involve potentially conflicting courses of action. With regard to the specific goal of enhanced student retention, decisions about mission alone will not be sufficient to determine which groups of students or forms of leaving should be the object of institutional action. At some point, institutions will have to ascertain not only how likely different forms of action are to yield acceptable returns in student retention but also which students are likely to benefit most from those actions. They will have to answer for themselves the question, What works in retaining-students?

The Principles of Effective Retention

The answer to that question, however, is not found in the listing of intervention strategies commonly employed in the treatment of dropout or in the description of their specific structural attributes.[3] It resides instead in the answer to the more important question of why particular forms of institutional action are successful in retaining students.

The fact is that there are many different types of successful retention programs. Among other things, programs differ in structure, form, mode of operation, and focus. At the same time, programs on different campuses differ because of the natural process by which they come to reflect particular contingencies. Nevertheless, a careful comparative analysis of successful programs on different campuses reveals that they are invariably similar in a number of important ways, specifically in the way they think about retention, in the sorts of emphasis they give their retention efforts, and in the ends to which they direct their energies. These commonalities, or what is referred to here as "the principles of effective retention," can be described as an enduring commitment to student welfare, a broader commitment to the education, not mere retention, of all students, and an emphasis upon the importance of social and intellectual community in the education of students. The "secret" of successful retention, if there is one, lies in understanding these principles and how they can be applied to the complex problem of the retention of different students in different institutional settings.

Institutional Commitment to Students

The first principle of effective retention can be stated as follows:

Effective retention programs are committed to the students they serve. They put student welfare ahead of other institutional goals.

One of the most evident features of effective retention programs is their enduring commitment to the students they serve. It is a commitment that springs from the very character of their educational mission. It is not a convenient add-on to other interests.

There is no programmatic substitute for this sort of commitment, no easy way to measure its occurrence. It is not the sole province of specific programs or of designated program staff but is the responsibility of all members of an institution, faculty and staff alike. As such it is reflected in the daily activities of all program members and in the choices they make as to the goals to which they direct their energies. The presence of a strong commitment to students results in an identifiable ethos of caring which permeates the character of institutional life. Student-centered institutions are, in their everyday life, tangibly different from those institutions which place student welfare second to other goals.

It is in this very important sense that institutions of higher education are like other human communities. The essential character of such communities lies not in their formal structures, but in the underlying values which inspire their construction. The ability of an institution to retain students lies less in the formal programs it devises than in the underlying orientation toward students which direct its activities. Communities, educational or otherwise, which care for and reach out to members and which are committed to members' welfare are also those which keep and nourish their members. Commitment to students generates a commitment on the part of students to the institution. Again, that commitment is the basis of student persistence.

Educational Commitment

The second principle of effective retention, one which derives from the first, can be stated as follows:

Effective retention programs are first and foremost committed to the education of all, not just some, of their students.

The secret of effective programs, if there is one, lies in the observable fact that their commitment to students goes beyond the concern for retention per se to that of the education of students. A commitment to that goal is the turn-key about which successful retention programs are built. Put in more direct language, effective retention programs do not leave learning to chance. They see it as an integral part of their mission that they actively pursue the goal of student learning. They require of themselves, their faculty and staff, and their students that each engage in activities to heighten the likelihood that learning arises within the college. To that end, successful programs direct their energies to insuring that new students either enter with or have the op-portunity to come to possess sufficient knowledge and skills to meet the aca-demic demands of the institution.

It is for this reason that effective programs concern themselves with the nontrivial question of the types of educational settings and faculty and staff skills that best promote student learning, especially during the critical first year of college. They pay particular attention to the construction of learning settings that actively involve students in the learning process. Active, rather than passive, learning is the hallmark of such settings.

It is for this reason as well that effective programs continually monitor student learning and provide frequent feedback to students in ways which promote, rather than hinder, their learning. This is particularly evident in the classrooms of the institution. It is there, more than in midterm reports sent through the mail or in end of year evaluations, that students can most effec-tively employ that information to alter their learning behaviors.

Social and Intellectual Community

The third and final principle of effective retention stresses the importance of community. It can be stated as follows:

Effective retention programs are committed to the development of supportive social and educational communities in which all stu-dents are integrated as competent members.

A third common feature of effective retention programs, indeed of institu-tions with high rates of student retention generally, is their emphasis upon the communal nature of institutional life and the importance of educational community, social and intellectual, in the learning process. They understand that student learning best occurs in settings that involve students in the daily life and provide social and intellectual support for their individual efforts.

Effective programs concern themselves with the integration of all individ-uals into the mainstream of the social and intellectual life of the institution and into the communities of people which make up that life. They con-sciously reach out and make contact with students in a variety of settings in order to establish personal bonds among students and between students, fac-ulty, and staff members of the institution. Particularly important is the continuing emphasis upon frequent and rewarding contact between faculty, staff, and students in a variety of settings both inside and outside the formal confines of the classrooms and laboratories of institutional life.

Effective programs see active involvement of students in the life of the classroom to be a key element. Among other things, they have looked to the construction of supportive learning settings in which students, individually and in groups, can become actively involved in the learning process. They see the development of "voice" in the classroom as the linchpin around which education is built. They employ faculty and peer mentor programs, frequent informal meetings between faculty, staff, and students, and specially constructed residential learning programs to heighten the degree and range of interactions that take place among members of the community outside the classrooms and laboratories of the institution. To have students become valued members of a supportive academic and social community is the goal of their actions.

The Principles of Effective Implementation

Having described the underlying principles of action that govern successful retention programs, we now turn to the principles of implementation that capture how successful programs have sought to put into practice the above principles. Our concern here is with the practical question of how it is that institutions have come, over time, to develop successful retention programs.

But we will not attempt to discuss each and every implementation strategy. That task is beyond the focus of this chapter. Rather our intent is to highlight some of the more important commonalities of implementation that mark the development of successful programs. Invariably, the best advice one can offer is that institutions considering the establishment of a specific retention program visit a number of programs of proven effectiveness that have been implemented in similar situations. The question one should pose of the individuals responsible for those programs is not merely what they do, but how, over time, did they come to do what they now do. That question frames the current discussion. As experienced administrators are all too well aware, the gap between the ideal and the reality of institutional action can be quite wide. In the final analysis, programs, however brilliantly conceived, stand or fall on their ability to be effectively implemented in the real world of institutional life.

It should be recognized, however, that the range of specific types of organization and implementation strategies is great. There is no one specific type of successful retention organization and/or successful implementation strategy. What proves to be effective in one setting may not prove equally effective in another. Each institution must seek to organize and implement its programs in the manner which best suits its own resources and particular situation. Nevertheless, it is the case that amid the variety of forms of organization and implementation which mark successful retention efforts, one is able to discern a number of common organizational and implementational themes. It is to these themes that we now turn our attention.

Successful implementation of retention programs can be described by seven action principles.

> *Institutions should provide resources for program development and incentives for program participation that reach out to faculty and staff alike.*

Institutional commitment to students is more than a slogan that is highlighted in catalogues and brochures. It is a pattern of activity that develops among *all* faculty and staff, not just those few whose job descriptions call for particular forms of student-centered activity (e.g., student services). It is a reflection of a *campuswide* orientation to serve students that occurs in the various contexts in which students, faculty, and staff meet on a daily basis.

That level of commitment rarely occurs on its own. Rather it is an outcome of an *intentional policy of incentive* that recognizes and rewards faculty and staff for the sorts of behaviors that are consistent with the institution's mission. Though there will always be, on any campus, a core of student-directed faculty and staff—or what one sometimes refers to as the retention choir—successful institutions have widened the circle of commitment through their incentive policies.

> *Institutions should commit themselves to a long-term process of program development.*

Successful institutions commit themselves to a long-term investment of resources required to insure that programs are able to grow and prosper in the diverse places in which they arise on campus.

Successful programs, however structured, invariably take many years to reach fruition. Typically, they start small, have pilot or demonstration stages, and grow and improve over time by continual evaluation of their effectiveness until they reach full development. Rarely are they one-shot affairs that arise overnight. Successful institutions understand that no matter how well-read and prepared faculty and staff are, there will always be a period of trial and error that marks the start-up stage of program development. At the same time, they know that it takes time to change deep-rooted habits and that final judgments as to program effectiveness should not be made before programs have had a chance to mature and reshape student, faculty, and staff behaviors.

In this context it should be observed that as they expand, successful retention programs often become centers of excellence on campus that serve to reshape the behaviors of people about them. Their successes serve both as models for the work of others and as inducements for the recruitment and involvement of other members of the institution into other efforts to enhance student education and retention. In doing so, these programs do more than simply re-arrange the surface veneer of institutional functioning or re-allocate the few committed faculty and staff to new combinations of offices and programs. They are successful because they serve as a catalyst for the re-orientation of the entire campus, faculty and staff, toward students. That sort of redirecting of institutional energy takes resources, incentive, and a long-term commitment. It requires a willingness from the top down and the bottom up to see such change through to its conclusion.

Institutions should place ownership for institutional change in the hands of those across the campus who have to implement that change.

Though successful institutions require leadership from those at the top of the institution, successful implementation requires that individuals who are charged with carrying out the program take *ownership* over those activities. To that end, incentives have to be structured so as to allow faculty and staff to become active participants in the process through which programs are developed. They have to be allowed to determine the specifics of program activity and the manner in which those specifics are implemented within their particular domains of responsibility. Programs have to be grounded in the class-rooms, offices, programs, and departments of institutional life. They have to built from the ground up if they are to be sustained.

The task for institutional leadership, then, is to provide the resources and incentives to make such programs possible and to establish the goals and standards for institutional action while at the same time seeing itself as a facilitator to the active involvement of others, faculty and staff, in the change process. And it must do so in a manner which includes, rather than excludes, the diverse elements the mark the campus terrain.

For long-term success, programs must involve the broad spectrum of faculty and staff and come to reflect the full diversity of institutional views that mark campus life. That, in turn, leads to wide-ranging implementation that comes, over time, to provide discrete solutions to the diversity of situations that different students, faculty, and staff face in their particular environments.

Here it bears repeating that in the same sense that there is no single cause of student leaving, there is no single program that institutions need refer to for the key to successful retention. Successful retention programs are invariably the result of wide-ranging actions of a diversity of faculty and staff who are charged with responding to the needs of students in the diverse settings in which they interact. Ground-up implementation over time is the vehicle through which that diversity of responses take form.

Institutional actions should be coordinated in a collaborative fashion to insure a systematic, campuswide approach to student retention.

Just as student leaving mirrors individual experiences in the total system of the institution, formal and informal, so too should institutional actions address the full range of student experiences in the social and intellectual communities of the institution. They should do so in a manner which recognizes the multiple ways in which experiences in one segment of the institution, formal or informal, academic or social, impact upon experiences in other segments of the institution.

But such diversity of effort should not be chaotic in nature. Coordination of the efforts of faculty within and between departments, and among faculty and staff, academic and student affairs, should be the norm, not the exception, of institutional action. Institutional action must be such as to enable individuals to transverse, in a collaborative fashion, the intra-institutional boundaries of campus life that typically separate individuals from each other. To that end, institutions should establish a series of collaborative committees or task groups from the departmental to the institutional level whose goal it is to share information and coordinate, where needed, the efforts of diverse members of the institution across the campus. Rather than working at odds, academic and student affairs must come to see themselves as working together, much like medical teams do, on behalf of student retention and the personal development it entails.

What this requires of institutions is that they develop a systematic, long-range plan for student retention that specifies the interplay between resources, personnel, and actions needed to achieve desired retention goals. In effect, it calls for institutions to take enrollment management and collaborative planning seriously as an integral part of their retention efforts (Kemerer, Baldridge, and Green 1982, Hossler, Bean, and Associates 1990).

Institutions should act to insure that faculty and staff possess the skills needed to assist and educate their students.

Staff training and development is an integral part of the successful implementation of retention programs. For that reason, institutions should require that all program faculty and staff are trained to effectively assist the students they serve. And they should invest the resources needed to achieve that goal.

Institutions should also work together with faculty to insure that all faculty, not just those involved in specific programs, come to acquire a broad repertoire of teaching and assessment skills appropriate to the task of educating all, not just some of, their students. This is the case, as argued earlier, because retention is ultimately the outgrowth of successful student learning experiences across a variety of educational settings. It is not simply the product of the work of several faculty and program staff associated with specific retention efforts or particular classes. In this fashion, faculty development, as much as staff training, is a critical element in the long-term success of retention efforts.

This is not to say that there are not many skilled faculty who are outstanding teachers. Rather it is to say that institutions of higher education, unlike those at the primary and secondary level, have not as a matter of practice instituted policies or committed resources to assist faculty in becoming more skilled in their work as teachers. Here there is much to do and much to be gained from consistent institutional action on behalf of student retention.

Institutions should frontload their efforts on behalf of student retention.

Given choices of where and when to invest scarce resources, institutions should frontload their actions on behalf of student retention, specifically to the first year of college. This is not to say that institutions should ignore students after that year. Rather it is to say that institutions should recognize that the first year, in particular, represents a strategic leverage point where the investment of scarce resources can yield substantial future benefits in both learning and persistence. As noted earlier, most leaving either arises during the first year of college or has its roots in the first-year experience.

Given that student persistence and learning are shaped by all aspects of the first-year experience and are influenced by students' very first encounter with the institution, it follows that institutions should begin to address student needs as early as possible so that potential problems do not become actual problems later in the student career. And they should work to coordinate the activities of all persons whose work shapes that year's character. For instance, institutions should coordinate the work of the faculty who teach freshman courses with those in admissions, orientation, counseling, learning support, advising, and, where appropriate, residential affairs, to insure that student academic and social needs are addressed from the very outset of their first year on campus.

Institutions and programs should continually assess their actions with an eye toward improvement.

Programs, indeed institutions generally, should invest in program evaluation as a requisite part of program development not only to ascertain to what degree and in what manner they are having the impact they intend, but also to obtain the information they need to become more effective over time. This orientation toward continued improvement is a hallmark of successful programs.

But while institutions require assessment of themselves and of their programs, they need not dictate how that assessment should be carried out. Following the principle stated above of ownership of action by those responsible for that action, so too should institutions allow program staff to determine, within reasonable limits, the specifics of assessment. This enables the institution to obtain the information it needs while allowing programs to creatively employ assessment for their own particular needs. As will be argued in the appendix on assessment, it matters less what form assessment takes than that it occurs and that it is directed toward the issue of program and institutional improvement.

As a corollary to the principle of assessment for program and institutional improvement, institutions should ask programs to share their work, its methods and outcomes, with other members of the institution. This is the case because the sharing of assessment information among colleagues, faculty and/or staff, is one of the most effective ways of widening the circle of innovation on campus over the long term.

What Works in Retaining Students

Having outlined the general principles of successful retention and of successful implementation of retention programs, we now turn to the question of how those principles can be applied to the practical task of student retention. What is it that institutions can do in programmatic terms to further the end of student retention?

As we answer that question, we will take seriously the fact that students with different reasons for leaving and possibly different types of students are likely to respond in different ways and at different times to different forms of institutional action. The art of successful institutional retention is to balance these varying needs in a coordinated, carefully timed program of action. Regrettably, past discussions of student retention have treated the issue of policy as if student leaving was largely unidimensional in character. As a result they have not provided the sorts of information institutions require for the establishment of specific retention policies.

We will also take seriously the fact that the situations facing different types of institutions, specifically two- and four-year, residential and nonresidential, are quite different and therefore require somewhat different forms of program activity. Unfortunately, most discussions of student retention have implicitly assumed that institutions are largely uniform in character and in mission and that the forms of their actions are or should be largely similar. Obviously this is not the case. It is hoped, however, that the current discussion can highlight some of the more important variants which affect the manner in which successful retention policies are formed.

But no one discussion of institutional policy, however detailed, can possibly speak to the needs of each and every institution of higher education. Though institutions can learn from one another, it remains the case that each institution must and should decide for itself what, in its present situation, is the appropriate course of action to treat student departure. Programs which may work well in retaining students in one institution may not be equally effective in another. Questions of mission aside, institutions differ, among other ways, both in the attributes of their students and staff and in the types of organizational resources they can bring to bear on the problem of student departure. More importantly, they may differ in the contextual forces which give rise to differing forms of student departure. The establishment of specific institutional policies must reflect the specific circumstances in which the institution finds itself. It is for this very reason that institutional assessment, as described here in an appendix, is a critical prerequisite for the establishment of institutional retention policy.

In this context it should also be observed that though all institutions share in a commitment to educate their students, it does not follow that the character of that commitment and the program it inspires need be the same for each and every institution. Quite the contrary. A program must reflect the unique educational mission of the institution. It is for this reason that it has been argued that the proper beginning point of institutional retention efforts is not the design of such programs, but the posing and answering of the question "What is the educational problem for which the institution is the proposed solution?" It is only in answering that question that institutions are able to decide which of many different programs deserve their attention.

In the sections that follow we will endeavor to make clear which types of actions may be taken at different times during the typical student career in response to different forms of leaving and indicate how those actions might differ for different types of student populations. For organizational purposes, our discussion of programs will begin with the very first contact the student makes with the institution, namely admissions, and proceed together with the student through the "typical student career" to degree completion.[4]

Recruitment and Admission to College: Setting the Stage for Retention

The beginning of the sequence of events leading to student departure can be traced to students' first formal contact with the institution, namely their recruitment and admission. It is during the process of seeking out and applying for admission to a particular institution that individuals form their first impressions of the social and intellectual character of that institution. The

importance of such impressions goes beyond the decision to attend the institution. Since pre-entry expectations influence the character of early experiences within the institution they also affect retention following entry. The
formation, for instance, of unrealistic or mistaken expectations about the
quality of social and/or academic life can lead to early disappointments.
These can, in turn, color subsequent interactions within the institution.
Without modification, they may lead to eventual departure by setting into
motion a series of largely malintegrative interactions based upon the perception by the individual of either having been misled or having seriously erred
in his/her choice of college.

It may also be the case that inaccurate information obtained during the
process of application may lead some individuals to enter an institution even
though they are likely to find themselves at odds with, that is, incongruent
to, the existing social and intellectual communities of the college. The issue
here is not simply unrealistic expectations, but incorrect choice. Such mismatches may occur either in the academic realm, when persons find themselves ill-prepared, or overprepared, for the existing level of academic work
or in the social realm, when persons discover to their dismay that they are
seriously at odds with the prevailing norms of the social communities of the
college. Had they had more accurate information about both the range of
formal programs and the variety of informal life on campus many might not
have applied or entered the institution. Other persons may have applied and
entered in their place. In any event, those who did enter would have done so
on the basis of more accurate and realistic information and therefore realistic
expectations about the character of institutional life.

It follows that one of the most obvious actions institutions can take to treat
a very early source of student departure is to insure that the materials it produces and distributes are accurate, complete, and openly reflective, within
reason, of the full range of intellectual and social life in the institution.
Whatever format information takes, honesty is the best policy. Though the
painting of a "rosy picture" may, in the short run, increase enrollments, it is
very likely, in the long run, to decrease retention by widening the gap between promise and delivery.

But honesty requires that an institution go beyond the presentation of the
more formalized "institutional" views of its own character to the provision of
the views of one or more "typical" students currently and/or very recently
enrolled on campus (e.g., students in different types of academic programs
such as the arts, sciences, and vocational programs and/or students who exhibit different patterns of educational participation). Such views, more than
those of administrators or faculty, are likely to capture the informal character
of the institution. Presenting information from the perspective of different

types of students may also give individuals a better idea not only of how student life varies across campus but also of how that variation may relate to their own particular social and intellectual interests.

All this does not mean that college information should ignore the hopes and aspirations of the college—what the college may become as opposed to what it is. It is important for admissions material to indicate to the prospective student the ideals and the hopes which guide institutional action. In particular it should clearly state the ideals that mark the institution's view of its particular educational mission. It is that view, as much as that of students, which frames the underlying intellectual current of the institution and the intellectual ethos which pervades it.

By the same token, admissions should be clear with prospective students about the expectations the institution holds for them. Standards of educational and social behavior should be plainly spelled out so that it is clear what the institution will expect of its students. Lest we forget, the most effective retention programs result in heightened, not lessened, standards. It is partly for this reason that a number of institutions such as Syracuse University have established contracts that specify at entry the expectations the institution holds not only of itself but also of its students.

The primary point of such informational exercises and agreements or contracts is quite simple. It is to portray as accurately and fully as possible the sorts of students, faculty, and staff and the types of social and intellectual communities which exist on campus and which are likely to be encountered by prospective students after entry. The more accurate and complete the information, the more informed, generally speaking, will individuals be in making their choice of college. Presumably the more informed the choice, the better the choice and the more realistic the expectations will be as to the character of the institution chosen. Also, students will be informed beforehand of the sorts of social and educational behaviors that will expected of them once they arrive on campus.

Of course no pre-entry information system, however sophisticated, is perfect or foolproof. Some persons will misread or not read materials, or read into them what they wish to find. There will always be some newly admitted students whose perceptions of the institution will be incorrect. No amount of effort, outside of detailed personal interviews, can totally eliminate such misconceptions. Nevertheless, it is the case that improved pre-entry information aimed at the needs of future students can be an effective tool in reducing, over the long run, student departure from institutions of higher education. It appears to do so by attracting to the institution better informed students who are less likely to find themselves at odds with the prevailing social and intellectual communities of the college. More importantly, it conveys to all students the perception that the institution is sufficiently committed to and respecting of student competence to provide them with accurate information for their own decision making.

In this regard, admissions officers have an important responsibility to both prospective students and to the institution which they serve. Though some critics argue that the interests of the institution to enhance enrollments places the admissions officer in the position of having to work against the interests of the student as consumer, this need not be the case. The responsibility of admissions officers to increase enrollments is but part of their larger responsibility to further the welfare of the institution generally. It is the view here and at institutions such as Westchester Community College (Seidman 1992) that the institution's welfare is best served by insuring that students who enter will be able and likely to complete their education within the institution. This goal is achieved only when admissions officers also see their work as serving the needs of students as consumers and act to provide students with the information they need for informed college choices. The work of admissions officers should entail counseling and advising as much as it does recruiting.[5]

By so serving student needs, admissions officers enhance the likelihood not only that more students will seek to enter the institution—as students tend to seek out such institutions—but also that those who do enter will be more likely to stay until degree completion. The underlying principle is one of commitment, commitment on the part of the institution to the welfare of students and the resulting commitment engendered on the part of students to the institution.

Student impressions of college are shaped by a host of other informational sources. Though one normally thinks of the catalogs, brochures, and application materials colleges commonly distribute to prospective students as being the primary sources of student views, one should not overlook the diverse ways in which the institution portrays itself to other segments of the communities and/or market area it seeks to serve. Media agencies, high school counselors, teacher organizations, high school newspapers, open campus days, college fairs, high school visitation programs, and alumni associations are some of the more obvious sources of information which may shape impressions and therefore decisions as to choice of college.

High school counselors, for instance, can be quite influential in students' choice of college. But often they may have outdated or even mistaken information and views as to the character of the institution. Though the use of college-data books, brochures, and computer-based college information systems may help, they often provide only more formalized narrow views of what different institutions are like. More importantly, the information they provide is not always relevant to the issues of individual congruency and integration into the life of the institution.

For that reason, it is not uncommon for institutions to invest in a series of visiting programs for high school counselors; programs which bring onto campus counselors from various school districts which the institution serves—or hopes to more effectively serve in the future. The point of such visits is not merely to provide firsthand information as to the character of the institution, but also to enable counselors to obtain an accurate, multidimensional picture of the daily life of that institution. It is for the very same reason, of course, that some institutions make it a point to encourage prospective students and parents to visit the campus prior to deciding on enrollment. The principle is the same: to provide them with accurate information about the formal and informal character of the institution.

As to visiting programs generally, a number of colleges have given a good deal of attention to the manner in which those programs can serve the long-term educational goals of the institution. Hood College (Maryland), for instance, has employed a one-day program for prospective students and parents referred to as the One-Day Admission Seminar. It is designed to expose both students and parents to the character of the college and the connection between its programs (mostly liberal arts) and adult careers. Its goal is not only to introduce families to the ongoing life of the college, but also to insure that they fully understand the particular mission of the college. In this regard, though the seminar has proven to be an effective recruiting tool, it also has yielded important benefits in the understanding new students have of the essential ethos of the institution.

Other institutions take a different approach to this problem by directing their energies to high school students in the form of credit-bearing college courses taken during the regular academic program of the high school. Syracuse University's Project Advance, the Secondary Student Training Program at the University of Iowa, and the Bridge Program of the Staten Island Continuum of Education (New York), for instance, enable high school students not only to acquire college credit but also to obtain firsthand insight into the character of academic life at an institution of higher education. Though not necessarily aimed at recruitment, it is not surprising that such programs report not only high rates of college attendance but also very high rates of college completion by those students who were enrolled in their courses. Project Advance, for example, reports degree completion rates of over twice the national average (Adelman 1984).

Since disadvantaged students face particular problems in obtaining information, a number of institutions have organized a range of outreach programs that seek to inform, encourage, and prepare disadvantaged youth to enter college. Programs at Clemson University and the University of Wisconsin-Parkside, for instance, concern themselves not only with the improvement of student skills, but also with helping students make intelligent college and career choices.

ORIENTATION: BRIDGING THE GAP TO COLLEGE

Not surprisingly, most orientation programs stress the provision of information. Most new students are quick to express their need for accurate and complete information about the character of institutional life and about the requirements of the academic system they will soon be entering. They simply want and need to know what is expected of them in order to complete their college degree programs. And they want to know where to find assistance when it becomes necessary to do so.

Nevertheless it is surprising how often institutions fail to provide the full range of information needed or fail to provide it in a form readily available or understandable to new students. While most institutions are not reluctant to provide new students with information, that information is most often quite formal in nature. In emphasizing, for instance, the formal institutional requirements, they frequently understate, if not entirely overlook, the equally important informal demands institutions make upon new students. Orientation programs often do not give incoming students an accurate glimpse of the informal character of the social and intellectual communities which exist on campus. Yet it is precisely that informal world of student life that many times spells the difference between staying and leaving.

More importantly, orientation programs frequently fail to provide information in a form which leads new students to establish personal contacts with the individuals and offices which are responsible for providing advising and counseling services and/or which can provide the types of informal information new students require. That is, they often fail to recognize the fact that students' ability and willingness to obtain much-needed information during the course of their academic careers depend upon their having established personal, nonthreatening contacts with the persons and agencies which provide that information.

Here in the realm of interpersonal affiliation lies one of the keys to effective orientation programs, indeed to effective retention programs generally. Namely, that they go beyond the provision of information per se to the establishment of early contacts for new students not only with other members of their entering class but also with other students, faculty, and staff. In this manner, effective orientation programs function to help new students make the often difficult transition to the world of the college and help lay the foundation for the development of the important personal linkages which are the basis for eventual incorporation of the individual into the social and intellectual life of the institution (Pascarella, Terenzini, and Wolfle 1985).

A variety of techniques are employed for this purpose. Some programs bring upperclass students, faculty, and staff to meet with new students in informal situations in order to discuss the sorts of hurdles they are likely to have to surmount during the course of their college careers. Other programs employ the same range of persons as program participants, individuals who are expected to play both a formal and informal role in orientation activities. Still others, perhaps the more successful programs, extend the participation of students and faculty beyond the orientation period to the academic year through the use of peer and faculty mentor (tutor) programs, as they do at California State University at Fullerton and the University of New Mexico. In these instances, student and faculty participants take on the role of mentors to a group of new students. During the first year (and in the case of the faculty sometimes for the entire four-year period), mentors serve as informal advisers, campus friends, and not infrequently important role models to new students. They help shepherd, if you will, the newcomers through the period of separation and transition to the life of the college and assist in their eventual incorporation as participating members in the communities of the college.[6]

PRE-ENTRY ASSESSMENT AND PLACEMENT: IDENTIFYING STUDENT NEEDS

The utility of orientation programs for student retention is not limited to their role in student integration. Like admissions, orientation programs can also provide the setting for the beginning stages of institutional assessment by enabling institutions to assess, at a very early date, the nature of student skills and the character of their needs and concerns. They can be used not only to identify and place students into appropriate first-year courses, but also more broadly for counseling and advising purposes before students begin their first semester. In Kent State University, for example, prospective freshmen meet in small groups with professional academic advisers who answer student questions, respond to their concerns, and help them register for the fall semester (Young, Backer, and Rogers 1989). In this fashion, pre-entry assessment enables the institution to respond to student needs and concerns before they materialize into significant academic or social problems (see Hall 1982). As a consequence, they can serve as linchpins about which a range of institutional services are provided to beginning students in an integrated and systematic manner.

Though employed for a variety of purposes, pre-entry assessment has been most commonly used for admission screening and selection, placement in pre-entry programs and freshman courses, and for freshman advising and counseling. A number of institutions have quite consciously sought to utilize admissions screening/assessment procedures to reduce at entry the numbers of students who are judged unlikely or less likely to complete their degree programs. These combine data from admissions with evidence from the experience of past student cohorts to produce estimates of "dropout proneness" of different groups of students. These institutions are, of course, in the minority. Only a small percentage of all institutions, 15 to 20 percent, are in the position of having a large enough pool of suitable applicants from which to select their students. For most institutions, the question of the use of selective admissions procedures is a moot one.

But even if it were not, there are a number of serious questions as to the value and wisdom of attempting to use screening procedures in order to enhance student completion rates. The most obvious of these concerns the effectiveness of such screening procedures. Given the quite variable roots of student departure it is unclear whether any selection procedure, however sophisticated, could accurately predict the likelihood that various applicants would complete their degree programs. Though one might be able to predict the probability of academic difficulties, it is unlikely that one could gauge the likelihood of value or goal change or the degree of intellectual growth that occurs during the course of the college career.

Even if one could "improve the odds" by so screening students, there is good reason to question the wisdom of doing so. The great danger of screening procedures is that they may lead not only to self-fulfilling prophecies but also to the constriction of opportunity for late-developing students and/or those individuals whose abilities are not easily captured on formal admission documents. Screening procedures tend, by their very nature, to heavily weight the past at the expense of the future. By so doing they may hinder the chances for admission of those persons who are "late bloomers" or who tend to flourish only after being admitted to particular types of intellectual and/or social climates. In a very real sense they may act counter to one of the presumed ends of the higher educational enterprise, namely the discovery and fostering of individual talent. It might also be added that screening devices can produce, over time, homogeneous student populations, populations whose limited variety may also serve to constrain rather than promote the attainment of the educational ends of higher education.

All this does not mean that admissions screening procedures cannot be used to enhance retention. They can. But they must be employed with great care. They can and have been utilized as part of an institutional "early warning system" to identify "high-risk" or "dropout prone" students who are likely to need additional assistance to complete their college programs. Though still fraught with many pitfalls, such pre-entry assessment can be gainfully employed in an integrated retention program by enabling the institution to target services to identified students at the very outset or even before the beginning of the first year. In that manner they may be able to address the needs of some students before they encounter difficulties in the first year.

In this latter mode, pre-entry assessment has been used to trigger the provision of academic assistance prior to the start of the first year as a way of bridging the academic gap between high school and college. Some institutions, such as Bunker Hill Community College, Georgia State University, and Syracuse University, place new students into "summer bridge" programs that, like orientation generally, are specifically designed to help students acquire the academic skills required for college work. These programs typically ask students whose prior academic preparation is insufficient to meet the demands of academic work to attend a several-week summer session prior to the beginning of the first academic year. The focus of that session is largely but not solely academic. Its goal is simple, namely to insure that no student is so far behind the body of entering students that they cannot participate in the regular curriculum.

In the same vein, pre-entry assessment utilizing tests of area competencies (e.g., ACT ASSET tests of reading, writing, and mathematics) have been used by many institutions (e.g., Maricopa Community College District) to place incoming students in appropriate freshman courses. Though we commonly think of such screening as serving the growing needs for remediation or developmental education, they have also been used over the years to identify high achieving students (e.g., the College Board Advanced Placement Tests) who are allowed to skip over entry level coursework if they so wish.

However used, they are only as effective as the predictive accuracy of the tests and the quality of the subsequent courses in which students are placed.[7] Regarding the former, debate continues over the fairness of many tests, especially when they are used among ethnically and racially diverse student populations. It is for this reason, and others, that a number of institutions have begun to employ multiple indicators of competency lest any one of them yield inaccurate or biased estimates of student abilities.

Regarding the latter, the experience of Miami-Dade Community College reminds us that the intent of the placement tests is to enable the institution to assist incoming students acquire the skill they need to do college-level work. In the final analysis, it is the quality of the courses in which students are placed more than the accuracy of the placement tests that should be central to institutional concerns. Unfortunately, the reverse is frequently the case.

Finally, pre-entry assessment, as noted above, has been successfully employed by a great variety of institutions as part of first-year advising and counseling programs. Typically tied to orientation programs, questionnaires are utilized to identify student needs, concerns, and interests. This in turn is used to trigger, where called for, specific forms of advising and counseling and the provision of information from a variety of institution and student groups. In effect, it enables the institution to "frontload" some forms of advising and counseling. But, as in the case of placement tests, the collection of data on students is only as useful as the quality of the advising and counseling they in turn receive. To be effective, institutions have to put into place the resources needed to quickly respond to students before the first year is well underway.

The First Year: Making the Transition to College

The next critical period in the student career occurs in the first year of college, especially during the first semester or quarter. It is that stage in the college career which typically calls for individuals to separate themselves from past associations and patterns of educational participation and to make the social and academic transition to the new and possibly much more challenging life of the college (Upcraft, Gardner, and Associates 1989). Many new students, especially those who are moving away from home, have difficulty in learning to fend for themselves in the adult world of the college. Others, whose prior academic training has not adequately prepared them for college-level work, may have difficulty in adjusting to the more rigorous academic demands of college. While many students soon adjust, others have great difficulty either in separating themselves from past associations and/or in adjusting to the academic and social life of the college.

Not surprisingly, the incidence of withdrawal is highest during this early stage of the college career. The individual is least integrated into and therefore least committed to the institution and thus most susceptible to the pains and doubts which separation and transition evoke. Deficiencies in prior academic preparation are most noticeable and most acutely felt. By the same token, however, it is during this transition stage in the student college career that institutions can do much to aid continued attendance. By providing much-needed assistance early in the student career, they can help students make the necessary transition and thereby insure that most students have at least a reasonable opportunity to complete their degree programs should they desire to do so.

At this stage, several types of institutional actions have proven to be effective in treating the early roots of student withdrawal. These fall into five broad categories of action: transition assistance, early contact and community building, academic involvement and support, monitoring and early warning, and counseling and advising.

TRANSITION ASSISTANCE

Transition assistance programs are designed to assist individuals overcome or at least cope with the many social and academic difficulties that arise in the transition to college. These typically stress academic, social, and/or residential issues.

For some students, transition assistance programs emphasize the academic component of college life. These commonly stress improving study skills (e.g., writing and reading skills), study habits (e.g., learning to apportion one's time to meet academic deadlines), academic preparation (e.g., high school mathematics), the use of libraries and other institutional resources, and the writing of college-level reports and term papers.

One of the more successful types of academic assistance programs, *Becoming a Master Student,* derives from the Learning to Learn tradition in which students are given a structured sequence of skill-building exercises, each attached to a concrete academic outcome (Ellis 1985). In this instance, students are asked, in a course format, to cover a range of academic, social, and financial issues. Though widely available, such courses are more commonly found in community colleges (e.g., Jefferson County Community College, Miami-Dade Community College, Sacramento City College, and Westchester Community College) and in state four-year colleges (e.g., Appalachian State University, Central Missouri State University, St. Cloud State University, South Carolina State College, and Stockton State College) which serve large numbers of first-generation college students and/or students whose prior academic preparation does not well suit them for college work.

Another widely used program is that drawn from the *University 101* program, established by John Gardner at the University of South Carolina (Gardner and Jewler 1985). In this case, institutions such as Clemson University and Yakima Valley Community College have taken the notion of orientation, as discussed above, and extended it to a first-semester course in which various aspects of adjustment, academic, social, and otherwise, are discussed and skills/strategies provided to assist students in dealing with the difficulties they characteristically encounter during that year (Upcraft, Gardner, and Associates 1989). Some institutions, for example Shelby State Community College, have integrated a semester-long "orientation" course with pre-entry orientation activities to form a year-long program that is as much developmental in character as it is "orientational" in the more common usage of the term.[8] The same can be said of the program at Winthrop College which uses discussion of critical issues as the vehicle to advance student cognitive development.

But not all transition programs are entirely or largely academic in character. Transition programs may also concentrate on the social adjustments new students are required to make in entering college. These will cover a wide range of topics appropriate to the particular college setting in which new students find themselves. Social adjustment, social responsibility, sexual behavior, discrimination, date rape, and self-protection are only a few of the many issues that are often discussed in such programs. Whatever the content, the goals of these programs are the same, namely to help young people acquire the social skills and adopt the social norms of behavior appropriate to membership in the diverse adult communities of the college.

In residential institutions such programs may also focus on the practical problems of fending for oneself and of making new friends in a strange environment. These range from the mundane art of doing one's own laundry to the somewhat more complex tasks of establishing financial and legal residence on campus and to the sometimes quite difficult matter of meeting and making new friends (Upcraft, Gardner and Associates 1989, 142–67). Lest we forget, in residential institutions at least, most students (still in their teens) are faced with the task of living on their own for the first time without the reassuring aid of parents. It is, as some will recall, both a stimulating and frightening period. Not surprisingly, many of these programs, such as those at Miami University of Ohio, St. Lawrence University, Stanford University, the University of Delaware, the University of Miami-Coral Gables, and the University of Michigan, operate out of the residential settings in which new students find themselves.

In the case of the University of Michigan, its 21st Century Program, like many others of its type, is aimed at the development of a supportive, inclusive residential community that draws students from a wide variety of backgrounds. While this is also true of the thematic residential programs at Stanford University, their Structured Liberal Arts Program, like that at St. Lawrence University, seeks to integrate academics with the residential experience. Like other "co-curricular" programs, an attempt is made to bridge the gap that typically divides students' academic life from that which takes place in the residence hall (Moffatt 1989)

EARLY CONTACT AND COMMUNITY BUILDING

Early contact/community programs are, as their name suggests, designed to provide new students with contact with other members of the institution and with the various communities that make up its daily life. Their long-term goal is the incorporation of individuals into the academic and social communities of the institution. These programs go beyond the mere formalities of college life and involve students, faculty, and staff in a variety of formal and informal interactions over a range of topics pertinent to the needs and interests of new students. Contact among students may be particularly important not only because it helps cement personal affiliations which tie the new student into the fabric of student culture, but also because it enables the newcomer to acquire useful information as to the informal character of institutional life. Information of this sort can only be obtained from other students who have already been successful in navigating the institution. It cannot be gained easily, if at all, from either faculty or staff, however sympathetic or competent.

As noted earlier, the evidence for the effectiveness of such interactions is quite clear. The more frequent and rewarding interactions are between students and other members of the institution, the more likely are individuals to stay. This is especially true for those contacts which take place between students and faculty. When those contacts also occur outside the formal domains of the institution and are seen as warm, receptive, and wide-ranging in character, that is, not restricted solely to the formalities of academic work, individuals are not only more likely to stay but also more likely to grow both intellectually and socially while staying. The faculty are key links to the intellectual life of the institution. Rewarding contact with them is an essential element in student development.

To encourage such interactions, contact programs have taken on a variety of forms. Many institutions, such as California State University at Fullerton, Canisius College, Colorado State University, Loma Linda University, North Seattle Community College, Notre Dame College of Ohio, University of California at Irvine, and Western New Mexico University, have established faculty and staff mentor programs where individual faculty and staff become advisers or mentors to beginning students. These programs run the spectrum from very formal programs, such as the Systematic Mentoring Process at the University of Nebraska, to very informal programs where faculty mentors serve as the student's person of last resort.

Other programs have sought to take advantage of interactions which arise in "naturally occurring" situations (e.g., outside classrooms), while others, such as the Freshman Forums at Syracuse University, have emphasized the use of formally organized seminars, dinners, and the like in a variety of settings including faculty homes and student housing. A number of programs are run as part of ongoing freshman-year residential programs. Frequently led by upperclass student, dorm, and faculty advisers, these programs use formal situations as jumping-off places for the more important personal matters which concern new students on campus. A more recent variation on the same principle is that of peer network therapy. In this form of peer contact, family network therapy techniques are applied to groups of first-year students. Though group discussions focus on common needs and concerns, the end product is the formation of a stable network of peers which provides intellectual and emotional support for its members (see Crouse 1982).

Among the more creative uses of naturally occurring situations is the case of one institution which distributed to each of its faculty and staff a coffee/tea cup which could be filled free of charge only at the student center. It was hoped and indeed it proved to be the case that heightened student-faculty interactions would follow. In another instance, an institution gave to its faculty college jackets which, if worn to sports events, would insure the wearer free entry. Again increased student-faculty contact is reported to have occurred. And the contact eventually extended beyond the localized situation of the student center and/or sporting event. Enhanced contact in one setting appeared to have fostered moré contact, both formally and informally, in a variety of other settings.

A particularly successful variation of some of these principles can be seen in the University 101 program at the University of South Carolina and many similar programs around the country. The program provides both special preparation for faculty to sensitize them to the intellectual and social needs of new students and orientation activities for new students which include listening and communication skills. Approximately one-third of the freshman class participate in the program, with special sections being offered to unique populations such as older students, undeclared majors, Upward Bound students, and handicapped students. A particular goal of that program is the breaking down of the barriers which keep people from communicating with one another, faculty and students alike. Its well-documented outcome has been a higher rate of retention even for those students who were initially less well qualified than students who did not participate in the program.

However structured, contact programs are often seen as logical extensions of orientation programs or as part of ongoing student/faculty mentor programs. More importantly, they are also viewed as an essential component of the intellectual and social life of the institution. For many institutions, rewarding contact among members of the institution, especially among students and faculty, is the primary task of the institution, not a by-product of other events. Not surprisingly, those institutions see the process of education as one of modeling, and faculty and staff as providing important role models in that process.

It should be observed, however, that contact programs, especially mentor programs, can place a great deal of strain on faculty and staff, many of whom are already burdened with full academic and administrative loads. In addition, such programs require staff training and the provision of information that would enable mentors to respond effectively to student needs as they are identified. Not surprisingly, a mentor, whether student, faculty, or staff, is frequently the first person to know of a student's problems. His or her ability to respond effectively is often critical to a program's success.

In this regard, it is ironic that during this first year of college, when contact with other students and faculty is so important to retention, so many institutions structure the first year, especially first-year courses, so as to discourage contacts. Freshman classes are frequently the largest on campus and, in university settings, often taught by graduate students rather than by faculty. One would think, given the evidence presented above, that the reverse ought to be the norm rather than the exception. The short-term economic gains thought to arise from greater efficiency in the allocation of resources (e.g., through large course enrollments) are often achieved at the expense of long-term losses in both retention and student development.

It is for this reason, among others, that an increasing number of institutions are establishing special educational programs or courses designed specifically for the beginning student. In some cases they are based on our growing knowledge of the particular learning situations best suited to education of beginning students (Erickson and Strommer 1991). In others, they are based upon the spreading recognition of the value of collaborative and cooperative learning for both student learning and retention (Goodsell, Maher and Tinto 1992).

In the latter case, scores of programs have been established in both four- and two-year colleges to more fully involve students, especially beginning students, as collaborative participants in the learning experience. At the University of Oregon, then at the University of Washington and other institutions, freshmen interest groups have been established: beginning students form groups based upon common academic and intellectual interests whose members enroll in the same set of courses during their first semester/quarter of college. In some cases, such as at the University of Washington, some of these groups have been joined to "linked courses" that in turn typically join a writing course to a content-area course—the former focusing on the content of the latter. Students in a freshman interest group will take these courses together during their first semester or quarter of college as a means of encouraging the formation of self-sustaining student communities that have an academic focus.

In other cases, such as Brown University, Evergreen State College, LaGuardia Community College, Long Island University-Brooklyn Campus, Seattle Central Community College, and Western Michigan University, programs based upon collaborative-learning models have been developed that call for students to become actively involved as collaborators in the learning process (see Gabelnick, MacGregor, Matthews, and Smith 1990, and Goodsell, Maher, and Tinto 1992). In the Coordinated Studies Program at Seattle Central Community College and the Learning Communities at LaGuardia Community College, students enroll in a block of courses, typically three, that meet as one community throughout the quarter. The faculty and students join together as collaborators in dealing with the content of the courses in a manner which provides both for thematic unity and synthetic wholeness.

In these instances, the *process* of collaborative learning is as important as is content. Though the latter is not insignificant, the primary intent of the course is to actively involve students in the learning process in a collaborative, rather than competitive, manner. Such programs seek through that involvement to promote both student learning and the development of academic and social communities in college. And they do so via the vehicle of the educational experience of the classroom, not despite it.

A different approach to the same end is found in the growing application of cooperative-learning teaching strategies to the college classroom setting (Bonwell and Eison 1991, Johnson, Johnson, and Smith 1992). Drawn from the extensive body of research on cooperative learning in elementary and secondary schools (e.g., Johnson, Johnson, and Holubec 1986, Slavin 1990), an increasing number of faculty at institutions ranging from the University of California-Dominquez Hills, Duquesne University, Gallaudet University, the University of Maryland, and the University of Minnesota to De Anza Community College, Florida Community College at Jacksonville, and MT. San Antonio College are training their faculty and restructuring their courses to require students to work together in structured cooperative settings. Unlike the collaborative programs noted above that frequently join together several faculty and courses, cooperative programs are commonly run by individual faculty within their own courses. In any case, they share a common concern, namely actively engaging students in a cooperative fashion in the learning process.

However structured, these education programs, when applied to the first year, seek to achieve the same ends. They strive to promote both student learning and retention through actively involving students in some cooperative/collaborative fashion that builds both learning and community membership. The transition they seek to bridge is the educational one from passive to active involvement, from spectator to active participant.

It should be pointed out here that such programs, whether collaborative or cooperative, are particularly important to nonresidential institutions and to commuting students whose attachments to the campus may be weak. For those institutions and students, learning communities are an effective response to the issue of academic involvement in situations that normally constrain involvement.

But not all students have the skills needed to participate in the regular coursework. Some require some form of remediation or what is more frequently referred to as developmental educational support. These "developmental" education programs are designed to assist students in acquiring skills needed for full college participation. Numerous colleges—Bunker Hill Community College, Chesapeake College, Johnson County Community College, LaGuardia Community College, the Maricopa Community College District, Miami-Dade Community College, Southern University, the State University of New York at Albany, and Tacoma Community College among many others—have established first-year programs designed to help "developmental" students acquire academic skills appropriate to college-level work. Like most programs that are targeted to specific segments of the entering class (e.g., adults, transfer students, etc.), these programs typically combine a range of efforts, from special coursework to advising and mentoring that typically follows the students throughout their stay at the institution (Tomlinson 1989). In many cases they are tied to summer bridge programs and other institutional services in an integrated approach to student development.

As noted in chapter 3, the most successful of these programs are administratively integrated in the mainstream of institutional life. Rather than being marginal to academic life, they are seen as an integral part of the institution's mission and therefore requiring a central administrative location. Indeed some states, most notably New Jersey, have made developmental education a centerpiece of state higher educational policy and have, in turn, provided incentive monies to help establish programs throughout the state.

Another approach to the issue of developmental education, one that does not pull students out into separate programs, is that of supplemental instruction. First developed at the University of Missouri-Kansas City, supplemental instruction calls for students needing extra assistance to attend "supplemental" study groups that are attached to regular coursework. These group sessions, typically led by student tutors, provide an informal, nonthreatening, yet course-attached setting for students to review course material and acquire the skills needed to meet course requirements (see Blanc, DeBuhr and Martin 1983). Unlike the broader reach of general developmental education programs, these programs are tied to specific courses and as a result are more dependent on the cooperation of faculty and program staff to organize course and group work to the students' benefit.

MONITORING AND EARLY WARNING

Given the importance of the first year to retention generally and learning growth in particular, institutions have also begun to put into place systems that monitor student progress. As part of that monitoring, some institutions have instituted "early warning systems." These are designed, in theory, to provide the institution and, in turn the student, an early indication of difficulty. In principle they are structured so as to insure that that "warning" or "academic alert" comes early enough to be useful, namely in the first five or six weeks of the first quarter or semester.

In some cases, monitoring is, as it is in Bunker Hill Community College, course specific. In other cases, as in the University of Wisconsin-Oshkosh and Walla Walla Community College, it is part of a broader monitoring system that encompasses the first year generally. In still other cases, early warning systems may be tied to computerized student tracking systems that enable the institution to monitor the progress of students throughout the institution. In the latter instance, there are several computer software packages available that can be used for this purpose.

However constructed, the principle of early warning systems is the same, namely that treatment of student needs and problems should occur as early as possible in the student career and should be approached in an integrated fashion. If we have learned anything over the years in our attempts to improve student retention, it is that the earlier one attends to a problem or potential problem, the easier it is to deal with that problem and the less likely it is that it will manifest itself in the form of student withdrawal.

Prompt feedback to students and to those who can assist students is an essential element in the effectiveness of these systems. In Walla Walla Community College, for instance, early warning begins during the fourth week of class, early enough for institutional services to reach students before the middle of the quarter. That system, like the one at the University of Wisconsin-Oshkosh, is initiated by faculty in their classrooms. They employ faculty developed monitoring forms to note the incidence of classroom behaviors (e.g., absences, failure to complete work) typically associated with academic difficulty. During the fourth week of classes, faculty use those forms to monitor student progress and inform, if necessary, both students and support staff of potential problems. Beyond the obvious benefits of quick institutional response to student needs, faculty initiated systems also put faculty into direct contact with students about their needs and difficulties. That contact, as much as the assistance it provides, underlies the success of faculty-initiated early warning systems.

Regrettably, many institutions employ indicators such as mid-term grades which, when finally recorded, come too late in the first year to be particularly useful. By the time the institution is able to respond, many students are already too deep in difficulty to be easily helped. Indeed many will have already given up and withdrawn from the institution.

COUNSELING AND ADVISING

The utilization of counseling and advising programs during the early part of the student career underlines the fact, evident to most counselors, that not all students enter college with clearly held goals.[9] And even those who have goals will often change them during the course of the college career. But as noted in chapter 3, neither initial lack of goal clarity nor changes in goals are of themselves objects of concern. It would be surprising indeed if all entering eighteen-year-olds were clear in their future plans and career goals. More surprising still would be the absence of significant changes in career goals during the course of college. One would anticipate that exposure to higher education would lead numbers of students to reconsider their plans. Temporary ambiguity about one's future is an expected, perhaps even desired, part of the maturation process. Lest we forget, many of us change career goals, indeed careers, several times during our working lifetimes.

Continuing failure to resolve one's goals is, however, another matter. Prolonged uncertainty about them often leads students to call into question the reasons for their continued presence on campus. In situations where the rewards for participation are minimal, it may lead students to withdraw from college. For that reason institutions have willingly invested in a host of "developmental" advising and counseling programs whose intent it is to help guide individuals along the path of goal clarification (Young, Backer and Rogers 1989). This is especially true for individuals who indicate at the outset that they are undecided as to the direction of the academic studies.

The effectiveness of such "developmental advising" for student retention appears to reside, however, not only in the availability of such services, but in the manner in which they are presented (e.g., Creamer 1980). They tend to be most effective when advising and counseling is required for students. Thus the growing use of what is referred to as "intrusive" advising (Glennen and Baxley 1985).[10]

The effectiveness of advising and counseling is further enhanced when they are an integral and positive part of the educational process which all students are expected to experience. This is especially evident among the growing number of colleges that have instituted freshman advising programs that target all first-year students. Institutions such as the University of Iowa, the State University of New York, and the University of Chicago all have established freshman advising centers that serve the advising and counseling needs of all freshmen. In most cases, departments take over advising in the second year, but in the case of the University of Chicago, the advising center continues to advise students throughout their college stay.

This view of advising and counseling as being an integral part of the college experience manifests itself on campus in several ways. On some campuses, such as Monmouth College, New Mexico Military Institute, Phillips County Community College, and West Chester University of Pennsylvania, one finds such programs housed in a central place. Not infrequently they are located in the student center or in another place that students naturally frequent. They are often bright, cheerful places staffed by warm, friendly, and of course competent persons who are visibly open to student contact.

Effective counseling and advising programs also tend to be systematically linked to the other student services and programs on campus, as they are in Monmouth College. Often they are part of an integrated network of programs aimed at student retention and are administratively tied to both admissions and orientation programs (Frost 1991). At the University of Denver and elsewhere, as well as at the University of Chicago, advising is seen as a comprehensive system which spans the entire four years of student life from admissions to graduation. In some cases this results from associational linkages between separate programs. In others, it arises from the existence of a campuswide retention program of which each subprogram is a component part. In either case, information from earlier programs is employed in the subsequent programs through a variety of feedback mechanisms to insure that student progress is continually monitored by the institution. When there are discrete programs concerned with different facets of student life, they also tend to be coordinated in their actions. The *whole* student is the focus of effective retention programs.

In some institutions, such as George Mason University, Loyola University of New Orleans, and Ohio State University, special intrusive academic advising programs are targeted to the undecided student. In other cases, such as Bloomfield College, Los Rios Community College District, and the University of California at Davis, they are directed at transfer students. In still other settings, such as College of New Rochelle, Cornell University, San Diego State University, special programs have been developed for particular segments of the student population ranging from students of color to science majors to adult students recently returned to higher education.

However directed, an increasing number of institutions are placing a greater reliance on professional advising staff. The extent to which they do so, however, varies considerably. In some institutions, such as the University of Chicago, professional advisers do much of the advising throughout the student's college career. In many other cases, indeed the majority of cases, a professional advising staff work together with specially assigned faculty. In institutions like the State University of New York at Albany, the University of Iowa, and York University in Toronto, carefully designed networks link professionals in an advising center to faculty in differing programs and departments. In some of these cases, such as at the University of Iowa, the advising center will, with the assistance of the faculty, take primary responsibility for advising first-year students, who are then "passed on" to faculty advisers in the respective departments in their second year.

However organized, institutions are beginning to take seriously the notion that advising is not a skill that comes "naturally." Certainly as it applies to the task of developmental advising, but increasingly for program advising as well, institutions such as Cecil Community College and the University of North Florida, among many others, are establishing training programs for all advisers regardless of background. This applies as well to those institutions such as Bunker Hill Community College, Cleveland State University, San

Diego State University, and Wesleyan College (Georgia) that also employ peer and/or faculty/staff mentors in the advising process.

Noteworthy, in this respect, is the growing popularity of computer-assisted advising (and registration), at such institutions as Brigham Young University, Georgia State University, Johnson County Community College, Miami University of Ohio, Pepperdine University, Purdue University, Syracuse University, the University of Minnesota-Duluth, and the University of North Florida. In these cases, computerized registration and on-line degree audit systems enable both students and advisers to obtain accurate and up-to-date information pertaining to the task of program planning. In the process, they help overcome the single greatest hurdle to effective program advising, namely the inability of advisers to provide students with consistent and accurate information about their program choices.

Integrated First-Year Programs: Putting It All Together

Thus far we have described several programs that are typically used alone or sometimes together with other programs in some fashion to frame a "retention program." In most cases, even when employed together, programs are run as discrete entities, each with its own specific sphere of authority. Though sometimes tied together through some coordinating agency (person, committee, or office), they remain little islands unto themselves.

That this is the case is frequently an artifact of how programs develop. Typically they arise from the initiative of specific individuals, faculty and staff, with particular spheres of authority and skill. There is, however, an alternative to this type of program development, namely that of integrated first-year programs. In this case, the question institutions pose is not what programs they need during the first year of college, but how that first year should itself be structured and directed.

In response to this question, several institutions, for instance King's College (University of Nova Scotia), St. Lawrence University, and the University of Notre Dame, have set aside part or even the whole of the first year of college for the development of the intellectual and social foundations for the remaining college years. In these instances a core program is established whose intent it is to help integrate individuals into the intellectual and social life of the institution and equip them with the skills needed to take advantage of the remaining college years. Rather than invest in highly segmented courses and/or experiences which tend to isolate students from each other and from faculty, foundation programs seek to provide a range of common, shared experiences wherein both students and faculty come to interact along a range of intellectual and social issues. Early separation into discrete areas of study is avoided, and community participation in intellectual and social discourse is stressed as a means of building the personal linkages which are the basis of competent intellectual and social membership in the life of the college.

In other cases, separate colleges such as the General College of the University of Minnesota and the University College of the University of Arkansas-Little Rock have been set up for the distinct purpose of providing education for segments of the freshman class. Though these have often been geared to the needs of developmental education students, as in the two cases cited above, the same principle has been applied more broadly to other segments of the entering student population, most notably to the brightest of entering students (e.g., the Lee Honors College at Western Michigan University). However directed, these colleges represent an administrative response that enables a smaller college with a distinctive mission to grow within a larger university. In effect, it enables the institution to serve several missions and therefore student audiences without undue conflicts in staff and faculty responsibilities.

Though such programs may not be either feasible or desirable in all college settings, their apparent success in the institutions where they have been used suggests that elements of that conception may be gainfully employed elsewhere. Specifically it suggests that attention be given during the first year to the establishment of the conditions which foster the integration of students into the intellectual and social life of the institution. Early contact and mentor programs, specific educational programs or courses, as already discussed, are but several of a number of possible mechanisms for that end.

In this respect, another approach to the issue of integration, one which has fallen into disfavor during the past several decades, involves the use of first-year ceremonies and rituals. Despite the claims of many of the critics of the sixties and seventies that such events were forms of indoctrination, there is much to be said for the value of ceremonies and rituals in helping integrate newcomers into the life of a community. Besides reaffirming the importance of commonly held values, they also serve to cement the personal bonds that are the continuing fabric of the community over time. Though such events are now commonly reserved for the end of one's college career, there is little reason why they should not be employed during and at the end of the freshman year. Freshman-year ceremonies and rituals can, if properly conceived, do much to assist new students over the difficulties of separation and transition which mark that year.

Incorporation into College: Long-term Actions for Retention

Beyond the early stages of separation and transition to college, student withdrawal is most frequent at the end of the first year and during the second, when numbers of students decide either to leave higher education altogether or to transfer to other institutions.[11] The causes of withdrawal and dropout during this period are many. A number of individuals may leave because they find the institution ill-suited to their needs and interests. Others may come to realize in the course of clarifying their intentions that higher education of any form is not in their best interests. Some students are unable to keep up with the academic demands of the college and are either dismissed or withdraw under the threat of eventual failure. Others find, however, that those demands are not challenging enough. They leave to participate in more stimulating environments. Still others may experience difficulty in making contact with other persons and establishing competent membership in the communities of the college. For them isolation is a primary cause of departure. And of course other students will not seek to become integrated because they find the available communities not to their personal liking. They withdraw in order to locate more compatible college communities.

Clearly no single intervention strategy will suffice to treat these quite varied forms of student departure. Though it is possible to conceive of early intervention strategies as applying to students generally, the same does not hold after the end of the first year. After that time, institutions have to consider a wide range of both general programs and highly differentiated ones specifically tailored to the needs of different types of students and student leavers. In this respect the formation of long-term retention policies is considerably more complex.

Here the issue of institutional choice is clearest. To repeat a point made earlier, it is simply unwise for institutions to presume to be able to effectively treat all forms of student departure. At some point institutions must address the complex question of what forms of departure they will define as dropout and therefore deserving of institutional action and what they will consider to be the perhaps unavoidable outcome of institutional life.

The focus of long-term retention programs. It is the view here that institutions should center their attention primarily on those forms of departure which can be understood by both the institution and the individual as representing educational failure. They should focus their actions on student dropout rather than on student departure generally. With this understood, it follows from our earlier discussions that long-term retention efforts beyond the first year should focus on three major sources of student departure: academic difficulties, the inability of individuals to resolve their educational and occupational goals, and their failure to become or remain incorporated in the intellectual and social life of the institution.[12] Accordingly, the focus of long-term intervention programs should center, on one hand, on continuing forms of academic assistance, advising, and counseling, and, on the other, on educational programs to further involve students in the life of the institution. More than retention alone, educational growth should be the goal of these programs.

The use of extended counseling and advising programs has proved to be particularly effective. Students' needs for advice and counsel do not end after the first year. In addition to the need of students to locate themselves in a major, many also need help in dealing with the sometimes difficult and often frightening task of deciding what to do after college. Upperclassmen frequently require special counseling as they deal with the unknowns of yet another impending separation and transition, namely that from college to the adult world of work.

In addition to meeting the continuing need for academic support services, some institutions have also turned to the development of educational programs that extend the logic of active involvement in learning during the first year to subsequent years of college. Following, for example, models of collaborative and cooperative learning and the use of learning communities (e.g., Evergreen State College), several institutions have sought to construct special academic programs that stress fuller participation in the intellectual life of the institution. In some cases, these programs take on the form of new majors, while in others they become special areas of study or interest. However constructed, they represent one more way in which colleges and universities have sought to broaden the range of educational communities in which students can find rewarding membership.

In this regard, an increasing number of institutions, for instance Earlham College and Xavier University, have turned to their upperclass students and have asked them to become involved with programs to assist other students as both peers and mentors. In this fashion they have sought to extend the notion of community membership to that of responsible citizenship and have asked continuing students to take some degree of responsibility for the welfare of newer members of the community. The benefits are not only increased retention for both groups, helper and helped alike, but also and more importantly, an enriched educational experience that goes beyond the confines of a prescribed curriculum.

Some institutions, such as Marymount College in California, have instituted senior-year programs, which seek not only to provide a capstone experience for seniors but also help orient graduating students to life after college. In the same way that pre-college orientation programs are designed to ease the transition to college, these programs are geared to helping the student make the transition from college to the adult world of work and broader community membership. Other institutions, such as Berea College, Iowa State University, Miami University, and Stanford University, have found that extracurricular programs can be gainfully employed in long-term retention programs (see Kuh, Schuh. Whitt and Associates 1991). Specifically, they have sought to encourage the growth of a variety of clubs, student programs, social and intellectual activities, and the like, as natural meeting places for both students and faculty. They have sought to have continuing contact arise as a naturally occurring outcome of activities which draw students, and students and faculty, together around a variety of common interests and needs. In so doing, institutions have also discovered that such efforts have significantly enhanced the social and intellectual life of the institution—an outcome of some educational importance.

However structured, the essential component of all of the various long-term retention programs is that they enable the faculty and staff to make continuing, personal contact with students. An important product of that contact is the building of the interlocking chains of human affiliations that are the foundation of supportive educational and social communities. Besides providing students with particular types of services (e.g., advice and career counseling, special activities), they serve to draw individuals into the social and intellectual mainstream of campus life. They act as a continuing demonstration of the institution's commitment to the welfare of its students—a commitment which is the necessary condition for the development among students of their commitment to the institution. Like healthy families, effective institutions are those whose various members reach out to one another in a variety of settings not strictly limited by the formal confines of academic life. They are institutions to which the term "community" is aptly applied, for they are collectivities of persons concerned with each others' welfare.

Stopout, Delay, and Student Retention

As noted in chapter 2, a growing number of students temporarily suspend attendance from college, or "stop out," work while in college, and/or shift their participation from full-time to part-time during the course of their college career. To the degree that these students are also more likely to withdraw permanently from college, so too have they become the focus of a range of retention programs.

Regarding stopout, we have already noted the fact, apparent to many college administrators, that changing financial needs and altered external commitments will force some individuals to leave college at least temporarily. What is not apparent is the willingness of institutions to make it possible for these students to return to college. Rather than leaving the issue of return to chance, some colleges have developed programs to attract these students back to campus. Here relatively simple actions, such as sending letters and/or newsletters to all stopouts in good academic standing, can yield substantial benefits.

The same can be said of services for working students and for those who shift from full-time to part-time attendance during the course of their academic career. Both groups of students, more certainly the latter, are in some degree less strongly attached to the institution. In the latter case, many students are, in fact, beginning a gradual process of detachment that eventually leads to full withdrawal from college. It is mainly for that reason that some colleges have targeted special advising and counseling services to those students or to particular segments of that group. The underlying assumption is that the institution has to make an effort to reach out in some special way to those students in order to keep them attached. Mailings, weekend and/or evening programs, such as the one at the College of Notre Dame of Baltimore, are typically part of those efforts.

Many institutions offer courses on weekends and during the evening to enable working students to attend classes. What they do not do as well is offer academic and student services during times available to students. Beyond the obvious impact on the likelihood of student success, such policies have the unintended, but very real, consequence of stigmatizing evening and weekend students as "second-class" citizens of the college. The success of the programs cited above lies, in large measure, in their adherence to a simple principle, namely that all students, regardless of their form or time of participation, should have access to equivalent forms of institutional services, in particular to those of academic and social support.

FINANCIAL ASSISTANCE AND STUDENT RETENTION
Before we go on to other matters, several comments are called for here concerning the role of financial assistance in long-term retention programs. Though it has been argued earlier that finances are not as important to student retention as is commonly thought, short-term fluctuations in finances can and do cause a number of students to withdraw from college. Though some of these departures will be temporary, others may not. In any case, even among the former it is usually the case that it is more difficult to finish a degree program after having "stopped out" than it would have been had one remained continuously enrolled.

As a result it is true that financial-aid programs can, in certain situations, help prevent departure by enabling students to overcome temporary financial difficulties (Martin 1985). North Seattle Community College, for example, has successfully utilized funds in an institution foundation to assist students with short-term financial needs (e.g., child care, textbooks). But it is also true that not all forms of financial assistance work equally well. For example, work-study programs can, when properly structured, enhance the likelihood of retention over that which might have resulted from direct financial aid. Within limits, on-campus work-study programs serve not only to provide additional income, but also help the individual make wide-ranging contact with other members of the institution. In this manner they may further retention by aiding the individual's incorporation into the life of the college. Of course, work-study programs can also detract from one's chances of completion. They may do so by either isolating the person from the life of the institution (e.g., as might occur in off-campus jobs) or by taking up so much of that person's time as to undermine academic work.

For most students, persistence is more reflective of the character of their social and intellectual experiences on campus than it is of their financial resources. Student loans often go unused, even when readily available. This does not mean that some students, especially those from less advantaged backgrounds, may not require or need financial assistance. Rather it suggests that individual response to financial stress is conditioned by other forces, namely those associated with the interactive character of student experience on campus. The more rewarding that experience is perceived to be, the greater, generally speaking, will be the person's willingness to withstand even great financial hardship in order to stay. Conversely, unrewarding experiences in the academic and/or social communities of the college may lead students to withdraw in the face of even quite minimal financial stress. The citation of financial stress as a reason for withdrawal is sometimes a polite way of describing one's displeasure with the character of one's social and/or intellectual life within the institution.

Retention Policies for Different Students

Thus far our discussion of retention policy has not made specific reference to the different students programs serve. Should we fail to do so, we run the risk of leaving the impression that successful institutional action is largely invariant across types of students served and that successful institutions treat all students the same. In fact, the opposite is the case. Successful institutional action necessarily entails the assessment of student needs and the fine-tuning of programming to the specific needs of differing students.

What then of our preceding discussion of institutional policy for student retention? In what ways would that discussion differ if the focus of policy was the retaining of students of color or those who are academically at risk? How might policy differ if it were applied to older students or to those who commute, attend part-time, and/or work in order to support families while in college?

As we turn to address these questions, it bears repeating that there is an unfortunate tendency in discussions of this sort to erroneously assign to one attribute of a group differences in persistence that reflect other attributes also affecting persistence. The most obvious example of this tendency has to do with discussions of differences in persistence among white students and students of color. Though it is the case that students of color as a group are less likely to persist than are white students as a group, we have already noted in chapter 2 that much of that difference reflects differences both in social origins and in prior quality of academic training of the two groups. As a group, students of color are more likely to come from poorer backgrounds and have experienced inferior education than are white students as a group. But not all students of color are disadvantaged, nor are all disadvantaged students those of color. Most disadvantaged students are in fact white. And several groups which can be classified as racial minorities (Asian Americans and Cuban Americans among others) have higher rates of educational success than do groups commonly classified as belonging to the racial majority.

At the same time, we must also avoid the tendency to assume that all members of a particular group have the same interests or needs. Though it is sometimes necessary for institutions to develop programs targeted to the needs of distinct groups of students, it is always the case that program action must be guided by the assessment of *individual* needs. Though this is obvious to any seasoned administrator, it is striking how often discussions, for instance of students of color or of older students, treat either group as if all its members share the same interests and needs. Nevertheless, to the degree that older students, for instance, tend, in the aggregate, to have somewhat different needs than do younger students, it follows that programs designed for those students must in some fashion reflect those differing needs.

This does not mean that programs designed for different types of students will differ dramatically in substance. In fact, most programs are very similar in the types of actions they take on behalf of student retention. This is the case because most students, regardless of attributes, encounter many of the same sorts of problems in seeking to persist in college. Rather than differing widely in types of efforts, programs for differing types of students will typically vary in the relative mix of efforts and in the emphasis they give to specific types of actions. For instance, some will give greater weight to social support, while other may emphasize financial aid or academic support.

The point of these comments is relatively simple but critically important, namely that while we need to recognize the need to design programs for different groups of students, we must never forget that college is an individual experience, one that is similar but never exactly the same for different individuals regardless of attributes that may be attached to group labels.

In the discussion which follows, we will speak to five different categories of students, specifically to academically at-risk students, students of color, adult students, honors students, and transfer students. Though our conversation could cover a much larger range, it is not our intent to deal with all possible variants in retention programming. Rather it is to highlight how retention programming may vary for a number of groups of students who are, today, objects of concern of institutional policy. Nor is it our intent to highlight every possible variant that may be applied to particular groups of students. Rather we will attempt to spotlight program components that are typically deemed "critical" to program effectiveness.

Programs for Academically At-Risk Students

The distinguishing components of programs for academically at-risk students are (1) an emphasis on intrusive intervention; (2) assessment, monitoring of academic progress, and early warning; (3) the enhancement of basic skills; (4) the development of study and learning skills; and (5) the development of appropriate learning settings (see Levin and Levin 1991).

PROACTIVE INTERVENTION

One of the clearest aspects of effective programs for academically at-risk students is their proactive orientation toward intervention. Simply stated, they do not leave academic improvement to chance. They expect, indeed often require, that at-risk students participate in a variety of programs. And they do so at the very outset of a student's entry into college. In many cases, this may require attendance during summer bridge programs that precede the beginning of the first year. However constructed, the principle of effective programs for at-risk students is that one does not wait until a problem arises, but intervenes proactively beforehand or at least as soon as possible.

ASSESSMENT, MONITORING, AND EARLY WARNING

It follows that such programs entail forms of assessment, monitoring, and early warning that enable the institution to identify academically at-risk students before the beginning of the first year and/or very early during the first year (Clewell and Ficklen 1986). As noted earlier, such assessment can be effected either by entry level testing carried out at the institutional level and/or by course-specific assessments carried out by individual faculty. However effected, the issue is the same, namely that the institution needs to assess for itself the skills of its entering students and continually monitor, especially at the classroom and program level, the progress of those students.

ENHANCEMENT OF BASIC SKILLS

Given assessment, effective programs proactively respond to the identification of academically at-risk students by requiring a range of basic skills courses, typically in reading, mathematics, and writing, that are designed to "bring entering students up to speed." This is to insure that all students accepted for entry possess sufficient skills to meet the minimum academic demands of the college.

Though these courses are frequently stand-alone courses that take place either before the beginning of the first year, as for example in the summer bridge programs at Syracuse University and the University of California-San Diego, and/or during the first year of college, some institutions have attached skill development units to individual courses. One such variant, noted earlier, is the University of Missouri-Kansas City Supplemental Instruction Program (Blanc, DeBuhr and Martin 1983). In this case, basic skills instruction is attached to the course in which those skills have to be applied and its activities sequenced to match the demands of the course. The principle here is one of placing academic enrichment in the context of the courses in which those skills have to be applied.

DEVELOPMENT OF STUDY AND LEARNING SKILLS

Beyond addressing the need for basic skills enrichment, programs for at-risk students have also emphasized the improvement of student study skills and student acquisition of effective learning strategies. In some cases separate programs are established, in other cases study skills are provided within the context of specific courses (Frierson 1986). In yet other situations, study skills and learning strategies are part of a freshman-year program designed for at-risk students (Ellis 1985).

For the most part, evidence suggests that skills are most effectively learned in a context that gives meaning to those skills as they might be required in a course situation or with regard to a domain-specific learning situation (Levin and Levin 1991, Frierson 1986). It is for that reason that institutions are increasingly turning to what is referred to as "integrated academic enrichment." Very much akin to supplemental instruction, additional units on skills acquisition and learning strategies are attached to specific entry level courses.

It should be noted, in this context, that part of the success of basic skills and study skills courses has to do with the effect on student self-concept of becoming successful in academic work (House 1992). Simply put, the more at-risk students come to develop mastery over previously difficult material, the more positive they become in their view of what is possible in the future. This, in turn, leads to heightened likelihood of future success.

DEVELOPMENT OF APPROPRIATE LEARNING SETTINGS

One other common element in effective programs for academically at-risk students is the development of learning situations specifically designed for the needs of at-risk students. These range from small-group tutorials to freshman seminars, summer bridge programs, and learning communities.

The use of small group tutorials, for instance as developed by Uri Treisman at the University of California-Berkeley, has now been widely emulated elsewhere (Levin and Levin 1991). Indeed it has become part of other academic programs, including summer bridge, skill development, and supplemental instruction. The principle is the same, namely that at-risk students learn best in supportive small groups that serve to provide both skills and social support to those who would otherwise be marginal to the life of the institution. The same can be said of the use of learning communities. Drawing upon the notion of learning communities as supportive settings in which faculty and students work collaboratively on class materials, a number of institutions, such as LaGuardia Community College in New York City, have established programs specifically for at-risk students.

Of course, the success of all such programs ultimately hinges upon the skills of the instructors who teach at-risk students. Thus the growing concern with the nature of staff development programs designed to train faculty and staff to work with these students. The issue here is not just a matter of pedagogical skills. It is also one of understanding the ways in which at-risk students make sense of academic work. Lest we forget, most faculty were themselves successful learners who never or at least rarely ever experienced the academic difficulties at-risk students have encountered. The difficulty most faculty and staff have in working with at-risk students is, in large measure, not being to able understand "where those students are coming from" and therefore not being able to put themselves in the students' place as the latter attempt to acquire what faculty deem to be simple concepts and basic skills.

Programs for Students of Color

As we turn to programs for students of color, it bears repeating that to the degree that institutional commitment to retention efforts generally is a precursor to program success, so too is institutional commitment to the retention of students of color a necessary condition to the success of programs for those students (Clewell and Ficklen 1986, Richardson 1987, Richardson, Simmons, and de los Santos 1987).

But it is not a sufficient condition for success. Among other things, program successes also requires that institutions integrate those programs within the mainstream of the institution's academic, social, and administrative life (Clewell and Ficklen 1986). Too often those programs, indeed programs for different students generally, are marginalized. Either by the assignment of part-time or lower-level staff and/or by administrative and

physical placement in remote locations on campus, programs are often segregated from the institutional mainstream. Segregation of that sort serves to
stigmatize both programs and students and tends to undermine the likelihood
of their success (Research Triangle Institute 1975). To restate a point made
earlier, to the degree that retention is everyone's business, so too is the retention of students of color everyone's responsibility, not just that of the few
administrative and support staff assigned to those programs.

As to the programmatic character of successful programs for students of
color, it is not surprising that those programs typically share many elements
of programs for at-risk students (Eddins 1982, Valverde 1985, Giles-Gee
1988, Wright 1987, and Levin and Levin 1991). This is the case because
students of color are, on the average, more likely to be academically at-risk
and to come from economically disadvantaged backgrounds than are white
students generally. But of course not all students of color are either disadvantaged or academically at risk. For that reason we will restrict ourselves now
only to those program elements that can be said to apply to students of color
regardless of their economic situation or academic skills. Specifically we
focus on elements that are distinct to the needs of students of minority status,
that is, to situations where students of color are a distinct minority on
campus. In these situations, programs for students of color commonly emphasize (1) advising and counseling; (2) social support; and (3) community
membership. At the same time, institutions that have been successful in enhancing the retention rate of students of color have also paid particular attention to issues of diversity and cultural awareness and the development of
inclusive campus climates.

ADVISING AND COUNSELING

One very evident component to successful retention programs for students
of color is the establishment of specialized advising and counseling services
(Mickey 1988, Wilkerson 1988, Giles-Gee 1988, Trippi and Cheatham
1991). Institutions such as Cornell University, Kennesaw College, and
Xavier University have established advising programs and frequently specially designated offices to which students of color go for advising and counseling.

Though having counselors and advisers of like ethnicity is not a requirement of those programs, experience tells us that students of color will be
more likely to utilize those services when the counselors and/or advisers
are of similar ethnicity (Sanchez and King 1986, Atkinson, Jennings and
Liongson 1990). And they are more likely, as are students generally, to utilize those services during their first year than in following years (Trippi and
Cheatham 1991).

BUILDING PERSONAL SOCIAL SUPPORT

To the degree that students of color represent a distinct minority on campus, they also face distinct problems in seeking to become incorporated into the life of what may be seen as a foreign college community (Fleming 1985, Attinasi 1989). In this case the use of special support programs and mentor programs has proven to be quite effective in increasing student retention (Lang and Ford 1988). In many instances those programs are designed to provide students of color with faculty mentors or advisers who take it as a particular responsibility to informally advise them. In other cases, faculty, and sometimes upperclass students, of similar ethnicity are asked to guide newly arrived students of color through the institution or at least through the first year of college.

While role modeling seems to be effective in retention programs generally, it appears to be especially important among those programs concerned with disadvantaged students of color. For them, more so than for the "typical" college student, the availability of like-person role models who have successfully navigated the waters of majority institutions appears to be an especially important component to their own success on campus. But given the availability of faculty of color on most campuses, it is not surprising that there are rarely enough faculty mentors to go around. In any case, to limit faculty mentors only to faculty of like ethnicity is a questionable practice if only because of the implicit message it conveys to students about the interests of other faculty. Again, the retention of students of color, as it is for students generally, is everyone's responsibility.

DEVELOPING SUPPORTIVE STUDENT COMMUNITIES

Programs for students of color also tend to stress the development on campus of a viable community of students of similar ethnicity. The need for such communities and the informal social and emotional support they provide is obvious. As Attinasi (1989) points out, those communities can help new students manage the difficult task of making the transition to the largely unknown world of the college.

Also apparent, however, are the dangers of excessive segmentation of institutional life that those programs may engender. There is no a priori reason why the concept of incorporation into the intellectual and social life of the college necessarily requires that all students of color be provided with separate and highly differentiated social and academic settings. At some point the obvious benefits of that particular attention may be outweighed by the price paid in the excessive fragmentation of campus life. It might be observed that the same logic is rarely applied to discussions of tracking in elementary and secondary schools. Quite the contrary. Mainstreaming and integration are the catchwords of the day.

BUILDING INCLUSIVE CAMPUSES

But of course, many of the difficulties that students of color encounter on a predominantly white campus reflect the behaviors and attitudes of the students, faculty, and staff about them. For that reason an increasing number of institutions have instituted programs designed to educate the broader community on issues of racism and the diversity of cultural traditions that mark American life. As it applies to faculty, some institutions have established programs to broaden the repertoire of teaching skills faculty bring to bear in the education of diverse student bodies. They have done so well aware of the critical importance of the classroom setting and of the many unintended ways in which faculty teaching behaviors may inadvertently hinder the education of students of color. These efforts, like those dealing with diversity generally, have given added weight to the important notion that to be fully effective, college communities, academic and social, must be inclusive of all students who enter.

Programs for Adult Students

When their institution is made up of largely young recent high school graduates and/or is primarily residential in character, older students, like many at-risk students and students of color, may experience a sense of being marginal to the social and intellectual climate of the college. At the same time, many may discover that their academic skills are quite rusty. Added to these problems is the fact that a disproportionate number of adult students have family and work responsibilities which limit the time they can devote to college work. For them, going to college is not a matter of doing college or something else, as it is for many younger students. Rather it is a question of doing college in addition to many other things.

For these reasons, programs for adult students combine many of the elements we have already discussed, namely possibilities for academic assistance, advising, counseling, and mentoring (Cross 1981, Pappas and Loring 1985, and Schlossberg, Lynch, and Chickering 1989). In addition, they also concern themselves with the construction of appropriate learning settings and the provision of classes and services at times most suitable to the schedules of adults.

Returning adult students face a number of other difficulties. Not the least of these has to do with the perception that one might be too old to do college work or that one is "out of place and out of tune" in the youthful environment of the college. When academic difficulties are experienced, it may be more difficult for older students to readily admit that they are having problems. They may be less willing to ask for assistance in making the transition to college. For that reason some institutions make it a point to have specific orientation programs (or portions of orientation programs) designed specifically for the needs of older students. Others establish specific organizational units whose task it is to advice, counsel, and when necessary assist older students. That assistance may range from the updating of possibly "rusty" academic skills to special forms of counseling for these students, many of whom are in the midst of a significant career and/or life-style change.

Again, we should not overlook the fact that many adult students are asked to juggle many roles (e.g., family member, parent, wife or husband, and worker) which may be in conflict not only with one another but also with the goal of college completion. Effective programs are generally very aware of those conflicts and are able to assist adults in managing the problems they produce. It is noteworthy, in this regard, that such programs (e.g., such as the one at the College of Notre Dame of Maryland) view their task not as preventing withdrawal but as reducing the barriers in the way of persistence.

Two of these barriers reflect family and work responsibilities. Since many adults also work and/or are responsible for their own families, many programs seek to encourage persistence by offering flexible and extended schedules and assisting in employer-work education agreements. Most typically, these involve the use of weekend seminars or educational gatherings to bring students together on campus for brief, but intensive, periods of interaction (e.g., at the College of Notre Dame of Maryland and the University of Oklahoma, Norman). They may also entail the institution's going to the students, that is, the offering of courses when and where students can most easily attend (e.g., weekend courses in branch locations). In either case, the principle is clear, namely, that there is no substitute for face-to-face contact among students and between them and members of the faculty and staff. Extended campus programs, degrees by mail, etc., often fail to provide for such contact.

In this respect programs for adult students, like those for working and/or commuting students, tend to share the view that one of the primary difficulties facing those students is the inability to spend time on campus and therefore the difficulty in making contact with faculty and other students on campus. In residential institutions, in particular, those students are often isolated from the life of the institution. Unless efforts are made to provide for their integration, their lack of significant on-campus participation may lead to a sense of personal marginality and isolation as well. Retention programs for those students seek, therefore, to encourage and provide channels for greater involvement in the educational process (Ashar and Skenes 1993).

Beyond the provision of specific services, a number of institutions have sought to provide appropriate educational settings in which adult students are more likely to become actively involved in learning. An institution which has long dealt primarily with adults, the New School for Social Research in New York, has applied many of the principles of freshman-year programs to the needs of adult students. In this case the adult's entire first year is taken up with interdisciplinary seminars which stress inquiry and inquiry-related skills characteristic of the major disciplines within the school. Other institutions, such as LaGuardia Community College and Seattle Central Community College, have established learning communities in which students work collaboratively, together with one or more faculty, on class material. Others, such as the University College at the University of Maryland, have employed principles of cooperative learning to classes for adult students (Millis 1991). However structured, the evidence is clear that collaborative/cooperative learning settings are more likely than traditional lecture settings to engage the energies of adult students.

Programs for Honors Students

Relatively little has been written about retention of honors students. Yet anecdotal evidence suggests that they, as much as "nontraditional" students, have special needs which go unattended in most college settings. Though those needs may be somewhat different, as these students need greater intellectual stimulation than do most other students, the forces underlying their departure are essentially the same. They may experience the same sense of marginality to the main currents of social and intellectual life of an institution and experience the same degree of isolation as might other nontypical students.

Though the departure of honors students from institutions has not gained the same national attention as has the leaving of students of color and disadvantaged students, a number of institutions have established programs specifically for their most able students (Long Island University, Washington State University, the University of Utah, the University of Iowa, Tennessee State University at Nashville, and Syracuse University among others). Similar programs have been instituted in quite large universities (e.g., Western Michigan University and the University of Georgia), in smaller colleges (e.g., Edinboro State College), and in community colleges (e.g., Community College of Philadelphia, Tidewater Community College, Virginia) and have been located in specific fields of study ranging from computer sciences (e.g., the University of Alabama) to the liberal arts (e.g., Swarthmore College).

Whatever their form, effective honors programs tend to share the common attribute of providing unusually able students with the sorts of social and intellectual climates appropriate to their particular learning needs. Typically these involve the use of alternative learning settings that actively engage students in the learning process and give them a say in their own learning. In the Lee Honors College at Western Michigan University and Long Island University-Brooklyn campus collaborative-learning techniques are a core part of an integrated four-year program for honors students. In the former, the program is capped by a senior-year thesis or project which focuses and applies learned skills to concrete settings.

Retention Policies for Transfer Students

One group of students which we have yet to speak of is that made up of persons who transfer to a college or university from another institution of higher education. Though transfer students as a group form a significant segment of the student population generally, and often a large segment of the population of individual institutions, they have received little attention in the discussion of retention policies. Yet there is every reason to believe that specially tailored programs will enhance the likelihood that they will finish their degrees in the institutions to which they transfer.

Though national statistics indicate that transfer students are less likely to complete their degree programs than are students of similar age who remain in their first college, there is no reason to suppose that that is largely the result of their having withdrawn from their initial institution and/or of individual shortcomings in either skills or motivation. It may also result from the many roadblocks that transfer students face when they move from one institution to another. Recall that many students who leave voluntarily are brighter, more motivated, and more concerned with education than are some persisters. Their departure, often to other institutions, sometimes mirrors a desire to find a more challenging education.

It follows then that one possible goal of retention programs for transfer students is the lessening of barriers which have commonly been placed in the path of such students. Articulation of coursework and transfer of credits are rarely smooth. Indeed these processes frequently penalize the transfer students (Prager 1988, Eaton 1990, and Wechsler 1989). Though a number of states and districts are now moving on this issue, few have done as much as the Miami-Dade and Maricopa Community College Districts.

But the barriers facing transfer students result as much from institutional omission as from deliberate policy. One of the most obvious of these reflects the failure of institutions to provide transfer students with their own orientation programs. Transfer students frequently face as difficult a transition to the life of the new college as do first-time college students. For some it may be even more difficult.

It follows that retention programs for transfer students should strive to provide those students with the same sorts of services and programs that first-time students typically receive. This means that orientation programs may have to be offered more than once a year so as to capture those students who enter the institution after the beginning of the regular school year. It may also mean that transfer students should be provided with orientation and contact programs specially tailored to their needs and interests, namely the meeting of students and faculty whom they are likely to encounter in their remaining years. Unfortunately, this is still not a common occurrence.

In the relatively few cases where transfer students are provided with orientation programs, it is more often the case that this orientation is the same one provided to incoming freshmen. Transfer students are often channeled through those programs together with freshmen as if their needs and interests were identical. Here at least there is much that remains to be done to assist student retention.

Retention Policies for Different Students: An Observation

It bears repeating that in discussions of this sort we must be very careful not to lose sight of the fact that what might be said to apply generally to a group of students need not apply equally well to every member of that group. In the same sense that departure is an individual event, so too must policy be based upon the needs of the individual. In all cases, institutions should assess the needs of each and every individual and treat those needs on a person-by-person basis. When categorical assumptions are made about the needs of "nontraditional" students and special programs designed for those so categorized, one runs the great danger of seriously constraining the options of some, if not many, of the persons so labeled. In the final analysis, effective retention policies are highly individual in character. They start and end with the premise that the institution exists to serve the needs of the individual, not the group.

Retention Policies for Different Institutions

We conclude this chapter with a brief discussion of how retention programs and policies may differ among different types of institutional settings. Though much of our prior discussion regarding policy generally has already referred to different types of institutions and to the different types of students that those institutions serve, we will now highlight some of the more important differences that frame how different types of institutions have constructed successful retention programs.

But rather than repeat material we have already covered, we will speak to some of the primary themes and concerns that mark retention policies in different types of institutions. Among the many possible categories of institutional types, we will limit our discussion to four types of institutional settings, namely nonresidential colleges, two-year colleges, urban colleges, and very large public universities.

Let us reiterate once more that questions of institutional policy are necessarily a reflection of the specific situation in which each and every institution finds itself. Though there is much to be gained from understanding how similar types of institutions have successfully addressed the issue of retention, it falls upon the individual institution to assess for itself the wisest course of its own action. For that reason the beginning point of any institutional policy consists of both an assessment of institutional mission and therefore of institutional priorities and an assessment of the nature of student attrition on campus.

Regarding the latter, institutions need to know not only who leaves but also what types of events and forces help shape that leaving. In particular they need to understand how their own actions, formal and informal, come to influence their students (Tinto and Froh 1992). In this manner, the assessment of student retention is both a beginning point for the development of policy, as it helps identify areas of possible action, and, as a system of ongoing evaluation and monitoring of action, an integral part to any retention policy (see appendix on assessment).

Retention in Nonresidential Colleges

Though it is apparent to any observer that student communities, academic or social, are neither as numerous nor as pervasive on commuting campuses as they are on residential campuses, it does not follow that student involvement in those communities is not important to both learning and persistence. But the practical avenue to the attainment of that involvement in nonresidential settings is necessarily somewhat different.

For this reason, as well as others, retention programming in these schools has, relative to residential institutions, paid particular attention to 1) the construction of classroom communities; 2) the strengthening of the student and faculty communities within the college; 3) bridging the gap between the world of the college and external communities; and 4) the timely provision of services to students.

CONSTRUCTING CLASSROOM COMMUNITIES

The one constant of student life on nonresidential campuses is that time on campus is normally quite brief. And when on campus, students spend most of their time in the classroom. The classroom (and perhaps the library) is the one most common educational experience shared by commuting students, especially those who work. It is the one place where the student and the institution most frequently meet.

Nowhere then is the importance of involvement more apparent than in the classrooms of the college and, given what little has been done to reshape the experience of the classroom, nowhere is the potential for involvement greater than in the classroom. It is for that reason that an increasing number of commuting institutions have turned to the classroom as a point of departure for their efforts to involve students in the life of the college, seeking to enhance both student learning and persistence.

One example of this concern over the character of the classroom experience is the growing popularity of collaborative- and cooperative-learning strategies in those colleges (Goodsell, Maher, and Tinto 1992). California State University at Dominquez Hills and the University College at the University of Maryland, among others, have employed cooperative-teaching strategies in a number of classes. As discussed earlier, these strategies serve to actively involve students in cooperative classroom group work that sometimes extends beyond the classroom boundaries. Cooperative classroom activities enhance learning and break down the boundaries among students that typically hinder the development of self-sustaining peer groups. Not uncharacteristically, students in those types of classrooms will tend to spend more time together outside of class working on class projects (Tinto, Goodsell, and Russo 1993).

STRENGTHENING CAMPUS COMMUNITIES

Despite the fact that students do not reside on campus and may in fact be on campus for only brief periods of time, it behooves such institutions to do what they can to encourage the development of on-campus communities whenever and wherever possible. Though nonresidential institutions will rarely have the same sorts of communities found on residential campuses, the importance of student involvement in those communities is the same, namely that they enhance the likelihood of persistence.

Two different approaches have been employed to this end. One requires students to periodically come onto campus to participate in planned activities. Another calls for the institution to attempt to simulate on-campus communities by creative utilization of different forms of communication which reach out to students beyond the campus. Several commuting institutions have established programs which ask students to come together on campus to participate in a number of shared social and intellectual activities. Beyond the obvious educational benefits of such activities, the periodic coming together of students and faculty serves to remind persons of and reinforce the existence of ongoing social and intellectual communities on campus. In this latter regard, one should not overlook the potential benefits of ceremonies and rituals in such gatherings. They serve not only to mark students' progress through the college but also help develop among students a shared community when one might not otherwise exist.

Commuting institutions have also sought to reach out to students off campus by using different forms of communication (e.g., radio, television, mail) to keep individuals informed of ongoing campus activities. When periodic visits to campus are unlikely, shared "news" can serve to link up individuals to the social and intellectual life of the institution. In this manner the use of communications is at least partially intended to simulate the social and intellectual communities which might otherwise exist were it possible for persons to be on campus. Linkages can be created which simulate, if you will, the integrative effect of personal contacts which would occur on campus. It might be pointed out in this context that a number of institutions manage to survive, indeed sometimes flourish, without a true campus. The Empire State College of the State University of New York is perhaps the most notable case of such an institution.

But despite the apparent success of these programs, it is the view here that there is no substitute for periodic personal contact between students and faculty. Nonresidential institutions should encourage faculty to meet, where possible, with each and every student outside the classroom during the time that the student is on campus. Moreover they should encourage both faculty and staff to make it a point to call, within reason, each of their students at least once during the course of a semester. While such periodic contacts cannot fully replace the value of continuing on-campus interactions, they do serve to remind individuals not only that they are part of a college community, but also that the community is concerned with their welfare. As in the case of residential institutions, that show of institutional commitment may be a necessary condition for the development of individual commitment to the institution.

BRIDGING THE GAP BETWEEN COLLEGE AND EXTERNAL COMMUNITIES

Another approach to the question of retention in nonresidential institutions involves the establishment of supportive linkages between the college and the external communities to which students belong. To the degree that student departure sometimes reflects the conflicting demands of those communities, it follows that actions to reduce those conflicts may also serve to enhance retention. For that reason a number of urban nonresidential colleges have developed a variety of outreach programs whose intent it is to develop support in the wider community for the various programs of the college. These include the holding of classes off campus, the wide distribution in the surrounding communities of information about campus activities, and the bringing onto campus of varying community groups. In this fashion it is hoped that the college and external communities come to see one another as being cooperative rather than conflicting members of the same general community.

As part of the desire to reduce, wherever possible, conflicts between college and external communities, institutions have also established flexible forms of educational participation which enable greater numbers and a greater variety of students to successfully complete their college programs. Applied as well to commuting and part-time students in residential institutions, these flexible programs permit students to earn credits at night and during the weekends in order to accommodate potentially conflicting work schedules. In some cases individuals can earn their degrees through the mail. In others, it is the institution rather than the individual that commutes. A number of colleges offer classes off campus in a variety of settings ranging from on-the-job locations to smaller satellite locations. College outreach programs often require that the college go out to the external communities to offer its programs. Though by no means new to higher educational practice, such programs are increasingly being used as part of coordinated efforts to both recruit students and retain them until degree completion.

But in speaking of these varied forms of participation, an important caveat must be offered. To the degree that institutions seek to reach out to communities and retain students by enabling them to avoid on-campus attendance, they also endanger their ability to produce some of the intellectual and social gains that are central to the mission of higher education. Even in technical-vocational programs and in those institutions whose mission is largely defined by those programs, one has to question the price paid by students who are unable and/or not required to spend time on campus as part of their degree programs. There are important forms of education which can only be acquired through face-to-face contact among students and between students, faculty, and staff. No degree of simulation can replace those experiences.

So also is it the case that institutions should avoid the temptation of making their programs so relevant to community needs that they lose the ability and capacity to call into question the manner in which we organize our daily lives. An institution of higher education, regardless of type and level, has an important responsibility not only to serve the interests of its students and communities, but also to provide them with the tools to alter their own existence. By that token one should never expect nor want institutions of higher education to be in perfect accord with the needs and interests of local communities.

TIMELY PROVISION OF SERVICES

Given the very varied patterns of student participation (e.g., part-time, evening, weekend) that typify commuting institutions, a fourth area of retention programming has focused on the timely provision of services to students. Institutions have taken services to the student where and whenever possible. This has led institutions not only to extend hours of service to evenings and weekends, but also to broaden their availability to different places on campus.

Some campuses and staff members have gone so far as to set up office in cafeterias or in commonly used hallways. Other campuses are beginning to employ computer technology (e.g., on-line advising systems, etc.) to provide services on a round-the-clock basis they otherwise could not afford. Other institutions have taken a more intrusive approach, at least for beginning students, by integrating services into required first-year courses (see earlier descriptions of freshman seminars). As with other efforts, they have turned to the classroom as the place in which students are most easily reached. Though the variants are numerous, the principle is the same, namely that the institution has to find a way of making it possible for students to obtain the services they need while on campus.

Retention in Two-Year Colleges

Most, if not all, of the preceding discussion can also be applied to the development of retention programs in two-year colleges. With few exceptions, they too are nonresidential and are frequently located in settings where the influence of external communities may be substantial. They also attract students whose forms of participation are quite varied and frequently part-time in nature. As a result, retention programming at two-year colleges has also emphasized the development of classroom learning communities, the strengthening of campus social communities, the bridging of college and external communities, and the timely provision of services. They have often been even more aggressive than many of their four-year counterparts in seeking out ways of assisting their students and providing a range of alternative ways of engaging students in the life of the institution.[13] Given these commonalities, we will focus here on two aspects of two-year colleges that distinguish them and therefore their retention efforts from those at four-year nonresidential institutions. These have to do with transfer and articulation.

ARTICULATION AND TRANSFER PROGRAMS

The context for retention at two-year colleges differs in a number of important respects from that at four-year nonresidential institutions. Not the least important of these is the fact that two-year institutions typically serve as jumping-off places for transfer to four-year colleges. These schools are likely therefore to experience a higher rate of student departure than are four-year institutions. To label such leavings as dropout is, as argued earlier, a mistake. For two-year institutions to expect to entirely eliminate such leavings is also a mistake, as it would require institutions to effectively deny one of their important educational missions.

Retention in two-year colleges can thus be enhanced by insuring that students can, if they so desire, receive two years of coursework which serves as the practical equivalent to two years of study in most four-year institutions. Consequently, two-year colleges should concentrate on improving the academic quality of their programs to match, if not exceed, those offered in the four-year sector (as did, e.g., John C. Calhoun Community College in Alabama). By so doing, two-year colleges may reduce the incentive for students to transfer to a four-year college prior to the completion of their two-year degree programs. Though some students will be unaffected by such policies, others may decide to use the full two years of a low-cost public education before moving into the more expensive four-year sector.

A different tack that might be considered is for two-year institutions to encourage, rather than discourage, such departures. They should take as a given the desire of some students to transfer whenever possible to four-year institutions and should strive to provide those students with the advice, counseling, and assistance needed to make those transfers possible. By being properly concerned with student interests over institutional interests, institutions may find to their surprise not only that more students stay but that many more are willing to first enroll in that institution rather than in a four-year institution. What is being suggested is that two-year institutions might be better served by treating certain types of departures, namely transfers, as a desirable form of behavior and by limiting their concept of dropout to the departure of those students who come to the institution for terminal degree programs.

In this regard, a number of states, for instance Arizona, California, New York, and Maryland, have been intensifying efforts to insure greater articulation between different levels of the public higher educational system. They have instituted programs (e.g., Two-Plus-Two programs in New York) that encourage the completion of a two-year degree with assurance in certain programs of transfer to four-year institutions. Some districts, most notably the Maricopa and Miami-Dade Community College Districts, have established quite detailed agreements among participating two- and four-year institutions that detail linking courses. And among institutions, a range of partnerships have been established between two- and four-year colleges to facilitate the tracking of students and the coordination of courses (Eaton 1992).

The Urban College: A Category unto Itself
Our discussion of retention at commuting and two-year colleges would be incomplete if we did not speak to the situation faced by many urban colleges, especially those in the major urban centers of the United States. Though our preceding discussion applies to these institutions as well, it does not capture

the unique character of either their mission or their plight. It does not capture, for instance, the fact that many urban colleges devote a major share of their budgets to remediation, to the extent that some colleges report over 60 percent of their students taking remedial courses and nearly one-third having their entire courseload made up of remedial courses. Nor does it adequately reflect the fact that the majority of their students are disadvantaged, often minority, and frequently attending college on a part-time basis while trying to provide for themselves and their families.

The magnitude of the problems these institutions face sets them apart from most other institutions of higher education. Though the policies cited above may help, they do not directly address some of the most pressing needs, namely to help students come to class and acquire the basic academic skills they need to begin work toward a degree program. Here the task of retention, as we have described it above, dwarfs the capacity of the institution. Like the inner-city high schools before them, these institutions are faced with the monumental task of trying to undo the accumulated damage of many years of inferior schooling and the multiple constraints of poverty.

This does not mean, however, that successful retention programs are not achievable. Though there are understandable limits to what can be accomplished in such situations, institutions like LaGuardia Community College, Hunter College of the City University of New York, and Seattle Central Community College are demonstrating that a commitment to students matched with a willingness to go beyond the bounds of "normal" academic practice can yield positive results. Equally important, their students are also demonstrating that, given a reasonable opportunity, individuals will be tenacious in their pursuit of further education and will continue with their studies over a period of ten years or more.

Regrettably, we are often insensitive to such behaviors and to the institutions which make them possible. By using degree completion as the yardstick by which we measure institution and program success, we inadvertently undervalue the contribution such institutions make to the education of a very important segment of our college student population. Moreover, we hold up to students a standard of comparison which is not necessarily that by which they judge their own behaviors. For many, obtaining full-time work, rather than completing a degree program, may be the primary purpose of having begun college.

The Large Public University

The primary distinguishing difficulty facing the very large public university is its size. Though students gain much from its diversity and extensive resource base, their involvement in the life of the institution, especially its academic life, suffers from the size of the institution and the physical remoteness of its faculty and staff. This is particularly evident among first-year students, who find themselves taking many of their classes together with several hundred other students. These large, remote, frequently uninvolving, lecture classes do little to elicit student interest.

Not surprisingly, a distinguishing theme of retention efforts at the very large public universities, relative to other institutions, is 1) the breaking down of the campus into smaller, more knowable parts; and 2) the development of alternatives to the large lecture hall.

BREAKING DOWN THE CAMPUS INTO SMALLER PARTS

One of the distinguishing marks of successful retention efforts at very large public universities is the focus on breaking down the campus into smaller, more knowable communities. This arises in a great variety of ways in both the academic and social systems of the institution. Not surprisingly, efforts at cutting the university down to size is most common in the first year and first semester of college when attachments are most tenuous.

In the academic realm, some institutions have sought to use programs such as the "freshman interest groups" at the University of Oregon and the University of Washington to provide beginning students with at least one small class unit, typically of no more than twenty students, that focuses on academic themes of mutual interest. At other institutions, such as Syracuse University,'freshman forums" have been established in which beginning students meet with a faculty member during the first ten weeks of a semester not so much to cover a predetermined curriculum as to enable students to get to know each other and a faculty member—and sometimes his/her family— in a way not otherwise possible. The topics of those forums, which range from the experience of being a new student in college, through the writings of modern social thinkers, to the character of social and cultural activities in the surrounding community, are not so important as is the small, informal setting. In some instances, the faculty members take on the role of first-year mentors, thereby furthering the sense of attachment the students may feel. In any case, faculty who participate in such programs typically become informal advisers and mentors to those students regardless of the existence of any formal program to do so.

In the social realm of campus life, orientation programs, residential life activities, and extracurricular activities among many others are used to break down the sometimes overwhelming sense of isolation that newcomers to large campuses commonly experience. For students of color on predominantly white campuses, the activities of ethnic/racial clubs and/or associations have also proven effective (Attinasi 1989). Not surprisingly, some of the academic initiatives noted above also impact upon social relationships.

Though fraternities and sororities are still an important part of the social fabric of university life and, in very large settings, a way in which students make attachments to their peers, their role has been somewhat curtailed in the past few years. Limits have been set which prevent those organizations from seeking pledges too early during the first year of college. In some cases, pledging can only occur during and after the second year. The point of doing so is not to prevent social attachments from being made, but to shield new students from the sometimes excessive social pressures they feel to pledge during the first year and thereby free them to discover the fuller range of social options that may exist on campus.

ALTERNATIVES TO THE LARGE LECTURE HALL

Large lecture classes, sometimes as large as eight hundred students, are standard fare for many first-year students on large university campuses. Though they need not be, they are frequently uninvolving, uninspiring, and uninteresting. Many students' view of these classes is aptly captured by the words of one student that "the large lecture classes are classes for cutting." Indeed, businesses have sprung up on or around many campuses that, for a price, allow students to avoid such classes. Typically they sell class notes to students who prefer to use their time more productively in other endeavors. On some campuses, note-taking services are operated by the student government, which, in turn, is subsidized by the institution. Thus the ironic situation that some institutions subsidize, perhaps unintentionally encourage, students to cut their classes.

This does not mean that institutions are unaware of the problem of large lecture halls or have not sought to address it. Some institutions have attacked it by requiring students in those classes to attend small study groups that are attached to the lecture class. Often run by advanced students or graduate students, such groups are used to engage a small number of students in discussions about class material and class assignments. Though these groups do not alter the experience of the large lecture class, they do provide an alternative or supplemental route to acquiring course material. A few other universities, typically private ones, have accepted the costs of smaller classes and have eliminated many of their very large lecture classes. There is a growing recognition that such classes are inherently flawed.

Though it is the case that very large lecture classes are far from ideal and are, in a number of ways, educationally flawed environments (Erickson and Strommer 1991), it does not follow that the typical student experience in those classes is solely the result of class size. It also mirrors the way such classes are taught. Excluding the infrequent case of the charismatic, spellbinding lecturer who is able to make large lectures "work," most large lecture classes remain just that, classes in which students are largely passive recipients of faculty lectures (Bonwell and Eison 1991, pp. 14–15).

This need not be the case. And among first-year students it should not be the case. There are many other techniques that can be used to involve students in the learning process (Gleason 1986, McKeachie 1986, Weimer 1989, 1990, Erickson and Strommer 1991). One that is drawing increased attention is the utilization of cooperative-learning strategies, in particular "base groups," to actively involve students in class discussions (Johnson and Johnson 1987). Institutions such as Harvard University and the University of Minnesota have used these techniques with considerable success in classes as large as six hundred.

Concluding Observations

There are no quick or easy solutions to the issue of student retention. Nor is there any ready substitute for the institutional commitment to students that is the foundation of successful retention programs. Such commitment springs not from brochures or formal presentations, but from the enduring commitment on the part of faculty and staff to the education of their students. It arises from and is demonstrated in the everyday interaction among students, faculty, and staff in the formal and informal domains of institutional life. In a very important sense, institutional commitment to students and students' commitment to the institution are mirror images of one another.

Although programs can be most helpful, they cannot replace the absence of a high quality, caring, and concerned faculty and staff. Institutions should therefore not be misled by the use of modern technology and marketing strategies. Nor should they be overly captivated by the sophisticated programs of high-cost retention consultant firms. The road to institutional commitment and thus to student commitment does not require very elaborate or high-cost interventions. Nor does it call for computers or special programs with long titles and extensive resources. These are merely the tools of retention. Rather, effective retention calls for sustained effort on the part of all institutional members to give to each and every student serious and honest attention on a daily basis. It requires, if you will, a continuing commitment to the education of students. No technology, however sophisticated, can replace that sort of commitment.

It follows then that successful retention programs must focus on the institution as well as on the student, and on the actions of the faculty and staff who are the representatives of the institution. Questions of the value of staff development aside, it is most often the case that successful retention efforts result, perhaps unintentionally, in widespread institutional renewal and revitalization. They frequently serve as the beginning point for an institution-wide process of renewal which reaches to the very core of individual membership in the social and intellectual communities of the college. By contrast unsuccessful retention efforts are frequently marked by the unwillingness of the institution to consider such renewal as either necessary or desirable. They barely scratch the veneer of institutional functioning. Often the students are seen as being the primary root of the problem. But if there is one lesson to be learned from our discussions here it is that this is simply not the case. In the interactive, reciprocal world of institutional life, student retention is at least as much a function of institutional behavior as it is of student behavior.

One may then ask what gain in retention rates should institutional officials expect from their programs. How much gain in retention is an acceptable and realistic goal by which to measure the success or failure of a program? Without trying to beg the question it must be stated that there is no readily defined "acceptable" gain. Each institution must judge for itself what is acceptable and what is not. Nevertheless, given the experience of many institutions we can say that, on the average, institutions which have been deemed by others and/or by themselves to have successfully attacked the issue of institutional retention have felt quite comfortable with a gain of 10 to 20 percent in the proportion of entering students who persist to degree completion.

Smaller gains are generally considered unsatisfactory. Gains of considerably larger amounts are infrequent and often extraordinary in nature. Where they occur, they are often seen to reflect temporary rather than enduring situations on campus: circumstances which happen to change during the course of the retention effort. To bring us back to Durkheim's analysis of suicide, in particular to anomic and altruistic suicide, it may be the case that large gains (or losses) in retention most often reflect short-term alterations in the norms and/or circumstances of college-going rather than changes in institutional action. Student riots, a series of crimes on campus, the existence of specific student subcultures which call for students to "drop out of college and drop into life," marked changes in the availability of jobs for college students, and/or alterations in external constraints to departure (e.g., cessation of the draft) may all yield short-term changes in student withdrawal from college irrespective of institutional action.

The point of these comments is to suggest that if major changes in institutional retention are possible, they very likely require major alterations in the very structure and functioning of the institution. But such changes, indeed revolutions, in institutional social and intellectual life are not frequent. Nor are they necessarily desirable. They do not always, by themselves, lead to an improved education of students so retained. To repeat a point made earlier, it is the education of students, their social and intellectual growth, that is the proper goal of retention efforts.

Finally, though it is essential that we recognize the centrality of education to the process of student retention, we must be careful not to trivialize the manner in which that educational goal is defined. Recent movements toward value-added higher education are a welcome trend. There is much to be gained from concerning ourselves with learning consequences of higher educational participation and the impact institutions make upon the learning of students. But here an important caveat should be offered. There are a number of possible movements which can serve to undermine rather than aid the intent of value-added education.

The concern for measurement of learning outcomes is quite understandable. The drive for accountability aside, there is an obvious need for institutions to obtain reliable measures of the learning growth of its students. The danger is not that they should acquire such measures, but that such measures may become the only way in which institutions think about student learning. In the practical world of tests and measurements, we frequently accept partial solutions to the complex question of how to measure learning. Rather than measure the entire range of learning outcomes of education, we often tap but a narrow part of the learning spectrum. Measures of learning tend to reflect the concrete rather than the abstract, the convergent rather than the divergent, and to emphasize content rather than process.

That this is the case is not in itself a problem. It is extremely difficult to measure learning in all its varied manifestations. Indeed it may be neither possible nor desirable to do so. Rather, the problem arises when we take such limited measures and accept them as being suitable indicators of the value of learning added by the institution. Not only do such measures distort the character of the learning process, they may lead institutions to structure their academic programs to those measures. In the process they may unintentionally allow minimum standards to become maximum standards of educational performance. Value-added movements may, in this fashion, undermine rather than reinforce the educational goals of higher education. Rather than encourage institutions and individuals to explore learning in its widest dimensions, it may lead them to focus on increasingly narrow measures of that important goal. While we should not deny the importance of the value-added movement in higher education, we should make sure that it adds to, does not detract from, the value of the education students receive.

—6—
Conclusions

We began our inquiry with a question, namely, What can be done to enhance student retention in higher education? That question led us to consider the character and causes of student departure from institutions of higher education. In doing so we have come to a new appreciation of the dynamic life of those institutions and the manner in which their multiple social and intellectual communities affect student retention. We end our inquiry with a series of comments which, taken together with the preceding chapters, provide an answer to that question.

Educational Communities and the Character of
Institutional Commitment

Institutions of higher education are not unlike other human communities, and the process of educational departure is not substantially different from the other processes of leaving which occur among human communities generally. In both instances, departure mirrors the absence of social and intellectual integration into or membership in community life and of the social support such integration provides. An institution's capacity to retain students is directly related to its ability to reach out and make contact with students and integrate them into the social and intellectual fabric of institutional life. It hinges on the establishment of a healthy, caring educational environment which enables all individuals, not just some, to find a niche in one or more of the many social and intellectual communities of the institution.

This view of the effect of institutions upon student leaving highlights the intricate web of reciprocal relationships which binds students to the communal life of the institution. Rather than single out any one action or set of actions as being the primary cause of student departure, it argues that student leaving is affected by most institutional actions regardless of their immediate referent. In the interactive system of a college, almost any institutional action, whether in admissions, counseling, advising, academic programs and classrooms, or student life, will eventually affect student persistence and will do so in often unintended and quite unexpected ways.

Departure also mirrors the students an institution recruits. In particular, it reflects the character of student commitments and the quality of effort students are willing to make on behalf of the goal of college completion. To single out the institution as being solely responsible for student departure, as do many critics, is to deny an essential principle of effective education, namely that students must themselves become responsible for their own learning.

Nonetheless, institutions of higher education do have a special responsibility in the domain of student retention. In accepting individuals for admission, institutions necessarily accept a major responsibility to insure, as best they can, that all students without exception have sufficient opportunities and resources to complete their courses of study should they so wish. Like human communities generally, institutions of higher education have an obligation to concern themselves with the welfare not only of the whole but also of each of the constituent parts—that is, of the individuals who are members of the community.

In the final analysis, it is this sense of obligation to students and the commitment it inspires which best capture the source of effective retention programs and help distinguish between those institutions which keep students and those from which students leave. It is in this very important sense that institutions of higher education are like other human communities. The essential character of such communities lies not in the formal structures and programs which they construct, but in the underlying values which inspire their construction. The ability of institutions to retain students lies less in the formal programs they devise than it does in the underlying orientation toward students which directs their activities.

Communities, educational or otherwise, which care for and reach out to their members and which are committed to their members' welfare are also those which keep and nourish their members. There is no programmatic substitute for this sort of commitment, no easy way to measure its occurrence. It is not easily ascertained in any one action or set of actions, but is reflected in the policy choices made by institutional officials. The presence of a strong commitment to students results in an identifiable ethos of caring which permeates the character of institutional life and sets it apart from institutions which place student welfare second to other goals.

But unlike most communities, institutions of higher education are first and foremost educational communities whose activities center about their intellectual life. Their commitment to students springs from a broader commitment to the educational goals of higher education, namely that students are educated, not merely retained until degree completion. A commitment to that goal is the core about which successful retention programs are built. The development of that commitment and of the orientation toward education it entails is both the beginning and end point of effective retention programs.

The obligation of institutions to educate the students they admit springs from a more fundamental social obligation of higher education—to serve the welfare and preservation of society by educating its members. In many respects this obligation is similar to that which Durkheim described in his essays on moral education. It is a requirement to educate individuals which takes on the character of a moral imperative, and, in this sense, our theory of student departure upholds the inherently moral character of the higher educational enterprise.

Our theory of educational departure is also a theory of educational communities. It stresses the centrality of the intellectual life of the institution and its educational activities to the continued learning and persistence of students. The actions of institutional members with regard to that life, faculty and staff alike, are central to an understanding of the institution's impact upon student learning and leaving. Though there will always be some students who are unaffected by the intellectual life of the institution, for most students the educational activities of faculty and staff within and without the formal confines of classrooms and offices are essential to their intellectual and social development and thus critical to their continuation on campus. Here, as elsewhere, action speaks louder than words. An institution's commitment to the education of its students must be translated on a daily basis by the actions of each and every representative of the institution, but especially by the faculty. And nowhere are those actions more clearly felt than in the classrooms of the institution where educational activities primarily occur.

Educational Mission and Institutional Commitment

But that commitment need not be narrowly defined or taken to be the sole province of a particular segment of the higher educational enterprise. The commitment to educate students is as important to two-year open enrollment colleges as it is to the elite liberal arts colleges. At the same time, though all institutions share in a commitment to educate students, it does not follow that the character of that commitment need be the same in all. Of necessity, it must reflect the unique educational mission of each institution and the needs of the students it serves.

That mission and the commitment it inspires brings with it a series of difficult choices. In moving toward a policy on student retention, institutions must first decide the character of their educational mission. More often than not, that will require of the institution a realization that it cannot hope or even wish to serve all possible students who might apply for admission or feel obligated to serve unsuitable students. A research university, for instance, should not have the same sort of commitment to its students as a liberal arts college. Institutions must be selective in their goals and discriminating in the manner in which they seek to attain those goals.

Institutions must be careful, however, to avoid being discriminatory in the way those standards are constructed or applied to the everyday tasks of educating students. Excessively narrow definitions of educational standards or unnecessarily rigid application of standards to the evaluation of educational performance may inadvertently restrict, rather than enhance, the educational growth of differing students. They may do so not only by limiting access of students to education but also by reducing the likelihood that some students can successfully complete their educational programs once entry is obtained. In the increasingly diverse world in which higher education operates, that commitment must be inclusive of all students. The educational communities we construct must be inclusive, rather than exclusive. They must allow, indeed encourage, the active involvement of all students as equal members.

There is a fine line to be traveled by institutions as they seek to navigate between these two potentially discriminating domains. Though the character of higher education requires them to be selective in their mission and discriminating in their educational judgments, they must avoid being discriminatory in their views and in the manner in which they apply their judgments to the daily task of educating students.

The Paradox of Institutional Commitment and the Limits of Institutional Action

This latter observation leads us to more carefully consider what might be termed the "paradox of institutional commitment": that institutions that are willing to encourage students to leave are also those that are more likely to have students who will stay. To unravel this paradox will require that we backtrack a bit and review some of our earlier discussions.

The problem facing institutions in addressing the issue of student retention is one of developing a view and policy which not only take into account the complex roots of student departure on campus but also provide a meaningful basis for subsequent student retention. Persistence arises from the social and intellectual rewards accruing to competent membership in the communities of the college and from the impact that membership has upon individual goals and commitments, especially commitment to the institution. Institutional commitment is simply another way of describing the sum effect of personal commitments which link the individual to representatives of the institution—students, faculty, and staff. Individuals who perceive themselves as having established competent membership, both socially and intellectually, and having grown in the process, are more likely to express a strong commitment to the institution which houses those individuals and communities.

The commitment of individuals to the institution appears to be directly linked to the quality of one's education broadly conceived. This is especially apparent when contacts are wide-ranging and occur with faculty and staff on a continuing basis both inside and outside of the formal domains of institutional life. In a very real sense the faculty and staff serve as both representatives and mediators of the social and intellectual life of the institution. Their actions are important indicators to students of both the quality of that life and the degree to which the institution is concerned with the life of students.

The mirror image of individual commitment to the institution is the commitment of the institution, as exhibited in the behaviors of its faculty and staff, to the individual. The corollary of individual integration into the social and intellectual communities of the college is the existence of communities on campus which seek to reach out and integrate, that is include, all individuals into their daily life. The key to that integration is that it goes beyond the simple question of continued presence on campus to that of the social and intellectual development of the individuals who stay. The problem institutions face in attempting to foster such educative communities is not simply one of effort. Rather, in being committed to student welfare and in seeking to serve the goal of their social and intellectual development, institutions may find themselves in the seemingly paradoxical situation of having to do so by encouraging some persons to leave when their needs and interests cannot be adequately served by the institution.

The paradox of institutional commitment is quite easily resolved if it is understood that the object of retention is not merely that persons stay but that they be further educated. As we have argued before, the proper beginning point of institutional retention efforts is not the design of such programs but the posing and answering of the question, What is the educational problem for which the institution is the proposed solution? It is only in answering that question that institutions can determine in which cases the retention of students is in the interests of both the individual and the institution. Those institutions which are committed to the education of their students and are willing to tell students when it is in their interests to leave are also those institutions that are more likely to have students who are committed to the institution. As a consequence, they will also retain more of their students to degree completion. Furthermore, those institutions that are committed to their students will very likely also be those that fare better in the more limited academic marketplace of the future. For it is to those institutions, two- or four-year, that bright, interested, and committed students will seek entry.

In the real world of limited resources, there is only so much that institutions can or perhaps should do to retain their students. This realization of institutional limits goes beyond recognizing the fact that not all students who enter the institution have the ability, skills, intention, and/or commitment to complete their degree programs. It is reflective, if you will, of the very character of the higher educational enterprise rightly understood and of the complexity of behaviors which give rise to student departure.

The limits of institutional action are also a reflection of the dialectical nature of human actions, namely that actions in one domain of human endeavor eventually give rise to opposite or countervailing actions in other domains of endeavor. In the case of college retention programs, it may well be that the efforts of institutions to retain a particular type of student or deal with a given type of student departure also serve to increase the likelihood of other types of student departure. For example, it is often the case that efforts to produce a more cohesive and tight-knit community of persons may induce persons who prefer greater independence to leave. Conversely, efforts to enhance individual independence and diversity often give rise to the call for greater efforts at community building. Once more the question of institutional choice arises. Once more it is apparent that the beginning point of effective retention efforts lies in decisions regarding educational mission.

Educational Excellence, Retention, and Student Involvement in Learning

Current concerns about excellence in higher education stress the importance of educational excellence and the need to actively involve students in their own learning (Bennett 1984, Astin 1985). As the quality and quantity of student involvement is seen to be directly related to student learning, it is argued that the "effectiveness of any educational policy or practice is directly related to the capacity of that policy or practice to increase student involvement in learning" (Study Group on the Conditions of Excellence in American Higher Education 1984, 19).

But getting students involved in learning is no simple matter. It is not easily achieved by formal programs or revised curricula. We have argued here that, rather than being the outcome of a specific policy, student involvement, or what we have referred to as student integration, is the natural consequence of the institution's involvement in the education of its students. If we wish to have our students become actively involved in their own learning, we must first be involved in their learning as well as in our own. And we must provide them with meaningful ways of becoming involved in learning, both inside and outside the classroom. If we want students to become committed to the goals of education, we must first demonstrate a commitment to those goals and to the students we serve. We cannot expect students to do what we are unable or unwilling to do.

It is for that reason that classrooms are central to the process of retention and the activities that occur therein critical to the process through which students come to participate in the intellectual life of the institution. Classrooms represent smaller communities of learning in which both faculty and students participate. Involvement in those communities can serve as a vehicle for further involvement in the life of the institution.

The issue before us then is relatively clear. If we fail to involve students as active participants in the learning process in the classroom, how shall we engage them beyond the classroom? For many, if not the majority, of students in higher education, the classroom is the primary, if not the only, place where they and the faculty meet over matters of academic and intellectual substance. If we overlook the life of the classroom and the skills faculty bring to bear to engage students in that classroom, where shall we turn to for enhanced retention?

Understood in this manner, our analysis of student retention can be seen as also applying to the question of student learning. It maintains that the success not only of retention programs but of education programs generally hinges on the construction of educational communities at the college, program, and classroom level which actively involve all students in the ongoing social and intellectual life of the institution. Educational communities which are committed to their students and which reach out and involve them in the community's educational life also generate student involvement in learning and eventually student commitment to the goals of education. Educational communities which are themselves striving toward educational excellence will in turn engender a similar striving among students.

It should be observed that the question we pose here is not whether colleges are communities or whether there are multiple communities, academic and social, in which students may participate. Rather the question is: What type of communities should these be? Our view should by now be evident, namely that if institutions wish to make substantial progress in educating and retaining more, especially those who have been under-represented in the higher educational system, their communities must involve all students. They must actively engage students in the life of the classroom and allow them to gain a valued voice in the educative process. To a very real degree, our failure to make significant improvements in learning and retention over the past several decades reflects the regrettable fact that student experience has not led students to become actively involved in learning. Instead they have been alienated from education, seeing the task of college completion as a barrier to be overcome, a ritual to endure, rather than an experience to be valued.

Leaving College and Other Forms of Departure

Educational departure is but one particular manifestation of a range of leaving behaviors that mark social existence. Our lives are constructed of numerous comings and goings, of varying passages from one form of social participation to another. To single out and add undue importance to one form of leaving is perhaps unwise. In speaking only of departure from college we may inadvertently undervalue the importance of the education which goes on outside the formal boundaries of our higher educational systems. The thing we call higher education is but a small part of a much wider enterprise which concerns itself with the social and intellectual growth of people. Leaving college should by no means be taken to mean that individuals terminate their involvement in higher forms of education. Sometimes the opposite is the case. More than a few persons leave the formal world of higher education in order to pursue education in ways not encumbered by the rules and regulations of college life. Let us hope that this will always be the case not only for those who leave without degrees but for those who receive a formal certificate marking the completion of a given course of study.

Education is both actualization and potential. Every leaving contains the potential for eventual return. As departures mount, so do the opportunities for continued education. There is an ever-increasing number of adults in society who have acquired some college education. As pressures in society mount for increased education, it is likely that the press among adults to return to college will also increase. But whether individuals return to college at a later time depends on a variety of factors, not the least of which is the character of the leaving which occurred in the first place. Institutions of higher education would best serve their own interests by reconsidering their view of and therefore their treatment of student leavers. Education is a lifelong process, and the movement of individuals in and out of institutions of higher education is but one stage in that process. Education need not, indeed should not, cease when college participation ceases. Nor should the potential for

additional college education end when initial college participation is termi-
nated. Rather than cut off ties with those who fail to earn a degree, institutions should reinforce those ties. Rather than penalize, in effect, both the
institution and the individual for the person's not having completed his/her
degree, the institution should leave open its doors to leavers by viewing their
stay as but one part of a longer process of social and intellectual development
which we hope knows no bounds.

A Concluding Observation

The answer to the question of student retention which we offer is not simple.
It identifies no single path to enhanced student retention, nor promises that
all admitted students can be retained. It argues that there is no hidden magic,
no unique formula or sophisticated machinery needed to retain students. Institutions need not look far afield to find the key to enhanced student retention. It is achievable within the confines of existing institutional resources. It
springs from the ongoing commitment of an institution, of its faculty and
staff, to the education of its students.

But such commitment requires institutional change. It requires that institutions rethink traditional ways of structuring collegiate learning environments and find new ways of actively involving students, as well as faculty, in
their intellectual life. It requires a deeper understanding of the importance of
educational community to the goals of higher education. The explication of
this view of departure has been one of the primary goals of this book.

Regarding the character of effective institutional policy, we must remember that people make a difference. Ultimately the success of our actions on
behalf of student learning and retention depends upon the daily actions of all
members of the institution, not on the sporadic efforts of a few officially designated members of a retention committee. Properly understood, institutional commitment is the commitment on the part of each and every member
of the institution for the welfare, the social and intellectual growth, of all
members of the institution. It is a commitment to the notion of education
broadly understood which is not limited by either time or place.

Our discussions have now come full circle. We end where we started, with
the educational goal of higher education. We hope that we do so with a
deeper appreciation not only of the educational character of student leaving
but also of how a commitment to that educational goal directs our actions on
behalf of the students we serve. The goal of enhanced student retention is
merely the vehicle to that more important goal.

— *Appendix A* —

The Assessment of Student Departure from Institutions of Higher Education

This appendix concerns itself with the character of effective retention assessment systems and the role they play in the development of student retention programs. It will focus on their content and structure and the modes of analysis they should employ in the assessment of student retention and departure. It will also describe some of the many ways in which those analyses can be utilized in the formation of effective retention programs. It will not, however, seek to describe in detail how institutions might devise and operate such retention assessment systems. That task requires a more complete discussion than is possible here.

In the pages that follow, we will first focus on the content of assessment, that is the sorts of data that should be collected in an effective assessment system. We will then speak to the methods that can be used to collect those data. In pointing out the strengths and weaknesses of those methods, we will argue that effective assessment systems must include multiple methods of data collection. We will next turn our attention to the structure of assessment systems. Among other things we will address issues of the timing of data collection and the need for longitudinal portraits of student experience. In this context, we will speak to the analysis of assessment data and indicate how different forms of analysis can be used to answer different types of research and policy questions regarding student retention. Finally, we will focus on the implementation of assessment systems and the ways in which assessment can further the needs of institutional change.

As we turn to our discussion of assessment, it bears repeating that our focus is institutional in character. We will speak to the concerns of institutional officials and the need for assessment to identify for institutional leaders how the institution writ large shapes the persistence of its students. Though we will point out the importance of program and classroom-level assessment in an overall assessment system, we will not concern ourselves with the specifics of those particular types of assessment.[1]

In effect, the question we pose in this appendix is one that asks how institutions can assess student departure in ways which support efforts to improve the quality of institutional life. As we have stressed the importance of institutional goal setting as a necessary precondition to institutional change efforts, our perspective on assessment is not unlike that currently referred to as "outcome-based" school management. It is a perspective driven by the recognition that assessment must serve to help the institution attain desired outcomes.

The Content of Retention Assessment Systems

The first and most obvious requirement for an effective retention assessment system is that it be student-centered, that is that it tap the nature of student experience and the impact the institution has upon that experience. This requirement calls for institutions to collect a range of student-related data. First it requires that institutions collect information on the attributes, intentions, and activities of each student who enters the institution (or a reasonably representative random sample thereof) such that a valid picture be obtained both of the students who enter (e.g., ability, study skills, social background, educational and occupational goals and commitments, needs, concerns, and pre-entry expectations about the quality of institutional life) and of the range and variety of their social and academic experiences within the institution following entry (e.g., the nature of student interactions with student peers and faculty both inside and outside the classroom). Where appropriate—for instance in commuting institutions—that picture should also describe the character of student experiences and/or obligations in communities external to the institution. This is the case because of the need, noted in previous chapters, to better understand to what degree forces external to the campus impinge on student life within the confines of the campus.

That picture should detail both the social and academic experiences of students as it is understood by students. Regarding the former, assessment should provide a portrait of the interaction patterns which arise on campus among students, faculty, and staff beyond the formal boundaries of the institution. In residential settings, it should tap the nature of social interaction among peers in the various settings in which they meet (e.g., residential settings, clubs, etc.). In nonresidential settings, it should also gauge the student's external commitments (e.g., family and work) that provide a backdrop against which college-going takes place. Regarding academic experience, assessment should carefully review student academic experiences, especially in the classrooms and laboratories of the institution. For many students (e.g., commuting students and/or students in nonresidential settings) the classroom is the primary, if not only, place where students and faculty come into contact.

In all instances, it is important that data should be collected on both the formal attributes of participation (e.g., degree of contact) and the quality of that participation as it is understood by students (e.g., student satisfaction with contact, perceptions of climate, etc.). In this manner, student-centered assessment of student retention will contain necessary subjective as well as objective information about student experiences.

Effective assessment should also gauge the diverse outcomes of the college experience. In addition to measures of persistence (e.g., re-enrollment, goal and degree-credit hour progress, and degree completion), information should also be collected on the quality of student effort, on student learning (e.g., course and area content), on student intellectual and social development during the college years (e.g., critical thinking, values), and, if appropriate, on student transfer to other institutions. Institutions need to ascertain not only whether students stay and make progress toward their degrees, but also whether they have grown, that is been educated, while in college (Erwin 1991). Recall that the two are intimately linked. Learning leads to persistence, its absence is a root of leaving.

Here several caveats are called for. First, it is the view here that current federal requirements on the reporting of institutional retention data do not capture, indeed may mask, the diverse character of educational missions that mark higher education. In many institutions, degree completion is not a primary goal of entering students. As noted in chapter 5, measures of retention must reflect the diverse goals that mark student decisions to enter higher education. For that reason, a more complete measure of persistence would in some fashion capture both student enrollment and degree progress as well as progress toward the attainment of personal educational goals (e.g., do students achieve the goals which brought them to the institution in the first place?). Though this latter measurement is far from perfect—individual goals change—it is still a better reflection of institutional mission than are simple ratios of persistence alone.[2] It might also be observed that the assessment of student goals, as opposed to simple credit progress, pushes the institution to inquire more fully about student hopes and aspirations and, in the process, engages the institution with its students in ways in which the "objective" tracking of degree credit progress does not.

Second, though the assessment of student learning is far from a simple matter, it is nevertheless a matter worth pursuing. Tests of content, area-specific skills (e.g., reading, writing, etc.), and general intellectual skills (e.g., critical thinking) are time-consuming and expensive to administer and collect. Measures of student social and moral development (e.g., values and citizenship) are no less complex. Nonetheless it is essential that institutions inquire about the education of their students. And rather than debate endlessly the complex issues of the correctness of different measures, it is better for institutions to obtain some measure of that education than to have no measure whatsoever.

In this regard, it is especially important for institutions to gain some sense of how student learning occurs within the classrooms of the institution. For that reason, institutional assessment systems must include classroom- as well as program-level assessment of student learning (Cross and Angelo 1988). Though the issue of how one assesses student classroom learning is also far from simple, it is the view here that it matters less how faculty assess student learning than it does that each and every faculty member engages in some form of assessment of learning in his or her classroom.[3] The very act of inquiring into student classroom learning changes the nature of the classroom experience and the character of the relationship of faculty to student, teacher to learner. Opening up the conversation about what is learned in class to students is itself an important educative experience for both students and faculty.

Finally, assessment should capture both the nature of student involvement in learning and the quality of effort students exhibit on behalf of their own learning. This is the case because those behaviors are not only shaped by institutional actions but also because those actions in turn come to shape student learning and persistence. As pointed out in chapter 5, enhancing involvement in learning and quality of student effort is itself a vehicle for the enhancement of student retention.

Methods of Data Collection

To be effective, retention assessment systems must employ multiple methods of collecting data. In addition to the need to accurately record, document, and describe student experiences and student progress, assessment must also capture both the complexity and richness of student experience and student understanding of that experience. For that reason, assessment systems are increasingly turning to both quantitative and qualitative methods to study the nature of student experience.

As to quantitative methods, assessment systems frequently employ sampling and survey methods to obtain representative portraits of how any group of students, for instance an entering class, experience college (e.g., Baird

1990). In addition to simple random sampling, institutions have commonly employed disproportionate stratified random sampling techniques together with survey methods to more accurately track the differing experiences of groups of students (e.g., studies of persistence among white students and students of color).

But only infrequently have they done so fully aware of the dangers that low response rates and nonrandom response patterns pose to the interpretation of survey data. Take for instance the case of institutional surveys of leavers as a tool to understanding the roots of attrition. Typically such surveys yield both low response rates (e.g., in the 20 to 30 percent range) and highly biased response patterns. Since the most dissatisfied leavers are least likely to respond to such surveys, the picture one obtains of "reasons for leaving" is highly skewed toward the less negative. It is for this reason and many others that survey methods are best used in situations where incentives exist or can be applied to heighten response rates (e.g., use of a lottery) and where follow-up methods (e.g., telephone interviews) can be employed to ascertain the views of a representative sample of survey nonrespondents.

Partially in response to such problems, assessment systems have also employed surveys in carefully constructed experimental and/or quasi-experimental situations where sampling occurs within selected student groups. When assessing, for instance, the effectiveness of a program such as a freshman seminar, institutions will typically sample from both program students and a representative sample of nonprogram students. To control for possible self-selection artifacts that confound such designs, they will either ask for volunteers who are then randomly assigned to program and nonprogram groups or collect data that tap attributes associated with student propensity to volunteer for new programs (e.g., plans, commitment, and so forth).

However designed, survey methods are not able to fully tap the complexity of student views and the character of their understanding of the quality of their experiences. For that reason, effective assessment of retention also requires the use of a variety of qualitative methods ranging from focus-group interviews to qualitative interview techniques to explore student perceptions of their experiences on campus (e.g. Attinasi 1986, 1991, Kuh 1990, Kuh and Andreas 1991, Patton 1991, and Scott 1991). Though such methods are typically unable to present representative portraits of student life—if only because of the cost and time associated with carrying out a sufficient number of interviews—they enable the institution to uncover how students make sense of their experience. And they do so in ways not constrained by prior judgments that sometimes frame the development of survey questionnaires.

It should be noted that some institutions, such as Syracuse University, have asked senior administrators to sit in on student focus groups' interviews as nonparticipating observers. They report that the experience of being able to hear student voices unfiltered by numbers and official reports has been particularly helpful in allowing them to get a better understanding how students view their college experience. And when this observing is complemented by quantitative studies, they say, they come to a fuller understanding of how the numerical relationships in those studies arise (Tinto and Froh 1992).

But interviews of any sort, focus group or individual, are not simple matters (Attinasi 1991 and Scott 1991). Great care must be taken in the collection of student perceptions to insure their validity. All too often insensitive or highly structured, directed questioning of students leads to self-fulfilling results which produce findings that serve more to reinforce prior institutional expectations than to accurately mirror strongly held student views. In this instance, trained student interviewers are often more effective than faculty or staff. In some cases, colleges have asked a small number of newly entered students to keep diaries of their first-semester or first-year experiences. With sufficient training on how to collect and record data and with adequate guarantees of confidentiality, such dairies can serve as very powerful tools for both students and for institutional officials seeking to better understand how students experience college. In part their power arises from the fact that student observers are less inclined than adult observers to filter their observations through the sometimes biased lenses that are used by institutional representatives.

Institutions have also utilized a variety of unobtrusive indicators in order to gain insight into the character of student views and the likely direction of future student behavior. The most common example of the use of such indicators is in the assessment of student classroom behavior and student life in residence halls. Regarding the latter, residence hall staff have sometimes been asked to note the frequency of visits home very early in the first year and the absence of wall-hangings and the like in student rooms. Quite often those objects which grace the walls and doors of student rooms are quite sensitive indicators of the sense of belonging or ownership the individual has regarding his/her immediate environment. Absence of a sense of ownership or belonging can, in turn, be an important precursor of individual decisions to withdraw. The same principle can, of course, be applied to the study of classroom experience. One particularly eye-opening form of assessment involves the random collection of student class notes.

Clearly, no single method, quantitative or qualitative, survey or interview, will suffice for the range of situations assessment systems face. Not only must they produce "objective" data for reporting purposes (institutional, state, or federal), they must also yield information that enables institutional officials to better understand how and why attrition arises on campus. For that reason, effective systems employ multiple methods in their assessment of student experience. And they do so in a complementary fashion so that one method supplements the other.

The Structure of Retention Assessment Systems

Since the process of student withdrawal is longitudinal in character, student assessment must also be longitudinal in structure. Data collection must be timed to obtain information at a number of different points in the student's passage through the institution and be structured to permit the tracing of student movements into and through the institution from entry to exit. More importantly, retention assessment systems must provide the longitudinal information needed to ascertain not only how differing individual experiences link up over time to different types of student withdrawal but also the ways in which individual and institutional actions differentially affect those outcomes.

To do so, retention assessment systems must collect data at different times during the course of the student college career. When applied to the use of survey research methods, this means that institutions frequently structure their assessment along the lines of longitudinal panel or cohort studies. That is to say they typically identify a representative group of beginning students and follow that group (panel) over the course of a given time period. In some cases, such as Syracuse University, subsamples of that panel are also interviewed in focus-group fashion at different times during that period (Tinto and Froh 1992).

Though most retention assessment systems begin collecting data on new students at the start of their first academic year, it is preferable that assessment be initiated prior to students' entry into the institution. Early assessment enables the institution to more accurately ascertain the character of pre-entry expectations, commitments, and concerns about college life untainted by early exposure to the institution. The point of doing so is twofold. First, it enables officials to identify early student concerns and needs before they arrive on campus. And it does so early enough to be of practical value. The early collection of student data gives the institution the ability to target institutional services for new students as soon as they arrive on campus. In that manner institutions may be able to address potential problems before they become actual problems. Second, the collection of pre-entry data also makes possible the separation of the effect of pre-entry attributes upon retention from those effects which arise after entry from individual experiences within the college environment. That is, it enables one to distinguish between what students contribute to the process of institutional departure and that which the institution in interaction with students may do to cause students to leave.

In so doing, assessment can furnish the types of information needed for the development of selective, rather than general, policies for enhanced student retention.

Ideally data should be obtained, via questionnaire, from all or a representative random sample of those who either apply for admission and/or who are accepted for entry. The collection of data from all applicants, as opposed to all admitted students, permits the institution to study the nature of the college marketplace and the demand for its services relative to other institutions. Equally important, it provides the institution with the capacity to carry out "lost inquiry" applicant studies. Together, such determinations enable the institution to monitor over time the manner in which the demand for its service is influenced by its own actions and those of competing educational opportunities.

That ability is achieved, however, at a price. The one serious constraint to pre-admission data is that in posing questions to individuals during the process of application for admission and often for financial aid, one may elicit only that information which the applicants deem best suited to the task of being admitted to the institution and receiving financial aid. Individual fears, doubts, and concerns about making the transition to college may therefore go unexpressed for fear of not being admitted and/or of not receiving financial aid. Though there are steps one can take to deal with this potential distortion of data, one cannot entirely eliminate the possibility of obtaining somewhat misleading information about student views from applicant questionnaires. For that reason a number of institutions limit pre-entry data collection to those persons who have already been accepted for admission and carry out separate studies of the academic marketplace. Often those data are collected soon after acceptance or during orientation when students first come to campus. Generally speaking, the earlier the data are collected, the more time the institution has to employ them in the development of programs for those students (e.g., specialized orientation activities for specific groups of new students).

Beyond the point of entry, information must also be obtained on the changing character of student experiences within the institution. In particular, assessment must be sensitive to the critical stages of separation, transition, and incorporation which typically mark the beginning of the college career. Especially important to the process of departure are the stages of separation and transition to college. Since these are normally experienced very early in the student career, typically during the first semester and year of college life, more emphasis should be placed on the collection of information about the quality of student experiences during the early, rather than later, stages of association with the institution. As in the case of pre-entry data, early data collection leaves open the possibility that actions can be taken to remedy problems before they result in withdrawal.

Data should also be obtained from those students who intend to leave and/or who have already left the institution either through graduation or withdrawal. Exit interviewing of current leavers and/or follow-up interviews with recent leavers may prove to be particularly useful. When effective, these interviews often reveal important information (not easily obtained during the course of the student career) as to the existence of recurring problems students faced in attempting to meet the academic and social demands of the college. Persons who have already left or are in the process of leaving the institution are frequently more willing to "bare their souls" than are those who are still enrolled in the institution. But they will only do so when the interview is seen as nonthreatening. Great care must be taken by interviewers to approach the interview not as an attempt to find fault but as an opportunity to help the student make the transition to another setting. It is of some interest that institutions which have invested in exit interviewing of this sort often find that those interviews lead a number of students to reconsider their decisions to withdraw. For some, the exit interview may be the first time they have talked at length with a member of the institution about matters that concern them as students.

Whenever collected, assessment should allow for the comparative study of student outcomes (Light, Singer, and Willet 1990).[4] That is to say, it should enable institutional officials to discern what attributes, behaviors, and situations distinguish between successful and unsuccessful outcomes. For instance as it pertains to student learning, it should allow one to discern what experiences and patterns of behaviors distinguish students who show learning gain over their college careers from those who do not. Observed differences, let us say in classroom experiences, between those two groups can then serve as the beginning point of policy discussions that aim to insure that all students have those sorts of experiences. Obviously the same principle applies to the comparative study of successful college completion and departure.

The Recursive Character of Retention Assessment

Retention assessment systems must also be recursive in structure so as to provide consistent information over time about the experiences of *successive student cohorts*. They must collect data over the life of not one but several cohorts or panels of entering students. Recursive comparative data of this sort enable institutions to trace out and compare the movements of several cohorts of students in order to insure that the resulting image of student departure captures its enduring as well as temporary character. Institutions are thereby able to distinguish between the long-term forces and processes which characterize institutional life and those which are short-term, often nonrepetitive, in nature (e.g., effects of recession or specific events of campus).

The distinction between the two, for purposes of policy, is not trivial. Not infrequently institutional policies are established on the basis of short-term events which, though intense in effect, are short-lived in duration. Though effective retention must be sensitive to such temporary variations, it must be based on the continuing, more enduring character of the life of the institution and the experiences of students within it. In this fashion, longitudinal data over several cohorts of students may act as a useful and quite sensitive "social indicator" of the continuing functioning of the institution by isolating the existence of institutional experiences which are repeatedly shown to be associated with patterns of student departure. For example, should longitudinal data indicate continuing displeasure among departing students with the quality of classroom teaching or with the frequency and quality of student faculty contact outside the classroom, it would follow that future institutional policies should seriously consider actions in those areas of institutional functioning. Similarly, if it is found that new students continue to enter the institution with largely inaccurate expectations about the character of institutional life and that those expectations are in turn related to subsequent departure, then investigation of recruitment and admissions procedures might follow.

The same principle of recursiveness can also be applied to the collection of qualitative data. Repeated qualitative studies of student views of college and university life can also be gainfully employed as a barometer of the health of the institution. Recurring and widespread dissatisfaction with one or more segments of student life may highlight significant problems in institutional functioning. For instance, dissatisfaction with the quality of teaching or with the accessibility of the faculty may be indicators of especially serious problems in the academic life of the institutions—problems which go beyond the question of retention to that of institutional reputation and the ability of the institution to attract students in the future.

The Analysis and Use of Retention Assessment Data

Given valid and reliable data obtained systematically over a sufficiently long period of time, it is possible to use retention assessment data to answer several important questions central to the issue of student retention policy. The first and perhaps most obvious is that of description, namely, what types of student departure arise on campus and what are their relative frequency of occurrence among the student population generally and among specific segments of that population. The answer to that question arises directly from the data collected on the movements of students of varying attributes through the institution.

The second question which retention assessment can address is that of explanation, namely, what events lead to differing types of departure among various segments of the student population. The answer to that question, however, does not result in any simple way from any one form of analysis. Rather it is the outcome of the combining of results from several types of comparative and case-specific analyses. It arises, in part, from the longitudinal analysis of the relationship between individual attributes, patterns of experiences within the institution following entry, and subsequent patterns of persistence and/or departure during the course of the college career. It is also the outcome of the insights one obtains from the collection of qualitative data (e.g., interviews, observations. etc.) on the nature of student experiences within the various domains of institutional life. In both cases, the analyses appropriate to the question of explanation entail the multidimensional longitudinal comparison of the varying experiences of differing types of entering students as they relate to varying forms of leaving and staying behaviors.

In this regard, an especially important form of analysis is that which focuses on the longitudinal relationships between entering levels of student intellectual and social development, patterns of interaction and involvement in the life of college, and both retention and subsequent levels of student development. Carefully structured comparisons among different students and varying patterns of involvement lead the institution to more fully ascertain to what degree its actions lead not only to retention but also to the more important goal of student education.

Here is a brief caveat is needed. The understandable tendency of such analyses is to treat all gains from entry to exit as "value added" by the institution. Unfortunately, this overlooks the likelihood that some portion of student growth is due to maturation and therefore would have taken place without institutional action. If we are to make substantial gains in our understanding of the impact of colleges and universities on student learning we must find ways of distinguishing between that growth which is due to maturation from that which may be attributed to the actions of the institution. This is no simple task.

The results of retention analyses can be put to several important uses. For example, they can lead to the development of institutional early warning systems which flag, at entry or very early in the student career, those students who may have unusual difficulty in completing their degree programs. The repeated association among past cohorts between varying attributes at entry (e.g., high school grades, goals, commitments), first-year experiences (e.g., unusually low grades, high rates of absenteeism, frequent visits back home), and high rates of departure can be used to develop probability functions which indicate the projected likelihood that similar categories of future entrants will persist or depart prior to degree completion. Individuals may be classified as "high risk" in that they possess one or more attributes which, in the past, have been associated with higher rates of departure. In large residential institutions, for example, it is sometimes the case that students from very small rural towns, especially those with only moderate commitments, tend to have greater difficulty in adjusting to college life than do other students. In such settings, they might be flagged as more likely to depart. Similarly, entering students whose high school grades are below a given level and who in the past have experienced difficulty in meeting the academic demands of the college might also be classified as being more "dropout prone" than other students.

Early warning systems can also be constructed from data collected very early in the year on student behaviors within the academic and social systems of the institution (e.g., Krotseng 1992). In some cases faculty are asked to report on the class performance and attendance of each student. Signs of academic problems or behaviors that suggest possible withdrawal (e.g., repeated absences, failure to complete homework) are then used to flag students for immediate attention. Peer mentors often serve a similar function outside the classroom by unobtrusively monitoring the progress of their students during the first semester of college. In residential settings, additional data can be obtained from dormitory monitors who report signs of social isolation (e.g., isolation, frequent trips back home, lack of wall-hangings) or personal problems among student residents. However obtained, such systems collect information on current, rather than projected, behaviors and employ those data to target services to enrolled students rather than to entering students.

The determination of high risk or "dropout proneness" can serve at least two important functions in institutional planning. On one hand, it may permit institutions with selective admission procedures to more carefully tune their admission procedures to possibly reduce the numbers of entering students who do not complete their degree programs. On the other, for the greater bulk of institutions, it can be used to target institutional services to students very early in, if not at the very outset of, the college career. Thus, to follow the example above, it may lead institutions to provide counseling and early assistance to those students from very small rural communities who are more likely to have difficulty making the transition to the large, seemingly impersonal world of the large residential university.

The identification of "high risk" students is not, however, without some dangers. In developing early warning systems and in using them to project dropout proneness, one must be careful not to assume that past events are perfect predictors of future behaviors. Nor should one suppose that categorical associations between given attributes and/or early experiences and high rates of departure mean that that association need apply for each and every individual sharing those categorical attributes. One must be continually attentive to the dangers of using early warning systems for the uncritical labeling of students and the development, therefore, of self-fulfilling prophecies in the treatment of different students. They must be used discreetly lest the students so identified become stigmatized as likely departures. It is for these reasons that institutions sometimes employ both forms of early warning systems in the determination of "high risk." They use faculty feedback methods to check on the accuracy of quantitative predictive methods.

Early warning systems, at best, are signals of the likelihood of potential problems, not predictors of their occurrence. Though they may be used to indicate the likelihood that certain types of entering students may experience difficulties not unlike those experienced by similar types of entering students in the past, it does not mean that all future students of similar attributes will necessarily share the same sorts of experiences. Nevertheless, to the degree that repeated longitudinal assessments point to similar observations among a range of different entering cohorts, the results of early warning systems can be employed to sensitize the institution to the likelihood that particular segments of its entering student cohort may be in need of particular types of institutional services. Moreover, when driven by faculty feedback data, they can be the basis of a therapeutic approach to student needs which views identification of "high risk" as an opportunity to help students when that help is called for.

Retention assessment data, especially those which arise from comparative analyses of student success, can also serve as the basis for the establishment of long-term policies directed toward institutional change. By locating differences between successful and unsuccessful students, whether on a course, program, or institutional level, the institution can then focus on policies that seek to have more students share the experiences of successful students. To repeat a point made several times about the importance of active involvement in learning and student-faculty contact, if it proves to be the case that those activities distinguish on campus successful from unsuccessful students, then it follows that institutional policy should strive to have greater numbers of students engage in those activities.

To the degree that they are recursive in nature, retention assessment systems can also serve to "monitor" the impact of their actions to reshape student experiences and enhance learning and retention within the institution. In this manner, they may be utilized as part of ongoing formative or summative evaluation programs which seek to alter and improve student outcomes. By comparing, for example, the differential outcomes of successive cohorts of students who experience different and changing programs (e.g., altered freshman-year program), the institution can assess to what degree program changes are having the intended impact. To take another example, namely that of the impact of different admission policies, it may be possible to discern whether changes in recruitment material result in substantial improvements not only in admissions but also in rates of degree completion.

The Implementation of Retention Assessment Systems

To be useful for purposes of institutional policy, retention assessment systems must be systematic and comprehensive in their study of student experiences. That is to say, they must obtain data on the full range of student academic and social experience on campus and, in some cases, on experiences external to the college as well (e.g., family and work responsibilities). They must do so in order to enable institutional officials to discern which experiences, more than others, are differentially important in shaping different types of outcomes.

Unfortunately, many institutions carry out piecemeal assessments and/or allocate responsibility for assessment to different administrative units each with their own specific domain of responsibility (e.g., housing, student affairs, advising). Unless carefully coordinated, such partitioning of assessment leads to discrete studies that do little to advance the need for institutions to obtain a comprehensive vision of the relative importance of differing areas of activity to different student outcomes.

It is for that reason that retention assessment systems must develop organizational linkages to other units within the institution that also collect information about student experiences on campus. The goal of such linkages is the sharing of a range of information about student life which is acquired from a variety of different organizational perspectives. The desired consequence of such sharing is the development of a fuller and possibly more reliable picture of the character of student experiences within the institution. Of no small consequence is the likelihood that such cooperation will also lead to wider-scale coordination in decision making affecting student life—a coordination of effort which is not always present on college campuses (see Tinto and Froh 1992).

Particularly important linkages are those with the office of admissions and that office responsible for freshman orientation programs. Their importance arises in part from the need to begin the data collection process very early in the student career, if possible before the beginning of the first semester. It also results from the fact that one can substantially reduce the costs of retention assessment by piggybacking data collection to that which is ongoing in other offices of the institution. As the process of admission normally requires collection of student data, substantial savings can be obtained by integrating data collection for retention assessment with that ongoing data collection process.

Linkages between retention assessment systems and other parts of the institution should be reciprocal rather than unidirectional in nature. They should be so structured as to insure that information obtained from assessment is sent, in usable form, to other units within the institution that have responsibility for student life. In that manner it is possible for retention assessment systems to become an integral part of the wider structure of student services that dot the institutional landscape. Their output serves as an important input to the process of decision making done elsewhere in the institution.

Finally, to the degree that retention assessment must also include the assessment of classroom experience by faculty, it must allow for, indeed provide incentives for, faculty to carry out their own assessments. As in the case of the implementation of retention programs, successful implementation of student-centered assessment systems requires that faculty take ownership over the process of assessment at least as it pertains to their classrooms and programs. But institutions need to strike a reasonable balance between the need for faculty to decide for themselves the assessment to be used in their own classrooms and the need for the institution to obtain a more systematic picture of what goes on in college classrooms. It is here that program-level assessment becomes a useful and much needed tool in the formulation of institutional policy.

Implementing Useful Assessment Systems

It should be evident by now that retention assessment systems, however employed, are only as effective as their use by the institution. Data unused, however complete, are data that are ineffective, if not counterproductive, to the long-term goal of institutional change. The importance of retention assessment systems lies in their being used by all members of the institution involved in the education and retention of students. It is for this reason that one typically begins a conversation about the development of an assessment system with the questions "What information do we want and how will we use that information for institutional improvement."

At a minimum such utilization requires that the data obtained through retention assessment be made available to different members of the college community (e.g., faculty, advisers, counselors, student services, and admissions) in formats which are meaningful and useful to those persons or organizations. Generally, the closer the match between assessment data and those which are normally employed by an organization, the more likely will those data be employed in the decision-making process. Usage, not mere availability, is one of the primary goals of the establishment of retention assessment systems.

It is not very surprising, then, that retention assessment systems have the greatest impact upon institutional functioning when they are fully integrated into the ongoing academic and administrative activities of the institution. In some instances retention assessment activities may serve to connect and integrate the efforts of diverse persons and units in the college concerned with student retention. They may act to integrate the diverse activities of disparate institutional elements by the very fact that they require those varying groups to work together on a common problem, namely, the retention of students.

Concluding Observation

However employed, retention assessment systems are a necessary beginning step in the process of formulating retention policies. Despite the wealth of data which may be obtained from the experiences of other institutions, each institution must ascertain for itself the particular attributes of its own situation. To repeat again a major theme of this book, student departure is more a function of what goes on within the institution following entry than of what may have occurred beforehand. Its occurrence and patterning on campus is more a reflection of the attributes of a given body of students within a particular educational and social setting made up of varying social and intellectual communities than it is of any broadly defined societal force which shapes the activities of all institutions. Though it is obvious that external forces affect student retention, especially in commuting and urban open-enrollment institutions, for most institutions those forces are not central to the question of the development of institution-specific policies for student retention.

Finally, it should be noted that another potentially very powerful use of retention assessment systems is the development of "expected versus actual" indicators of institutional functioning. Let's take institutional rates of degree completion as a case in point. The specification of actual graduation rates is easy enough. The problem, certainly for the purposes of reporting to state and federal government, is of determining whether that rate is higher or lower than one would expect for similar institutions. Given the nature of student inputs and institutional circumstance, the question may be posed whether it is reasonable to expect that the institution's rate of graduation should be higher.

One way of responding to that question is to compare the actual rates of graduation with that which would be predicted on the basis of student inputs and institutional type and circumstance (expected rates of graduation). That latter rate can be determined by the use of available national data and multiple regression equations which predict rates of graduation for similar types of institutions (e.g., four- or two-year, mode of control, size, and location) using different student inputs (e.g., ability, social class, race, gender).

In effect the comparison of expected versus actual rates of graduation allows the institution to ascertain whether its performance on this measure is higher or lower than that expected of other similar types of institution whose students are of similar character. By doing so, it also provides the institution with a reasonable response to the demands of state and federal agencies that institutions improve their rate of graduation. Namely, it allows them to specify what is a reasonable goal of institutional efforts to improve graduation rates.

— *Appendix B* —

Toward a Theory
of Doctoral Persistence

In most countries, the more selective the level of education, the higher the rate of student completion. In the United States the reverse is true. The higher, the more selective, the level of education, the lower the rate of completion. In the nonselective secondary schools of America, approximately 25 percent of all students fail to graduate. In more selective four-year colleges and universities, between 35 and 40 percent of entering students fail to obtain a degree. In the most selective institutions, the graduate and first-professional schools, our best estimates is that up to 50 percent of all beginning students fail to complete their doctoral degree programs.

These data are striking for a variety of reasons, not the least of which has to do with the terrible loss of high-level manpower that continues to take place at the most selective levels of our educational system. In the educational sector that is frequently seen as contributing most to the advancement of our society, we do least well in enabling our most able students to complete their degree programs.

Given the importance of graduate education, it is surprising that so little research has been carried out on the process of graduate persistence. Relative to the knowledge acquired from the extensive body of research on the process of undergraduate persistence that we have detailed in chapters 3 and 4, we have gained little insight into the forces that shape graduate persistence.

That this is the case is not merely a reflection of the absence of research—

indeed, research on graduate education is not uncommon (e.g., Becker et al. 1951, Benkin 1984, Cook and Swanson 1978, Girves and Wemmerus 1988, Matchett 1988, Ott, Markewich, and Ochsner 1984, and Zwick 1991). Rather it mirrors the fact that research on graduate attrition has not been guided either by a comprehensive model or theory of graduate persistence or by the methodological strategies that have been successfully employed in the study of undergraduate persistence.[1]

This appendix is directed toward the goal of advancing our knowledge of the process of graduate persistence. Specifically, it seeks to begin a conversation about the possible outlines of an institutional model of doctoral persistence, one that is drawn from that for undergraduate persistence, with the hope that that conversation will lead to a much needed body of research on the character of graduate persistence.[2] Furthermore, it suggests a series of studies that would have to be pursued in order to bring clarity to the character of that process.

In the sections that follow we will first direct our attention to the application of a theory of educational communities, derived from our just concluded conversation of undergraduate persistence, to the problem of doctoral persistence. Having done so, we will turn to a discussion of the longitudinal character of that process and to the possible stages that mark it over time. These two discussions will then lead to the specification of the broad outlines of a longitudinal model of graduate persistence. The appendix then concludes with suggestions as to the sorts of research that would have to be carried out in order to better understand the character of the doctoral completion process and the sorts of policies that might be considered to enhance rates of doctoral completion.

A Theory of Graduate Communities and Doctoral Persistence

As a beginning point for our thinking about the possible character of a theory of graduate persistence we take the theory of persistence that we described in chapter 4.[3] We do so not merely because it seems plausible that the process of persistence at the graduate level would be somewhat similar to that at the undergraduate level, but also because recent research on doctoral persistence yields a number of findings that are quite similar to those at the undergraduate level (Thomas, Clewell, and Pearson 1987, 1991). Specifically, it suggests that graduate persistence is also shaped by the personal and intellectual interactions that occur within and between students and faculty and the various communities that make up the academic and social systems of the institution.

A theory of graduate persistence must recognize that the primary reference groups for doctoral students, as opposed to undergraduates generally, are the more local student and faculty communities that reside in the schools, programs, and departments that house the specific fields of study in which the doctoral degree is pursued (Girves and Wimmerus 1988).

This localization of communities gives rise to several obvious differences between the process of doctoral persistence and that of undergraduate persistence. First, the character of doctoral persistence is likely to be much more a reflection of the particular normative and structural character of the specific field of study and the judgments that describe acceptable performance than a reflection of the broader university. As a result, one can expect significant differences in that process to exist within the university, between different fields of study (Malaney 1988, Nerad 1990, Zwick 1991).[4] Indeed these differences may be so large as to overwhelm possible institutional effects. Though there are undoubtedly some broader institutional effects, as reflected for instance in the normative orientation or traditions of a particular institution, one can reasonably expect the process of doctoral persistence in some fields to be much more similar across institutions than it might be among some fields of study within a particular university (Zwick 1991).

Second, the process of doctoral persistence, relative to undergraduate persistence, is more likely to be reflective of, and framed by, the particular types of student and faculty communities that reside in the local department, program, or school. In this respect, the notion of social integration at the graduate level is more closely tied to that of academic integration than it is at the undergraduate level. Social membership within one's program becomes part and parcel of academic membership, and social interaction with one's peers and faculty becomes closely linked not only to one's intellectual development, but also to the development of important skills required for doctoral completion. In a very real sense, the local community becomes the primary educational community for one's graduate career.

The effect of that community, however, is likely to change over time. Specifically, it is likely that the process of doctoral persistence, especially in the later stages, will be much more a function of the behaviors of a specific group of faculty or of a particular faculty member (e.g., one's adviser) than it is of the local community generally (Clewell 1987, Girves and Wemmerus 1988). As such, the process of doctoral persistence is more likely to reflect the specific character of student-faculty interactions than is undergraduate persistence generally (Thomas, Clewell, and Pearson 1991). Indeed, the experiences of students within a department, though tied by field of study and departmental norms, can vary considerably if the behaviors of the faculty also vary considerably. In this manner, the experience of any particular doctoral student, regardless of field, will always be somewhat idiosyncratic.

This is not to say, however, that local communities exist in isolation from the rest of the university. They are necessarily tied to the wider community of the university not only in practice (i.e., via organizational rules and regulations), but also in orientation. In part this reflects the probable link between the broader attributes of the university and the types of people who are likely to apply and attend the schools and departments within the university. It also mirrors the fact that students and faculty within departments come to join other communities that cross-cut departmental boundaries. They become members of several communities, departmental and university.

At the same time, local graduate communities are also part of broader external professional communities that frame the field of study. This is the case not only because faculty members are themselves members of such associations, but also because graduate students are frequently preparing to enter the profession representing their particular field of study.

To extend the logic of this line of reasoning a bit further, a theory of doctoral persistence is but an early stage of a more general theory of professional career attainment, completing one's degree but one step of many to success in those professions for which that degree applies. In this regard, our conversation about the process of graduate persistence at the doctoral level can be understood as being analogous to the conversations sociologists have about processes of socialization to work and the role normative reference groups play in that process.

Graduate persistence is thus possibly influenced by several normative reference groups, local and external, to which students orient themselves. And to the degree that it is seen by students as providing entry to a particular field of work, it is also shaped by processes of anticipatory socialization. Doctoral students, in seeking entry to a profession or field of work, are likely to orient themselves toward the norms that they perceive as determining success in that field of work. When the norms of the local communities are understood as congruent with the norms of the larger national communities, the process of socialization is straightforward. Socialization to the local community serves to prepare the individual for entry to the larger national community in which that local community is a member. When the norms are incongruent, difficulties may arise. Doing well in the institution, that is persisting, may not be equally conducive to doing well in the field of study after graduation.

Students also belong to other external communities, such as those of family and work. Though these may intersect institutional and departmental communities, their functioning is largely independent of the institution. As a result, they too may give rise to conflicting demands upon student time and energy. Here also the student has to find a way to resolve or at a minimum manage or negotiate those conflicts. Unfortunately, not all students can easily negotiate such "role conflicts." Membership in one community may require giving up membership in another.

The demands of external communities may also serve to limit one's involvement in the communities of the department. The difference between full-time and part-time attendance, in this regard, is not merely a difference in time commitment. It is also a difference in the degree to which one is able to become involved in the intellectual and social life of the student and faculty communities that undergird graduate education. Whereas the former may serve to extend time to degree completion, and only indirectly constrain persistence, the latter acts directly to undermine persistence by isolating the person from the intellectual and social life of the department.

Though it is not the intent here to explore this issue in depth, the way in which the student resolves the conflict between the demands of internal and external communities at least partially reflects the attributes of the person and those of the institution within which the program is housed. On one hand the ability of the person to negotiate different norms hinges in part upon a willingness to play out different roles—for example, the experience of females in male-dominated fields of study (Hartnett 1981, Berg and Ferber 1983). On the other, it is conditioned, among other things, by the capacity of the local community and institution to insure access to the field of work (i.e., the "status conferring" ability of the program/institution). For example, when the perceived ability of the program/institution to insure entry to the field of work is high, the individual is more likely to want to negotiate those conflicts in order to complete the degree program.

Nested and Intersecting Graduate Communities

These observations lead us to argue that it is possible to visualize the process of doctoral persistence as reflecting an interactive series of nested and intersecting communities not only within the university, but beyond it to the broader intellectual and social communities of students and faculty that define the norms and structure of the field of study at a national level.[5] Though the process of doctoral persistence is primarily shaped by the specific local student and faculty communities that frame departmental life, it is also conditioned by the external communities within which those communities are nested.[6] And it is also influenced by the intersecting external communities to which the student may have membership. Graduate persistence is, at one and the same time, both more local and more national in character than is undergraduate persistence.

This notion of nested and intersecting communities and the experience of doctoral students as anchored in the local communities of the department leads us to a somewhat more complex, yet more restricted concept of academic and social integration and the mechanisms through which that integration is achieved. On one level, the person's academic and social integration is much more narrowly defined by the immediate communities of the department and the limited number of people who inhabit the department. At another level, it is also shaped by the normative and structural attributes of the field of study that is represented by the department. In this manner, student integration is more broadly defined by the nature of work and therefore patterns of interaction that mark the field, be it professional or disciplinary.

Stages of Graduate Persistence

The process of graduate persistence, like that at the undergraduate level, is longitudinal. Events are continually being shaped by past events and, to some degree, molded by the anticipation of future events. Unfortunately, we have little empirical evidence that documents the time-dependent character of that process because most research on graduate persistence has not been longitudinal in character. By focusing on easy to acquire cross-sectional data, past research has, with few exceptions, failed to document how student experiences come, over time, to shape the completion of the doctoral degree (Peters and Peterson 1987). Regrettably, the few studies that have viewed graduate persistence as a longitudinal process have greatly oversimplified the process that leads to graduate degree completion. On one hand they have considered only part of the process of persistence may span as many as ten years. On the other, they have implicitly assumed that the process of persistence at the doctoral level is largely invariant in character over the course of the graduate career, that is to say that events that shape persistence early in the graduate-student career are essentially the same as those that shape persistence later in that career.[7]

Yet there is much anecdotal evidence and some recent qualitative evidence from studies at Syracuse University to suggest that this is not the case (Tinto and Wallace 1986). Rather than being uniform in quality across time, the process of doctoral persistence seems to be marked by at least three distinct stages, namely that of transition and adjustment, that of attaining candidacy or what might be referred to as the development of competence, and that of completing the research project leading to the awarding of the doctoral degree.[8]

The first stage of the process of doctoral persistence, here referred to as the stage of transition, typically covers the first year of study. It is during this time that the individual seeks to establish membership in the academic and social communities of the university. As such it mirrors both the development of personal affiliations with other students and faculty within the department and the judgments individuals make about the nature of those communities (whether or not their norms are consonant with the student's own). Consequently, this stage of the doctoral persistence process will be shaped by social as well as academic interactions, both formal and informal,

that occur in the communities of the institution, in particular in the department or program in which the degree is sought (Goplerud 1980).

Persistence at this early stage will also be influenced by the character of
individual commitments to the goal of doctoral completion and by specific
career goals (Zwick 1991). Given the implicit tie between graduate study at
the doctoral level and the attainment of career goals, continuation at this
stage will mirror individual goals and commitments as well as individual
perceptions as to the relevance of institutional programs to those goals. In
this manner, the movement from transition to subsequent membership involves a series of individual judgments about the desirability of membership
and the likely costs and benefits of further involvement.

The second stage of graduate study, that leading to candidacy, entails the
acquisition of knowledge and the development of competencies deemed
necessary for doctoral research. Culminating as it does in doctoral comprehensive exams, successful completion of this stage mirrors both individual
abilities and skills and the character of personal interactions with faculty
within the academic domain of the institution. The development of recognized competencies, rather than community membership per se, is the critical issue during this period. As a result, interactions within the classroom
and department/program pertaining to issues of academic competence are
likely to play a central role in student persistence. But in this instance the
distinction we typically make between the role of academic and social integration becomes somewhat blurred. Insofar as the students' academic and
social communities are localized within the department, interactions within
them tend to become intertwined. Social experiences become part of one's
academic experiences and vice versa.

In this manner, social experiences within the local communities of the department, peer and faculty, are likely to play a more important role in the
development and determination of academic competencies than is the case
generally at the undergraduate level. A student's social experience within a
community of peers and faculty comes to influence not only the development
of academic competencies, but also the judgments significant others make
about those competencies. This results, in part, from the particular character
of graduate-student peer groups and the way social experiences within those
groups come to influence the development of academic skills (e.g., the role
of midnight bull sessions over academic issues). It also mirrors the fact that
faculty judgments as to student competence within the classroom are necessarily conditioned by social judgments arising from interactions beyond the
classroom—in the hallway and offices of the department. The experience of
minority students, of some older students, and in some fields of some female
students will, to some degree, always be conditioned by the nature of social
judgments made by faculty as to the requisite characteristics of student membership in a given field of study.[9]

The final stage of doctoral persistence, that of the completion of a doctoral dissertation, covers that period of time from the gaining of candidacy, through the completion of a doctoral research proposal, to the successful completion of the research project and defense of the dissertation.[10] As such it is likely to reflect not only the nature of individual abilities but also the direct role individual faculty play as mentors and advisers (Clewell 1987).

During this stage of doctoral persistence the nature of faculty interaction shifts from that involving a number of faculty within a department to the specific behaviors of a very few faculty.[11] In many cases, it may involve a specific relationship between the candidate and one faculty member who takes on the role of dissertation adviser and with several faculty who comprise the dissertation committee. Consequently, persistence at this stage may be highly idiosyncratic in that it may hinge largely if not entirely upon the behavior of a specific faculty member.

It might be observed that experiences during this stage of the doctoral completion process are likely to play a significant role in later attainment. Especially in those fields where the faculty have a good deal of influence upon entry to work and later job performance—as they do for persons who seek university faculty position—the character of student-faculty interactions may influence not only later faculty sponsorship but also the quality of what is learned about the nature of the profession or field. Simply put, an informed and influential adviser may be invaluable to the early occupational success of the candidate.

Finally, it is the case that for some students the role of external communities will gain in importance during the last stage of doctoral persistence. The character of the candidate's commitments to those communities, such as families and work, and the support they provide for continued study may spell the difference between success and failure at this stage. The documented difficulties that women with families face is just one example of the differential impact families, and in turn social norms, may play in doctoral persistence (Hartnett 1981).

The Role of Finances in Doctoral Persistence

We have delayed until now talking about the role of financial aid in doctoral persistence. This is not because financial aid is not important to persistence. Quite the contrary. It is quite evident that the completion of a doctoral research dissertation requires that candidates have sufficient financial resources to complete their studies and devote a major portion of their time to the completion of the research project. But while finances matter, it is not clear that they matter in the same way at different stages of the doctoral completion process. For example, it is likely that one of the primary effects of limited financial resources during the first two stages of persistence is to lengthen the time to the attainment of candidacy (e.g., attendance part-time and/or working while attending graduate school). As a result, the impact upon the likelihood of persistence is largely indirect. That is to say, the longer the degree takes, the less likely are individuals to finish the degree.

During the later stage of persistence, however, the primary effect of limited financial resources upon persistence may be largely direct in that it may reduce one's ability to devote the time required to successfully complete a research process (Ehrenberg and Mavros 1992). Unlike many other possible projects, a dissertation project requires a good deal of concentrated effort over an extended period. To the degree that limited financial resources detract from that effort (e.g., so that a student has to work while trying to complete a dissertation), so too do limited resources directly affect the likelihood of completing the degree (see Tuckman 1990, and Tuckman, Coyle and Bae 1990). Of course, the sum effect of limited financial resources is not only a reduction of the likelihood of persistence but also a lengthening of the time required to complete a doctoral program—now estimated to be upward of ten years in some fields of study (Abedi and Benkin 1987, Nerad 1990). Little wonder then that the probability of completion may diminish over time for some types of graduate students (e.g., married, working adults and disadvantaged students).[12]

The form that financial assistance takes may also play a role in doctoral persistence. The difference, for instance, between aid in the form of a fellowship and that in the form of a graduate assistance may not be trivial. Indeed, it may be the case, at least during early stages of doctoral persistence, that an assistance, especially one involving research, may be more conducive to persistence than an outright fellowship. Whereas the former serves to involve the student in the intellectual life of the department and enables that person to work together with faculty, the latter may have no such impacts. It is for this reason that it is sometimes argued that a fellowship, given early in the graduate career, may be counterproductive to long-term persistence. During the last stage of doctoral persistence, however, the reverse may be true, since the demands of an assistance may limit the time the person can give to his/her own research project.

A Longitudinal Model of Graduate Persistence

Unlike undergraduate persistence, the process of graduate persistence cannot be easily described by any one simple model. This is the case because models of graduate persistence are likely to differ somewhat across fields of study and across periods of time. The factors that appear significant at one stage of persistence may not be significant later on. And some factors, like student-faculty interaction, may change over time in the manner in which they influence persistence.

Given that caveat, we have attempted in figure B.1 to describe the general dimensions of a model of institutional doctoral persistence as it is mapped across the different stages.[13] At the outset, the model posits that individual attributes, most notably gender, age, race, ability, and social class, and individual educational experiences prior to entry to graduate school help shape individual goals (educational and career) and commitments (goal and institutional) at entry. These help specify the orientations individuals bring with them to the task of completing a doctoral degree and, in turn, establish the conditions within which subsequent interactions occur.[14] Their impact upon persistence, though indirect, may be important in the long run. For instance, individuals whose educational and career goals are such as to require the completion of a doctorate—as in the case of a person wishing to become a university faculty member in the physical sciences—are more likely to finish than other persons whose goals are not so linked.

At the same time, the model also specifies the nature of external commitments (e.g., work and family responsibilities) and financial resources available to the individual at entry (e.g., type and amount of financial aid). Together with goals and commitments, these establish the parameters of the student's participation in graduate school, in this case as measured by full- or part-time attendance and by place of residence (on or off campus). As in the case of commitments and goals, participation patterns have an important, though indirect, impact upon persistence. In this instance they condition the nature of subsequent academic and social interactions the student has with other members of the institution/program.

Following entry, during the early stage of doctoral persistence, the student interacts, in varying degrees, with students, faculty, and staff within the institution, largely if not entirely with those within the department or program in which the degree is sought. The terms "academic system" and "social system" are used here to distinguish those events that occur within and have to do with the academic domain or system of the institution from those that are primarily social in character. Of course, the two are never totally distinct, as events in one are influenced by and influence in turn events in the other. Thus the simultaneous path joining the two.

These interactions, conditioned as they are by individual commitments and goals and by the person's form of participation, serve to mold individual perceptions not only of community membership (i.e., integration), but also of the desirability of that membership and its value for one's career goals. Among other things (e.g., finances and external commitments), issues of community membership, relevance of academic programs for specific career goals, and expected benefits of those programs come into play at this point in time. Thus the interim outcomes of academic and social integration, and goal and institutional commitment.

Beyond the stage of transition, the individual is faced with the task of ac-

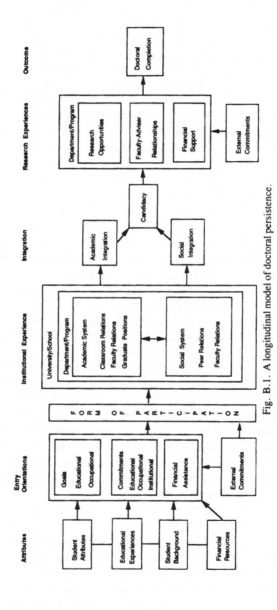

Fig. B.1. A longitudinal model of doctoral persistence.

quiring the skills and competencies required of a doctoral candidate. During this second stage of doctoral persistence interactions within the academic domain of the department/program (in the classroom, laboratories, and hallways of the institution), together with individual abilities, play a central role in student learning and the attainment of candidacy.

It is also during this stage that the individual forms specific affiliations with faculty within the department/program. These affiliations are important for at least two reasons. First, they are essential to student learning and persistence. Second, they lead to the development of specific relationships from which emerge the faculty/mentor associations so important to the completion of the dissertation beyond candidacy. In this manner, the quality of formal and informal contact with faculty lays the foundation for subsequent attainment following candidacy.[15]

Finally, having attained candidacy, the individual seeks to identify a dissertation topic, successfully carry out a doctoral research project, and defend that dissertation at a formal hearing. Here specific affiliations with one or more faculty come to shape the persistence process. Though other interactions may matter, it is the faculty-mentor relationship that is most likely to shape completion.

At the same time, the completion of this final stage of doctoral persistence calls for the availability of financial resources, both personal and institutional, that enable the candidate to devote the time needed to complete the research project. Yet it is here that resources are the most difficult to come by. Most graduate financial aid packages are frontloaded. They are designed to allow people to begin graduate study but not configured to enable them to finish.

A Research Agenda

Though there are reasons to believe that the model posited here may be useful, we do not yet have the sorts of longitudinal research we need to ascertain whether this or other possible models best explain that process. Until we do so, all of the above is merely informed speculation. To move beyond speculation, we need to invest in a range of research studies that empirically document the scope and varying character of the graduate persistence process.

Among the wide variety of possible studies, several seem most necessary at this point in time. First, it is evident that we must carry out a full longitudinal panel study of graduate work that traces out over time the experiences and differential outcomes of a representative sample of beginning doctoral students. That panel would have to be constructed so as to enable us to discern not only the degree to which the underlying character of persistence varies across the differing stages of graduate study, but also the manner in which experiences at one stage, for instance that during the attainment of candidacy, conditions experiences in later stages.

It follows that we must also shed light on the manner in which different forms of institutional behavior, in particular that of the faculty, come to shape the likelihood of doctoral completion at different points in time. Given the nested quality of graduate communities, the simple rubric of "student-faculty interaction" will not suffice at the graduate level. We need to uncover the nested effects of different levels of faculty-student interaction and eventually the specific role of faculty-mentor relationships upon the likelihood of completion (Williamson and Fenske 1992). And we must do so in a manner that highlights the differential experience of differing students, especially the experiences of students of color and persons of different age and gender.[16]

We also need to carry out a series of studies that would enable us to contrast the varying experiences of students in different fields of study both within and across graduate institutions of education. It is important to tease out the distinct, yet interactive, effects of field of study and institutional contexts upon graduate persistence. For instance, we must discern to what degree the effects of fields of study cut across or are conditioned by the broader institutional context within which those studies are carried out. Do the norms of a particular field of study override the institution and/or department specific norms of the particular context within which that study is being pursued? Since it has been argued that much of the difference between completion rates in the physical sciences and the social sciences or humanities reflects their differing structure of work—the former stressing apprenticeship/collaborative work, the latter stressing work that is individualistic—the question should be asked whether collaborative work, either in classrooms or in research, serves to increase student integration and thereby enhance the likelihood of persistence to degree completion.

At the same time, we must also come to better understand how other commitments and communities, as defined for instance by family and work, come to influence graduate persistence. The experience of older graduate students, especially those who work and/or have dependent families, would be a necessary focus of future inquiry. In this regard, we must also shed light on the ways in which institutional policies, for instance those concerning residency requirements and financial aid, differentially impact upon students with differing external commitments.

In these and other possible studies, we must employ both quantitative and qualitative methods. The former are needed not only to trace out the longitudinal linking of experiences at one time with varying outcomes at a subsequent time, but also to establish reasonable claims about the degree to which results from any set of studies can be generalized to a broader population of individuals and institutions. The latter methods, especially that of grounded ethnography, are needed to probe the meanings differing individuals attach to their experience as they take place within an observable sphere of personal interactions. Those understandings, more than any set of longitudinal path equations, help us to make sense of why it is that particular types of experiences lead to differing types of outcomes. They also enable us to uncover the complex ways in which the social context of academic studies (e.g., the prevailing social norms of a given field of study and the values of people within the communities of those fields) come to condition the impact of academic experiences upon student success.

Finally, our research, like that for undergraduate retention, must also enable institutions to address the policy question of how they can act to enhance graduate persistence and completion. Research in the assessment mode rather than the theoretical mode must be part of our research agenda. In the same way that we can compare successful and unsuccessful student experience, we can and should compare successful and unsuccessful doctoral programs. We should have the same sorts of case studies at the graduate level that we have had at the undergraduate level (e.g., Richardson Jr. 1987, and Richardson Jr., Simmons, and de los Santos 1987).

A Concluding Observation: The Link between Theory, Research, and Policy

The debate regarding the nature of graduate persistence is not merely of theoretical importance—a matter of the correctness of our conceptual models. It is also a matter of substantial interest in that distinctions such as those implied by the notions of local communities and stages of completion are essential to the development of institutional policies to enhance rates of doctoral completion. It is to this latter goal, as much as the to the former, that this conversation has been directed.

— *Notes* —

Chapter 1

1. There appears to be an intimate relationship between entry into higher education and the consequences of not finishing higher education. As a greater portion of the population enters higher education, the cost of not going to college increases even as the benefits of doing so diminish. When large numbers of persons go on to college after high school, college-going is increasingly seen by both employers and employees alike as the norm for occupational advancement, and it becomes the norm of educational attainment. But as it does so, the absolute value of higher education for occupational advancement declines, since more people acquire similar degrees in the marketplace.

This gives rise, parenthetically, to the possibility that increasing numbers of students enter higher education as much from a fear of the penalties of not doing so as from an appreciation of the benefits of that education. Unlike other college students, such individuals are likely to see themselves as captured by external pressures. Rather than take an active part in their education, they are more likely to be passive and to resist any efforts at change.

2. As the pool of available students has decreased, the competition for those students has intensified as more institutional officials become more skilled in using new marketing and recruitment techniques. Whereas the reception of a polished, student-oriented brochure by a potential applicant was formerly the exception, it is now the rule.

Chapter 2

1. This distinction is not trivial. Not a few studies of departure have tended to confuse the two. Quite often they will draw from aggregated national data inferences

as to the character of departure as if it were institutional in character. Thus Astin's (1975) study speaks of the effect of individual attributes upon departure as if those variations, derived from nationally aggregated data, applied as well to students in individual institutions.

2. Not surprisingly, the greatest diversity in time of entry is in the two-year sector. Many two-year institutions enroll a sizable proportion of their students in the first several days following the beginning of the academic year. Participation in the four-year sector is, by comparison, marked by a somewhat more "regular" pattern of entry.

3. The National Longitudinal Survey of the activities of the 1972 high school graduating class indicates that nearly 10 percent of that cohort entered college for the first time a year or more after graduating from high school (Eckland and Henderson 1981).

4. It should be pointed out that the use of college entrant cohort analysis is useful in its own right. As it focuses only on the activities of persons who enter college at the same time, it permits the holding constant of the possible effects of societal conditions upon student departure. In so doing, such analysis allows us to center our attention on the specific roles individuals and institutions play in the departure process. Though institutional conditions may change after entry, they are assumed to apply equally to all students. Of course, it does not obviate the need to take account of the changing circumstances of various individuals. Rather, it enables us to consider these varying effects as they apply to individuals as opposed to different cohorts of students.

5. Derived from U.S. Department of Education, the Digest of Education Statistics (1991), table 170, p. 177.

6. These figures are generated as follows. We take the mean of the range of first-year attrition rates for public and private four- and two-year institutions as our benchmark for full-time students. We increase these by 20 percent to get our estimates of first-year attrition among part-time and nonmatriculated students. Then from the proportion of full- and part-time enrollments drawn from the most recent U.S. Office of Education statistics (Digest of Education Statistics, 1991, table 166, p. 172) we calculate the overall rate of first-year attrition by multiplying full- and part-time rates by their proportional representation in each sector.

7. This is likely to be the case if only because of the development of statewide articulation agreements between public two- and four-year institutions. Though far from perfect, these agreements ease the movement of individuals between institutions.

8. Derived from Eagle and Carroll (1988a) by comparing information in table 3 (p. 20) with the proportion of 1972 high school graduates who entered four-year colleges and universities immediately after high school.

9. Estimates derived from Eagle and Carroll (1988a).

10. Data for figure 2.2 was derived from Carroll (1989).

11. Recent research by the author, not reported here, looked at the variation in rates of four-year degree completion over the period 1890-1980 (Tinto and Lentz 1986). Time-series analyses indicate that despite massive growth in the size of the higher educational enterprise and therefore in the number of persons obtaining four-

year college degrees, the proportion of entering students who do so has seemingly remained quite stable. Rates of degree completion at the turn of the century were also about 45 percent of the entering student body and have, since that time, not varied by more than plus or minus 8 percent. Interestingly, those analyses also support the notion that economic forces are largely responsible for the year-to-year variations in system departure which are observed over that period. Shifting economic conditions appear to influence rates of departure directly by affecting decisions regarding continued attendance and indirectly by altering the distribution of attendance at two- and four-year colleges.

12. Derived from data in Eagle and Carroll (1988b).

13. It might be observed in this context that the character of participation of delayed entrants differs considerably from that of "regular" entrants. Among other things, the former are more likely than the latter to enter via the two-year sector, to be enrolled part-time, and to be employed at least part-time while attending college. It follows, as noted earlier, that delayed entrants are therefore not only more likely than immediate entrants to require more time to complete their college degrees but also more likely overall to depart the system without so doing.

14. Though it is not yet the place to speak of the role of policies which emphasize the use of financial incentives in student retention, it might be pointed out in passing that our view of the importance of financial assistance in the completion process may be distorted by our tendency to confine our view of completion to a rather narrow "standard" time period and to a limited cohort of entering students.

15. Derived from calculations by the author of the 1972 NLS and 1980 HSB survey data (not shown).

16. But it does not follow that the association between ability and departure is merely the result of the inability of individuals to maintain adequate grades in college. Using the same data, Eckland and Henderson (1981) found that college grades were relatively unimportant in determining departure among the NLS cohort. Only 6 percent of all first-year students in the sample fell below a self-reported grade point average of between C and B.

17. The same conclusion is reached by Nettles et al. (1984) in a multi-institution study of progression of black and white students in ten southern and border states. Though aggregate rates of departure for blacks were higher than those for whites, they were nearly the same after controlling for differences in prior academic preparation.

Chapter 3

1. In those cases where researchers focus on dropout defined as academic dismissal, it is not surprising that ability proves to be inversely related to the likelihood of leaving (e.g., Panos and Astin 1968, Taylor and Hanson 1970, Astin 1972). But when they focus on dropout as voluntary withdrawal, it is sometimes observed that ability is directly related to leaving (e.g., Coker 1968, Vaughan 1968, Hackman and Dysinger 1970, Rossmann and Kirk 1970, Fenstemacher 1973, Nicholson 1973). In those instances when the two forms of leaving are captured together, it is not uncom-

mon for studies to report little or no relationship between ability and leaving (e.g., Mock and Yonge 1969, Chase 1970).

2. Cross-sectional studies of student departure such as those by Ammons (1971), Krebs and Liberty (1971), Yuker et al. (1972), and Nicholson (1973) typically compare the attributes of entering students with those who graduate, while others, such as those by Chase (1970) and Snyder and Blocker (1970), concern themselves with descriptive profiles of students who leave.

3. In the synthesis which follows, no attempt will be made to catalog each and every piece of research on student leaving. Only the more useful studies will be cited and sometimes described. Nevertheless, the reader will find that the references provide a relatively wide-ranging and detailed picture of current research on student departure from higher education.

4. Given the obvious relationship between intentions at entry and subsequent departures, it is surprising how infrequently institutions ask their incoming students about the character of their intentions, educational or occupational. Yet it is evident from those institutions that have done so that such information, collected before entry or during the first semester, can be quite a useful predictor of eventual departure from the institution.

At the same time, it is clear that new requirements for the reporting of retention data have put increased importance on data which accurately captures student intent. It is in the institutions' interests not to have their retention figures include persons who did not intend to stay.

5. Goal uncertainty among college students has received a good deal of attention over the past several decades (Ashby, Wall, and Osipow 1966, Baird 1967, Elton and Rose 1971, McGowan 1977, Lowe 1981, Gordon 1985). Two major types of undecided students have been identified, namely, those who change majors while in college and those who have yet to decide on a major when entering college (Titley, Titley, and Wolff 1976, Foote 1980, Slaney 1980). Some degree of uncertainty no doubt reflects the varying levels of development of young adults (Chickering 1969, Perry 1970, Rose and Elton 1971, Peterson 1992), but it also mirrors the failure of institutions of higher education generally to assist students in making important career decisions (Sheffield and Meskill 1974).

6. For some students, especially younger students, parental encouragement may also play a role in aiding early persistence (Bean and Vesper 1992).

7. Interestingly, both Demitroff (1974) and Astin (1975) report that leavers who fail academically are much more likely to characterize their own study habits as poor or below average than students who remain in college. It would seem as if a relatively simple questionnaire at entry would do much to enable institutions to identify new students who require some form of academic assistance early in their collegiate careers.

This is not to say that the current use of entry assessment tests of student skills is not desirable. Quite the contrary. Rather it does say that those tests may not capture all the students who might require academic assistance.

8. It also follows that some institutions which serve such students are more likely to experience higher incidence of academic dismissal than are other institutions. In the urban two-year institutions, in particular, this has resulted in the growth of large-

scale remediation programs which enroll a sizable proportion of entering students (U.S. Department of Education 1985).

9. It is difficult to gauge what proportion of persons classified as voluntary withdrawals are in fact leaving because of they think that academic failure is eminent. Discussions with academic advisers at different institutions lead one to believe that that proportion varies greatly among different types of institutions and is generally highest in those institutions which have very high academic standards and at the same time enroll large numbers of less well prepared students. Estimates range from 10 to as high as 30 percent of voluntary withdrawals leaving for largely academic reasons.

10. There are a few situations where this may not hold. Research on voluntary withdrawal from the University of California at Berkeley, for example, argues that voluntary withdrawals need not be intellectually at odds with other members of the institution (Simpson, Baker, and Mellinger 1980). Rather those voluntary withdrawals who were interviewed tended to exhibit value orientations which deviated from society generally, especially on the question of the value of education in a changing society. In this instance, many leavers reflected the particular belief, characteristic of that period in American youth culture (1960s), that dropping out of college was akin to dropping in to life.

However, this research is clearly a reflection of a particular period of American society and of a particular institution (the University of California at Berkeley) more than it is of events characteristic of the higher educational system generally. It reflects the manner and degree to which broader intellectual and social movements may, over short periods of time, overwhelm institutionally specific forces which also shape student departure. Compared to the students of the 1960s and 1970s, the students of today are demonstrably much more accepting of the importance of higher education even though that acceptance may be primarily governed by their highly pragmatic concerns regarding extrinsic effects of education upon adult occupations.

11. Though college teaching has long been recognized as a central part of the work of faculty, only recently has it been given serious scrutiny by researchers and policy planners alike (Axelrod 1973, Centra 1979, Levinson-Rose and Menges 1981, Tobias 1982, Doyle 1983, Shulman 1985, Wittrock 1985, McKeachie, Pintrich, Lin, and Smith 1986, Erickson and Strommer 1991).

12. There are a few exceptions to this rule. The most notable are the military academies. In those institutions individuals are more likely to leave either very early in the first year or at the end of the second year. At the later point in time individuals are required, as a condition of continued enrollment, to sign a letter of obligation stating their willingness to serve in the military after college graduation. Not surprisingly, the incidence of dropout in those institutions is high between the end of the second year and the beginning of the third.

13. The same conclusion also seems to apply to those situations where female students are a distinct minority on male-dominated campuses (see Brown Project 1980).

14. The concept of center and periphery is drawn from Shils (1961).

15. The difference between positive and negative effects of parents and families appears to depend, in part, on the nature of the family group and the specific relationships the person has with members of that group. Benjamin's (1990) very careful

study of freshmen's daily experiences identified four different family types, each of which had a somewhat different impact upon first-year college experience. Those from "fragile dependent families," for instance, tended to be highly involved with their parents and typically quite dependent upon them, while those from "affectionate independent families" had flexible and quite autonomous relationships with their families.

16. There is a growing body of research on the question of student choice (e.g., Bishop 1977, Dresch and Waldenberg 1978, Jackson 1978, 1981, Manski and Wise 1983, Zemsky and Oedel 1983). Regrettably, much of that work is still conceived within the framework of labor market and/or price differential responses to educational opportunities. Little has been directed to the construction of ethnographic histories of student choice. Though common experience tells us that the process of student choice is recursive—that is, it comprises a series of longitudinally linked choices (e.g., the decision regarding college going presumably precedes that concerning the choice of college)—surprisingly little research has been done to elaborate the stages of student choice. While considerable attention has been paid to the determinants of college going, we have given little time to the study of the determinants of individual choice sets (i.e., the sets of colleges to which individuals apply). Yet what little evidence we have suggests that those sets are surprisingly stable and much less susceptible to external forces than we have commonly assumed (Tierney 1984).

17. The reader should refer to studies such as Carrol's (1978) and Wright's (1985) studies of native American students; London's (1989) and Billson and Brooks-Terry's (1987) studies of first-generation students; Wiseman, Emry and Morgan's (1988) study of disabled students; and Stinson, Scherer and Walter's (1987) research on deaf students.

18. The failure to find a positive effect of social contact upon persistence in two-year colleges may also be due to the manner in which quantitative research on student retention has been carried out. Most frequently, such research has employed standard survey questionnaire techniques to follow the activities of random samples of incoming students. While these procedures may be useful in developing a general picture of departure, they may mask important events which mark the leaving of particular subgroups of students. Similarly, the quantitative analyses commonly utilized by such studies, namely longitudinal path analyses, are subject to errors in measurement and limitations in variance among measured variables which affect their ability to detect important relationships among independent and dependent variables. If the overall levels of social contact of two-year college students are low, there may not be sufficient variance in that measure to ascertain a significant relationship between contact and departure for the population generally and for specific subgroups in the population.

19. This leads to the finding that the incidence of remediation among entering two-year-college students is often quite high. In some urban two-year colleges, for example, as many as one-third of the entering students' course load is entirely remedial in character and over half are in some form of remediation. It is not surprising therefore that the incidence of academic dismissal is high in those situations.

20. It might be expected that departure from technical institutes and professional

schools would resemble that from institutions like the Coast Guard Academy. Yet a recent study of departure among nursing students indicates that their leaving is determined by factors not very different from those observed elsewhere—namely, by patterns of social and intellectual integration and by the frequency and quality of contact with faculty outside the classroom (Munro 1980, 1981).

Chapter 4

1. Oosterbeek (1989) argues that the failure of economic theories to explain student retention lies, in part, in the type of data employed to study student leaving decisions. Specifically, he suggests that expected earnings may be a better measure of student decisions than are the commonly employed data on realized earnings (p. 26).

2. Besides the obvious differences in the organization and composition of the two settings, attendance is largely compulsory in one and voluntary in the other. Attendance in high school is required by law until the age of sixteen or seventeen. No such legal compulsion exists for college attendance. Furthermore, students in high school rarely reside away from home, while nearly half of all college freshmen do so (Astin, Hemond, and Richardson 1982). Moreover, though virtually every member of an age cohort enters high school, slightly less than half enter higher education. Attendance at high school is entirely open, that in the higher educational system is not. For many institutions it is highly selective. As a result the typical high school "dropout" is quite unlike the typical college leaver. Though it would be difficult, it is not impossible to describe "typical" college leavers, as their attributes are a function both of the institution and of the mode of leaving adopted. It is not inaccurate to say that the average high school dropout is more likely to be a person from a poorer family, a member of a racial minority, and a resident of a large urban area than is the average college leaver. More importantly, though those who voluntarily withdraw from college are frequently of higher ability than the average persister, this is rarely the case with the high school dropout.

3. Much of the discussion which follows is drawn from the author's earlier work laying out a theory of student departure (Tinto 1975, 1981). Nevertheless, it differs in a number of ways which reflect the development of that theory and the manner in which empirical tests of its validity have shed light on its strengths and weaknesses (e.g., Terenzini and Pascarella 1977, Pascarella and Terenzini 1979, Pascarella, Duby, and Iverson 1983).

It must also be noted that that work owes much of its original form to the work of Spady (1970, 1971). It was he who first sought to apply Durkheim's theory of suicide to the study of student departure. The reader is urged to refer to that work as well as to those cited above.

4. Solon Kimball, in his introduction to the English translation of *Rites of Passage*, argues that Van Gennep's "scheme du les rites de passage" might be more appropriately translated as "dynamics of the rites of transition" with the term *dynamics* implying a sense of both process and structure (see Van Gennep 1960, v–xix). In his view, Van Gennep was concerned as much with the process of transition as with the structure of the rituals and ceremonies which mark the transitions.

5. As a theory of membership applied to educational settings, the notion of rites of

passage has been used by Leemon (1972) to study the highly ritualized process by which individuals come to be full members in college fraternities.

6. There is much to be said for the use of analogy in social science. Insofar as the character of human behavior does not vary greatly, if at all, among the differing spheres of human existence (family, schools, work, etc.), we can assume that theories and/or models of behavior which have been used effectively to explain behaviors in one sphere can be used, within reason, to study behavior in another. That is precisely what we have done here. In doing so we frequently gain new insight into problems which, heretofore, appeared closed to further inquiry.

7. Though we have yet to extend this line of research to the issues of involvement, effort, and persistence, there is little reason to believe that the same conclusions would not apply as well to those critical outcomes.

8. Finally, near the end of the college career, concerns about the next step beyond college are likely to take center stage. As they do, students are likely to focus on future external communities and the social and intellectual demands those may impose. As they anticipate and/or "get ready" for their future associations, they begin to shift their orientations from the local communities of the college toward the future communities (work, graduate school, etc.) into which they expect entry.

Chapter 5

1. In addition to the obvious, namely calling individuals at each of the cited institutions, the reader is urged to identify the various organizations and associations that are in some way involved in issues pertaining to student retention. Many of these organizations hold annual meetings in which noteworthy programs are either recognized (e.g., NACADA award winners) and/or asked to present information about their programs. Attending these meetings is another valuable way of identifying programs. In all cases, make a point of talking to people involved in those programs. In the same way that they are directed toward helping students, they are also directed toward helping other faculty and staff become more effective in helping their students.

2. This is not to say, however, that such judgments are a simple matter. The literature is replete with discussions of the many pitfalls of trying to assess individual competence in a fair and equitable manner. Nevertheless, we do mean to argue that institutions must, at some point, make those decisions, however difficult. To avoid them is to avoid, in effect, one of the primary responsibilities of institutions of higher education.

3. The issue of retention policy has already received considerable attention elsewhere (e.g., Astin 1975, Cope and Hannah 1975, Noel 1978, Beal and Noel 1980, Kemerer, Baldridge, and Green 1982). Though some of this work has proved to be of value, much has not. Despite the great wealth of information on retention programs, that body of accumulated experience and research has yet to be synthesized in a form readily translatable into action by individual institutions of higher education. The regrettable fact is that much of the work on student retention policy has been flawed in its conception and/or is of such a general sort as to be of little practical use to institutions faced with the practical task of devising their own policies.

Astin's (1975) national study of some 358 institutions of higher education, for instance, relied upon institutional samples of approximately three hundred students whose movements were tracked over a four-year period following college entry. Dropout was defined not as the failure to earn a degree from one's original institution but as the failure to complete a degree from any institution of higher education. A systemic, rather than institutional, definition of dropout was thus employed in the study. Given this definition, detailed analyses were performed and policy recommendations made as to how institutions can go about the task of improving student retention.

Unfortunately one cannot use analyses of system dropout to speak to questions of institutional policy. Many of the persons defined as completers by Astin were in fact persons who left their original institution to finish their degrees elsewhere. As a result Astin's very detailed analyses of patterns of dropout and the resulting policy recommendations which were drawn from those analyses prove to be of dubious validity. Though the analyses may be of considerable value for an understanding of the broader systemic perspective of dropout, they have quite limited value for the purposes of institutional policy.

The studies done by Noel (1978), Beal and Noel (1980), and Noel and Levitz (1985) are, in this regard, of greater institutional value, as they are based upon institutional self-reports of experiences with retention policy. Unfortunately, those experiences are reported in such a general way that it is difficult for any individual institution to know how those recommendations may apply to its own particular situation. More importantly, those recommendations do not take account of the variable nature of student departures and the diverse experiences which characterize the careers of different types of students. Nor do they point up the longitudinal character of the process of student departure and the resulting need to time different actions to the particular stage in the student career when those actions might be most effective. Accordingly, those and other studies of the same type fail to point up the need for institutions to tailor different forms of actions to different modes of student departures and/or types of students among whom those departures occur. In short, they have not provided the specific sorts of recommendations that different types of institutions need in order to attend to the quite variable nature of student departures. This does not mean that these studies have been wrong in their recommendations. Rather it argues that they have not gone far enough.

4. It should be noted that the phrase "typical college student career" is used largely for heuristic purposes. We know that there are a number of different "typical" college career paths which mark the movement of individuals into and through the higher educational system (see chapter 2). Since it is not our intent here to detail each of these dominant modes of college career development, we will focus only on that which is most common, namely that which exhibits a relatively regular flow of movements from prior educational contexts to full-time entry into an institution of higher education at the beginning of the normal academic year, namely, in the fall of any given year.

5. For a discussion of the role of admissions in student retention see Tinto and Wallace (1986).

6. Not infrequently new students who participate in such mentoring programs become student mentors in future programs. In this way institutions often find that such programs become self-generating over time. More importantly, their impact tends to expand over time much like the circular ripples in a pond caused by the dropping of a

pebble. Over the long run, mentor programs can serve as an important regenerating force in the social and intellectual life of an institution.

7. Predictive accuracy speaks to the degree to which pre-entry assessment tests predict the success students will have in the courses for which they serve as screening devices. In their most common usage, test scores are used to place students in different levels of first-year courses, from those requiring substantial remediation to those that call for minor enrichment.

8. As with the Becoming a Master Student program, conferences on University 101 programs are held in various regions of the country. These conferences highlight both the concept of the programs and the various ways in which they have been employed in different institutional settings. Among other benefits, the conferences provide valuable examples of how such programs can be structured and implemented and enable interested parties to make contact with individuals who have had experience running such programs on campus.

9. Readers interested in the area of advising and counseling are urged to contact the National Academic Advising Association (NACADA). Their annual conferences are invaluable sources of information on a variety of issues concerning academic advising and counseling in higher education. In addition, each year they recognize, via awards of excellence, outstanding advising/counseling programs in higher education. The annual awards booklets that describe those programs is a very valuable resource for any institution contemplating establishing an advising system.

10. When presented in a negative fashion, however, that is where advising and counseling are required only for persons "in trouble," they are considerably less effective. That is so because use of such services serves, in the minds of students, to stigmatize the individual as being less able or less successful than one's peers.

11. There are, as noted in chapter 3, exceptions. The most obvious are the military academies that require a commitment to service at the end of the second year of college. It is also true that some students will leave very late in their careers not because they have not been earning college credits but because they have not been making progress toward a major. In these instances, advising or rather the lack thereof is the primary contributing cause to leaving.

12. We have assumed that academic problems arising from having to make the transition to the academic life of the college have for the most part been attended to during the first year. This does not mean that academic assistance programs should not be a continuing part of retention programs. Rather it suggests that they are no longer preeminent in the operation of retention programs. Recall that over the course of the college career and certainly after the first year of college, departure arising from academic failure is a minor part of withdrawal generally.

13. Perhaps this reflects the fact that many four-year commuting institutions also have graduate functions attached to them. Unlike most faculty in the two-year sector, whose sole responsibility is teaching, many faculty in four-year institutions have taken on other responsibilities, not the least of which is research and publication.

Appendix A

1. Both program/department and classroom level assessment are important to any successful institutional assessment strategy. They serve two important purposes.

First, they enable faculty and staff responsible for courses and program requirements to become involved in the assessment process. Second, they allow those persons to determine what types of assessments are better suited to the needs of their own program and/or courses.

2. The problem many institutions face is tracking their students beyond college departure. It is very difficult and very expensive to determine if and to where each and every nongraduating student transfers. For this reason, it is in each institution's interest, certainly those in the public sector, that states develop comprehensive student tracking systems that quickly identify who is going where to college.

3. This does not mean that form of assessment does not matter. Clearly it does. But in the short run endless debates about appropriate measures and methods are counterproductive if the faculty do not acquire the norm of assessing learning in the classroom. It becomes a question of substance only after the faculty become involved and take ownership over assessing learning in their classes. It is for that reason that institutions should concern themselves with incentives to broaden faculty participation in assessment before they worry too much about the "correctness" of the assessments being carried out.

4. This principle of comparative analysis of successful outcomes is the same one that underlies the successful Harvard Seminar on Assessment (Light 1990). It is an institutional experience in using program assessment for institutional improvement that is well worth heeding.

Appendix B

1. This is overstating the point somewhat. The work of Ott, Markewich, and Ochsner (1984), and Girves and Wemmerus (1988) among others has begun to lay out a range of possible models of graduate persistence. It is the contention here, however, that those efforts, with the possible exception of Girves and Wemmerus (1988), have not yet moved toward the sort of comprehensive theory of graduate persistence needed for institutional assessment and policy.

2. It is important to distinguish between institution models of persistence and those that might be understood as system models of persistence. Whereas the former are generally concerned with explaining differential persistence within a specific institutional context, the latter seek to understand differential rates of success as they occur across institutions of higher education. Though the latter may be reduced to institutional contexts, they do not typically focus, as do the former, on institution specific forces in attempting to explain persistence.

3. There are, of course, a variety of possible starting points in the construction of a theory of graduate persistence. One can, for instance, follow the lead of the human-capital school of thought that envisions the process of persistence as primarily shaped by economic forces (e.g., Heath and Tuckman 1986, and Tuckman, Coyle, and Bae 1990). One can also pick up on that strain of work within the literature on social stratification that views persistence as being conditioned by the overriding structure of mobility in society and the control different groups exert on that process (e.g., Turner 1961). Similarly one can draw upon studies of socialization that argue that persistence is largely a matter of the successful adoption of social roles within particular social contexts (e.g., Becker et al. 1961, and Stein and Weidman 1990).

4. Some, if not much, of these differences may reflect the differences in the structure of work in different fields of study. While one can characterize research training in the physical sciences as following the "apprenticeship" model, training in the humanities, arts, and social sciences is highly individualistic. In those fields, students are more likely to conduct research alone. It is also the case that students in the sciences generally begin actual research immediately upon beginning graduate school. This is rarely the case in the arts, humanities, and the social sciences.

5. Lest we forget, doctoral training also entails attendance at meetings of one's professional association and the presentation of papers and sometimes publication of research articles in journals that represent the views and judgments of the field. As this typically applies both for faculty as well as doctoral students, there is an immediate, if somewhat weakened, relationship between the behavior of the larger national community of scholars and that of individuals, both faculty and students, in the local department.

6. When the expectations of the field are at odds with those of the local department—as they might be for a person at a research university seeking entry into an applied field of work—the tension between the present and the future may cause some stress. Indeed, the behaviors that lead the person to succeed in the present may themselves prove to be counterproductive to successful performance in the future. Regrettably, the expectations, indeed skills, of faculty in a research university, who are themselves researchers, are not always the same as those that mark the field of work when that field is applied (e.g., the difference between the experience of a doctoral candidate in educational administration with that of a successful administrator in a school).

7. That this is the case reflects at least two errors. First, most researchers have adopted models of persistence that assume that the process of persistence is invariant across time. Second, they have employed data and methods of analysis that do not permit differentiation between different stages of persistence across time.

8. The use of the term "stages of persistence" in this context is different from that employed in current theories of undergraduate persistence. In the latter case, the concept "stages of departure" refers to the early stages of passage through which a person goes as he/she moves from membership in pre-college community to membership in the academic and social communities within the college. As such it should be understood as most commonly describing the experience of new students during their first year of college. In this case, that is of doctoral persistence, the term "stages of persistence" refers to discrete stages that mark qualitatively different periods leading to the completion of the doctoral degree. In this manner our conversation here is not very different from Girves and Wemmerus's distinction between persistence and degree progress (see Girves and Wemmerus 1988, p. 166).

9. Insofar as the very character of the field of study is conditioned by social judgments about the norms of the profession, attainment of candidacy can be viewed as a form of social initiation into a group whose members have a vested interest in maintaining the norms of that group. And to the degree that that initiation requires prescribed social behaviors and beliefs, it can also be argued that successful completion of a doctoral degree calls for the successful performance of a social role called "graduate student" (see Tinto and Wallace 1986)

10. The issue of what constitutes candidacy is, however, not simple. Though all

institutions have a formal procedure that marks entry to candidacy, the events leading to candidacy may differ widely. In any case, the point here is that this stage of doctoral persistence has its own characteristic demands and requirements that qualitatively set it apart from prior stages.

11. While this is the case, the student may also become increasingly influenced by the norms of the wider external community that defines the profession or field of work to which the student seeks entry. In anticipating entry to that field, the student may become even more sensitive to the norms that govern it. At the same time that the student seeks to complete the requirements of the dissertation as defined locally, he/she may also strive to fulfill the expectations of the field in the expectation that doing so will assist in gaining entry to it.

12. It might be observed that the typical pattern of financial support for doctoral study is frontloaded. That is to say that monies are more generally available during the early stages of persistence and more difficult to obtain afterward. The logic of this analysis suggests, however, that the reverse pattern of support may make more sense (see Pruitt and Isaac 1985).

13. We have made no attempt here to distinguish between those persons who enter with a master's degree and those who enter either from college directly or from other areas of endeavor without an advanced degree.

14. Recent research (Zwick 1991) indicates that, given entry to doctoral study, subsequent persistence is not significantly related to differences in individual ability as by Graduate Record Examinations (Verbal and Analytic). This finding, however, should not be taken to suggest that ability does not matter. Rather it says that given the already high levels of ability among entrants and given the very limited range of ability that typically occurs within that population, that measured differences in ability do not help explain differences in completion. Of course, limitation in variance in ability alone can explain that finding.

15. Here the notion of "sponsored mobility" may be used to describe the actions of the faculty on behalf of the student (Turner 1961). That is to say that faculty may be seen as "sponsoring" their students as they seek entry to the occupation. In this regard, there is a link between the sponsoring capacity of the individual faculty and that of the institution to which we referred earlier when we spoke of the "status conferring" abilities of the institution.

16. Without belaboring the obvious, the issue of minority persistence in graduate education is simply too important not to warrant our immediate attention. Among other things, we must understand the institutional dynamics that characterize successful minority doctoral completion (Thomas, Clewell and Pearson 1991) and make better sense of the particular attributes of advisers and mentors who are successful in assisting minority doctoral completion.

References

Abedi, J. and E. Benkin. 1987. The effects of students' academic, financial, and demographic variables on time to the doctorate. *Research in Higher Education* 27: 1–14.

Abel. W. H. 1966. Attrition and the student who is certain. *Personnel and Guidance Journal* 44: 1024–45.

Adelman, C. 1984. *Starting with students: Notable programs, promising approaches, and other improvement efforts in American postsecondary education.* A report prepared for the National Commission on Excellence in Education. Washington, D.C.: National Institute of Education.

Alexander, K., and B. Eckland. 1974. Sex differences in the educational attainment process. *American Sociological Review* 39: 668–82.

Allen, W. 1985. Black student, white campus: Structural, interpersonal, and psychological correlates of success. *Journal of Negro Education* 54: 134–47.

Allen, W., et al. 1982. Black student educational experiences and outcomes at predominantly white universities. Paper presented at the annual meeting of the American Educational Research Association, New York.

American College Testing Program. 1983. Data compiled from the ACT Institutional Data File for 1983. Iowa City: Iowa: American College Testing Program.

———. 1986. Data compiled from the ACT Institutional Data File for 1986. Iowa City, Iowa: American College Testing Program.

———. 1990. Data compiled from the ACT Institutional Data File for 1990. Iowa City, Iowa: American College Testing Program.

———. 1992. Data compiled from the ACT Institutional Data File for 1992. Iowa City, Iowa: American College Testing Program.

American Council on Education. 1984. *A fact book on higher education.* Compiled by C. Ottinger. Washington, D.C.: American Council on Education and Macmillan Publishing Co.

Ammons, R. M. 1971. *Academic persistence of some students at St. Petersburg Junior College.* Report by the Office of Testing Services, Saint Petersburg Junior College, St. Petersburg, Fla.

Amos, Arthur K., Jr. 1990. *Effort and gain: The UC Davis undergraduate experience.* A report of Student Affairs Research and Information, University of California, Davis, August.

Anderson, K. L. 1981. Post high school experiences and college attrition. *Sociology of Education* 54: 1–15.

———. 1988. The impact of colleges and the involvement of male and female students. *Sociology of Education.* 61: 160–77.

Ashar, H., and R. Skenes. 1993. Can Tinto's student departure model be applied to nontraditional students? *Adult Education Quarterly* 43: 90–100.

Ashby, J., A. Wall, and S. Osipow. 1966. Vocational certainty and indecision in college freshmen. *Personnel and Guidance Journal* 44: 1037–41.

Astin, A. W. 1964. Personal and environmental factors associated with college dropouts among high aptitude students. *Journal of Educational Psychology* 55: 219–27

———. 1972. *College dropouts: A national profile.* American Council on Education Research Reports. Washington, D.C.: American Council on Education.

———. 1975. *Preventing students from dropping out.* San Francisco: Jossey-Bass.

———. 1979. *Four critical years.* San Francisco: Jossey-Bass.

———. 1984. Student involvement: A developmental theory for higher education. *Journal of College Student Personnel* 25: 297–308.

———. 1985. *Achieving educational excellence.* San Francisco: Jossey-Bass.

———. 1991. What really matters in general education: Provocative findings from a national study of student outcomes. Address presented at the Association of General and Liberal Studies Meeting, Seattle.

———. 1993. *What matters in college: Four critical years revisited.* San Francisco: Jossey-Bass.

Astin, A. W., M. K. Hemond, and G. T. Richardson. 1982. *The American freshman. National norms of fall 1982.* Los Angeles: Graduate School of Education, University of California.

Astin, A. W., W. S. Korn, and E. R. Berz. 1990. *The American freshman. National norms for fall 1990.* Los Angeles: Graduate School of Education, University of California.

Atkinson, D. R., R. G. Jennings, and L. Liongson. 1990. Minority students' reasons for not seeking counseling and suggestions for improving services. *Journal of College Student Development* 31: 342–50.

Attinasi, L. C., Jr. 1986. *Getting in: Chicano students' perceptions of their college-going behavior with implications for their freshman year persistence.* Unpublished doctoral dissertation. Arizona State University, Tempe.

———. 1989. Getting in: Mexican Americans' perceptions of university attendance and the implications for freshman year persistence. *Journal of Higher Education* 60: 247–77.

———. 1991. Phenomenological interviewing in the conduct of institutional research: An argument and an illustration. *The Association for Institutional Research Professional File* 38: 1–8.

Axelrod, J. 1973. *The university teacher as artist.* San Francisco: Jossey-Bass.

Baird, L. L. 1967. *The undecided student—How different is he?* American College Testing Program Research Report, no. 2. Iowa City, Iowa: American College Testing Program.

———. 1990. Campus climate: Using surveys for policy-making and understanding. *New Directions for Institutional Research,* no. 68 (Winter): 35–46.

Bandura, A. 1977. Self-efficiency: Toward a unifying theory of behavioral change. *Psychological Review* 84: 191–215.

Baum, S. 1987. Financial aid to low-income college students: Its history and prospects. A paper prepared for the Institute for Research on Poverty, University of Wisconsin.

Beahan, L. T. 1966. Initial psychiatric interviews and the dropout rate of college students. *The Journal of the American College Health Association* 14: 305–8.

Beal, P. E., and L. Noel. 1980. *What works in student retention.* Iowa City: American College Testing Program and the National Center for Higher Education Management Systems.

Bean, J. P. 1980. Dropouts and turnover: The synthesis and test of a causal model of student attrition. *Research in Higher Education* 12: 155–87.

———. 1982. Student attrition, intentions, and confidence. *Research in Higher Education* 17: 291–320.

———. 1983. The application of a model of turnover in work organizations to the student attrition process. *The Review of Higher Education* 6: 129–48.

———. 1990. Why students leave: Insights from research. In *The strategic management of college enrollments,* edited by D. Hossler, J. Bean, and Associates. San Francisco: Jossey-Bass.

Bean, J. P., and B. S. Metzner. 1985. A conceptual model of nontraditional student attrition. Paper presented at the annual meeting of the Association for the Study of Higher Education, Chicago.

Bean, J. P., and N. Vesper. 1992. Student dependency theory: An explanation of student retention in college. A paper presented at the annual meeting of the Association for the Study of Higher Education, Minneapolis.

Becker, H., et al. 1951. *Boys in white: Student culture in medical school.* Chicago: University of Chicago Press.

Benjamin, M. 1990. *Freshman daily experience: Implications for policy, research and theory.* Student development monograph series, vol. 4, University of Guelph, Ontario, Canada.

Benkin, E. 1984. Where have all the doctoral students gone: A study of doctoral attrition at UCLA. A Ph.D. dissertation, The University of California, Los Angeles.

Bennett, W. J. 1984. *To reclaim a legacy.* Washington, D.C.: National Endowment for the Humanities.

Berg, H. M., and M. A. Ferber. 1983. Men and women graduate students: Who succeeds and why? *Journal of Higher Education,* 54: 629–648.

Billson, J. M., and M. Brooks-Terry. 1987. In search of the silken purse: Factors in the attrition among first-generation students. *College and University* 58: 57–75.

Bishop, J. 1977. The effect of public policies on the demand for higher education. *Journal of Human Resources* 12: 285–307.

Blanc, R. A., L. E. Debuhr, and D. C. Martin. 1983. Breaking the attrition cycle: The effects of supplemental instruction on undergraduate performance and attrition. *Journal of Higher Education* 54: 80–90.

Blanchfield, W. C. 1971. *College dropout identification: A case study.* New York: Utica College.

Bligh, D. M. 1977. Are teaching innovations in post-secondary education irrelevant? In *Adult learning: Psychological research and applications,* edited by M. J. A. Howe, pp. 249–66. New York: John Wiley and Sons.

Bonwell, C., and J. Eison. 1991. *Active learning: Creating excitement in the classroom.* ASHE-ERIC Higher Education Reports, edited by Jonathan Fife. Washington D.C.: George Washington University.

Boshier, R. 1973. Educational participation and dropout: A theoretical model. *Adult Education* 23: 255–82.

Bowen, W. and T. A. Finegan. 1969. *The economics of labor force participation.* Princeton: Princeton University Press.

Bowles, S., and H. Gintis. 1976. *Schooling in capitalist America.* New York: Basic Books.

Boyer, E. L. 1987. *College: The undergraduate experience in America.* New York: Harper and Row Publishers.

Braxton, J. 1990. How students choose college. In *The strategic management of college enrollments,* edited by D. Hossler, J. Bean, and Associates. San Francisco: Jossey-Bass.

Braxton, J., and E. Brier. 1989. Melding organizational and interactional theories of student attrition: A path analytic study. *The Review of Higher Education* 13: 47–61.

Breneman, D., and S. Nelson. 1981. *Financing community college: An economic perspective.* Washington D.C.: Brookings Institution.

Brower, A. 1992. The "second half" of student integration. *Journal of Higher Education* 63: 441–462.

Brown, F. G. 1960. Identifying college dropouts with Minnesota Counseling Inventory. *Personnel and Guidance Journal* 39: 280–82.

Brown Project. 1980. *Men and women learning together: A study of college students in the late 70's.* Office of the Provost, Brown University.

Cabrera, A. F. 1987. *Ability to pay and college persistence.* An unpublished doctoral dissertation, University of Wisconsin.

Cabrera, A.F., M.B. Castaneda, A. Nora, and D. Hengstler. 1992. The convergence between two theories of college persistence. *Journal of Higher Education* 63: 143–164.

Cabrera, A.F., A. Nora, and M. Castaneda. 1992. The role of finances in the persistence process: A structural model. *Research in Higher Education* 33: 571–593.

Cabrera, A. F., J. O. Stampen, and W. L. Hansen. 1990. Exploring the effects of ability to pay on persistence in college. *The Review of Higher Education* 13: 303–36.

Cage, M. C. 1992. Fewer students get bachelor's degrees in four years, study finds. *The Chronicle of Higher Education* 38 (July 15): A29–A36.

Campbell, R. T. 1980. The freshman class of the University of Wisconsin 1964. In *Longitudinal perspectives on educational attainment,* edited by A. Kerckhoff. Greenwich, Conn.: JAI Press.

Carrol, R. 1978. Academic performance and cultural marginality. *Journal of American Indian Education* 18: 16–36.

Carroll, D. 1985. *Postsecondary status and persistence of high school graduates of 1980.* Longitudinal Studies Branch, National Center for Educational Statistics, U.S. Department of Education. Washington, D.C.: U.S. Government Printing Office.

———. 1987. Student financial assistance and consequences. A paper presented at the annual meeting of the American Statistical Association, San Francisco.

———. 1988. *The effects of grants on college persistence.* Washington, D.C.: U.S. Department of Education, Office of Educational Research and Improvement.

———. 1989. *College persistence and degree attainment for 1980 high school graduates: Hazards for transfers, stopouts, and part-timers.* Washington, D.C.: U.S. Department of Education, National Center for Education Statistics.

Centra, J . 1979. *Determining faculty effectiveness.* San Francisco: Jossey-Bass.

Chacon, M. A., et al. 1982. *Chicanas in postsecondary education.* A report to the Ford Foundation, Center for Research on Women. Palo Alto, Calif.: Stanford University.

Chacon, M. A., E. G. Cohen, and S. Strover. 1983. Chicanas and chicanos: Barriers to progress in higher education. Paper presented for the Conference on the Latino College Student. Princeton: Educational Testing Service.

Chaney, B., and E. Farris. 1991. *Survey on retention at higher education institutions.* Higher Education Surveys Report, Survey Number 14. A report written for Planning and Evaluation Service, Office of the Undersecretary, U.S. Department of Education.

Chase, C. I. 1970. The college dropout: His high school prologue. *Bulletin of the National Association of Secondary School Principals* 54: 66–71.

Chickering, A. W. 1969. *Education and identity.* San Francisco: Jossey-Bass.

———. 1974. *Commuting versus resident students.* San Francisco: Jossey-Bass.

Christie, N. G., and S. M. Dinham (1991). Institutional and external influences on social integration in the freshman year. *Journal of Higher Education* 62: 412–36.

Clark, B. 1960. The "cooling-out" function in higher education. *American Journal of Sociology* 64: 569–76.

Clark, B., and M. Trow. 1966. The organizational context. In *College peer groups: Problems and prospects for research,* edited by T. M. Newcomb and E. K. Wilson. Chicago: Aldine.

Claxton, C., and R. Murrell, 1987. *Learning styles: Implications for improving educational practices.* ASHE-ERIC Higher Education Reports, edited by Jonathan Fife. Washington D.C.: George Washington University.

Clewell, B. 1987. Retention of black and hispanic doctoral students. GRE Board Research Report No.83-4R, *ETS Research Report 87-10.* Princeton: Educational Testing Service.

Clewell, B., and M. Ficklen. 1986. *Improving minority retention in higher education: A search for effective institutional practices.* Princeton: Educational Testing Service.

Coker, D. 1968. *Diversity of intellective and non-intellective characteristics between persisting students and non-persisting students among campuses.* Washington, D.C.: Office of Education Report, BR-6-2728.

Coleman, J. S. 1961. *The adolescent society.* New York: Free Press.

Coleman, J. S., T. Hoffer, and S. Kilgore. 1982. *Achievement in high school. Public and private schools compared.* New York: Basic Books.

College Board. 1984. *College bound seniors 1983.* A report of the College Board, New York.

Collins, R. 1971. Functional and conflict theories of educational stratification. *American Sociological Review* 36: 1002–12.

Cook, M., and A. Swanson. 1978. The Interaction of student and program variables for the purposes of developing a model for predicting graduation from graduate programs over a 10-year period. *Research in Higher Education* 8: 83–91.

Cope, R., and W. Hannah. 1975. *Revolving college doors.* New York: John Wiley and Sons.

Cosgrove, T. J. 1986. The effects of participation in a mentoring-transcript program on freshmen. *Journal of College Student Personnel* 27: 119–24.

Creamer, D. 1980. Educational advising for student retention: An institutional perspective. *Community College Review* 7: 11–18.

Cross, K. P. 1971. *Beyond the open door: New students to higher education.* San Francisco: Jossey-Bass.

———. 1981. *Adults as learners: Increasing participation and facilitating learning.* San Francisco: Jossey-Bass.

Cross, K. P., and T. Angelo. 1988. *Classroom assessment techniques: A handbook for faculty.* Ann Arbor: National Center for Research to Improve Postsecondary Teaching and Learning.

Crosson, P. H. 1988. Four-year college and university environments for minority degree achievement. *The Review of Higher Education* 11: 365–82.

Crouse, R. 1982. Peer network therapy: An intervention with the social climate of students in residence halls. *Journal of College Student Personnel* 23: 105–8.

Cutrona, C. E. 1982. Transition to college: Loneliness and the process of social adjustment. In *Loneliness: A sourcebook of current research, theory and therapy,*. edited by L. Peplau and D. Perlman. New York: John Wiley and Sons.

Darkenwald, C. G. 1981. *Retaining adult students.* Information Series, no. 225. Columbus, Ohio: Educational Resources Information Center Clearinghouse on Adult, Career, and Vocational Education, ED 205 773.

Demitroff, J. F. 1974. Student persistence. *College and University* 49: 553–57.

Donovan, R. 1984. Path analysis of a theoretical model of persistence in higher education among low-income black youth. *Research in Higher Education* 21: 243–52.

Doyle, W. 1983. Academic work. *Review of Educational Research* 53: 159–200.

Dresch, S., and A. Waldenberg. 1978. *Labor market incentives, intellectual competence and college attendance.* New Haven: Institute for Democratic and Economic Studies.

Duncan, 0. D., D. L. Featherman, and B. Duncan. 1972. *Socioeconomic background and achievement.* New York: Seminar Press.

Durkheim, E. 1951. *Suicide.* Translated by J. A. Spaulding and G. Simpson. Glencoe: The Free Press. Originally published as *Le suicide: Etude de sociologie.* Paris: Felix Alcan, 1897.

Eagle, E., and C. D. Carroll. 1988a. *A descriptive summary of 1972 high school seniors: Fourteen years later.* National Center for Educational Statistics, Report CS 88-406. Washington D.C.: U.S. Government Printing Office.

———. 1988b. *Postsecondary enrollment, persistence, and attainment for 1972, 1980, and 1982 high school graduates.* National Center for Educational Statistics, Report CS 89-301. Washington, D.C.: U.S. Government Printing Office.

Eaton, J. S. 1990. Strengthening the transfer function: From "zero-sum" game to a "win-win" situation. *Leadership Abstracts* 3: XY–YZ.

———, ed. 1992. *Faculty and transfer: Academic partnerships at work.* Washington, D.C.: National Center for Academic Achievement and Transfer of the American Council on Education.

Eccles, J. et al. 1983. Expectancies, values, and academic behaviors. In *Achievement and achievement motives: Psychological and sociological approaches,* edited by J. Spencer. San Francisco: W. H. Freeman and Company.

Eckland, B. K. 1964a. A source of error in college attrition studies. *Sociology of Education* 38: 60–72.

———. 1964b. College dropouts who came back. *Harvard Educational Review* 34: 402–20.

———. 1965. Social class and college graduation: Some misconceptions corrected. *American Journal of Sociology* 70: 36–50.

Eckland, B. K., and L. B. Henderson. 1981. *College attainment four years after high school.* Report prepared for the National Center for Educational Statistics, Office of Educational Research and Improvement, U.S. Department of Education. Research Triangle Park, N.C.: Research Triangle Institute.

Eddins, D. D. 1982. A causal model of the attrition of specially admitted black students in higher education. Paper presented at the annual meeting of the American Educational Research Association, New York.

Ehrenberg, R., and P. Mavros. 1992. Do doctoral students' financial support patterns affect their times-to-degree and completion probabilities? Working Paper No. 3. Institute for Labor Market Policies, School of Industrial and Labor Relations. Ithaca: Cornell University.

Elliott, D., and H. Voss. 1974. *Delinquency and dropout.* Lexington: D. C. Heath.

Ellis, David. 1985. *Becoming a master student.* 5th ed. Rapid City: College Survival, Inc..

Elton, C., and H. Rose. 1971. A longitudinal study of the vocationally undecided male student. *Journal of Vocational Behavior* 1: 85–92.

Endo, J. J., and R. L. Harpel. 1982. The effect of student-faculty interaction on students' educational outcomes. *Research in Higher Education* 16: 115–35.

Erickson, B. L., and D. W. Strommer. 1991. *Teaching college freshman.* San Francisco: Jossey-Bass.

Erwin, T. 1991. *Assessing student learning and development.* San Francisco: Jossey-Bass.

Ethington, C. A. 1990. A psychological model of student persistence. *Research in Higher Education* 31: 279–293.

Featherman, D. L., and R. Hauser. 1978. *Opportunity and change.* New York: Academic Press.

Fenstemacher, W. 1973. College dropouts: Theories and research findings. In *Tomorrow's imperatives today,* edited by R. Cope. Seattle: Association for Institutional Research.

Fetters, W. 1977. *Withdrawal from institutions of higher education: An appraisal with longitudinal data involving diverse institutions.* Longitudinal Studies Branch, National Center for Educational Statistics. U.S. Department of Education. Washington, D.C.: U.S. Government Printing Office.

Fleming, J. 1985. *Blacks in college.* San Francisco: Jossey-Bass.

Flores, J. L. 1992. Persisting hispanic american college students: Characteristics that lead to baccalaureate degree attainment. A paper presented at the annual meeting of the American Educational Research Association, Chicago.

Foote, B. 1980. Determined and undetermined major students: How different are they? *Journal of College Student Personnel* 21: 29–34.

Forrest, A. 1982. *Increasing student competence and persistence.* A report of the College Outcome Measures Project. Iowa City: American College Testing Program.

Frank, A. C., and B. A. Kirk. 1975. Differences in outcomes for users and nonusers of university counseling and psychiatric services. *Journal of Counseling Psychology* 22: 252–58.

Friedlander, J. 1980. *The importance of quality of effort in predicting college student attainment.* An unpublished Ph.D. dissertation, University of California, Los Angeles.

Frierson, H. T., Jr. 1986. Two intervention methods: Effects on groups of predominantly Black nursing students' board scores. *Journal of Research and Development in Education* 19: 18–23.

Frost, S. 1991. *Academic advising for student success: A system of shared responsibility.* ASHE-ERIC Higher Education Reports, edited by Jonathan Fife. Washington, D.C.: George Washington University.

Gabelnick, F., J. MacGregor, R. Matthews, and B.Smith. 1990. *Learning communities: Creating connections among students, faculty, and disciplines.* New Directions for Teaching and Learning, no. 41. San Francisco: Jossey-Bass.

Gardner, J., and A. J. Jewler. 1985. *College is only the beginning.* Belmont: Wadsworth Publishing Company.

Garrison, D. R. 1985. Predicting dropout in adult basic education using interaction effects among school and nonschool variables. *Adult Education Quarterly* 36: 25–38.

Getzlaf, S. B., et al. 1984. Two types of voluntary undergraduate attrition: An application of Tinto's model. *Research in Higher Education* 20: 257–68.

Giles-Gee, H. F. 1988. Increasing the retention of Black students: A multimethod approach. *Journal of College Student Development* 30: 196–200.

Girves, J., and V. Wemmerus. 1988. Developing models of graduate student degree progress. *Journal of Higher Education* 59: 163–89.

Gleason, M. 1986. Better communication in large courses. *College Teaching* 34: 20–24.

Glennen, R., and D. Baxley. 1985. Reduction of attrition through intrusive advising. *National Association of Student Personnel Administrators* 22: 10–14.

Goodsell, A., M. Maher, and V. Tinto. 1992. *Collaborative learning: A sourcebook for higher education.* University Park: National Center on Postsecondary Teaching, Learning, and Assessment.

Goplerud, E. 1980. Social support and stress during the first year of graduate school. *Professional Psychology* 11: 283–90.

Gordon, V. 1985. Students with uncertain academic goals. In *Increasing student retention,* edited by L. Noel and R. Levitz. San Francisco: Jossey-Bass.

Gosman, E., et al. 1983. Predicting student progression: The influence of race and other student and institutional characteristics on college student performance. *Research in Higher Education* 18: 209–37.

Grace, H. A. 1957. Personality factors and college attrition. *Peabody Journal of Education* 35: 36–40.

Gurin, G., et al. 1968. *Characteristics of entering freshmen related to attrition in the literary college of a large state university.* Final report, University of Michigan, Project No. 1938, U.S. Office of Education.

Guthrie, L. F., G. P. Guthrie, and H. Tokunaga. 1991. *Minority achievement and retention: Evaluation of the California State University summer bridge and intensive learning experience programs (1985–1991): Final report.* San Francisco: Far West Laboratory for Educational Research and Development.

Hackman, R., and W. S. Dysinger. 1970. Commitment to college as a factor in student attrition. *Sociology of Education* 43: 311–24.

Hall, B. 1982. College warm-up: Easing the transition to college. *Journal of College Student Personnel* 23: 280–81.

Haller, A. 0., and J. Woelfel. 1972. Significant others and their expectations: Concepts and instruments to measure interpersonal influence on status aspirations. *Rural Sociology* 37: 591–622.

Hannah, W. 1971. Personality differentials between lower division dropouts and stay-ins. *Journal of College Student Personnel* 12: 16–19.

Hanson, G., and R. Taylor. 1970. Interaction of ability and personality: Another look at the drop-out problem in an institute of technology. *Journal of Counseling Psychology* 17: 540–45.

Hartnett, R. T. 1981. Sex differences in the environments of graduate students and faculty. GRE Board Research Report, no. 77-26R, Research Report 81-15, June.

Heath, J., and H. Tuckman. 1986. The effects of tuition level and financial aid on the demand for advanced terminal degrees. *Economics of Education Review* 6: 227–38.

Heilbrun, A. B. 1965. Personality factors in college dropouts. *Journal of Applied Psychology* 49: 1–7.

Hill, C. 1979. Capacities, opportunities and educational investments: The case of the high school dropout. *Review of Economics and Statistics* 61: 9–20.

Hood, D. W. 1990. A look at retention of afro-american male students at a predominantly white institution. Paper presented at the annual meeting of the American Educational Research Association, Boston.

Hossler, D., J. Bean, and Associates. 1990. *The strategic management of college enrollments.* San Francisco: Jossey-Bass.

House, J. D. 1992. The relationship between academic self-concept, achievement related expectancies, and college attrition. *Journal of College Student Development.* 33: 5–10.

House, J. S. 1981. *Work stress and social support.* Reading: Addison-Wesley.

Husband, R. L. 1976. Significant others: A new look at attrition. Paper presented at the seventh annual meeting on Future Solutions to Today's Problems sponsored by the Association for Innovation in Higher Education, Philadelphia.

Iffert, R. E. 1956. Study of college student retention and withdrawal. *College and University* 31: 435–37.

———. 1958. *Retention and withdrawal of college students.* Bulletin 1958, no. 1. U.S. Department of Health, Education and Welfare, Office of Education. Washington, D.C.: U.S. Government Printing Office.

———. 1965. *College applicants, entrants, dropouts.* Bulletin 1965, no. 29. U.S. Department of Health, Education and Welfare, Office of Education. Washington, D.C.: U.S. Government Printing Office.

Irvine, D. W. 1966. Multiple prediction of college graduation from preadmission data. *The Journal of Experimental Education* 35: 84–89.

Iwai, S. I., and W. D. Churchill. 1982. College attrition and the financial support systems of students. *Research in Higher Education* 17: 105–13.

Jackson, G. A. 1978. Financial aid and student enrollment. *Journal of Higher Education* 49: 548–74.

———. 1981. *Sociologic, economic and policy influences on couege-going.*

Program report no. 81-B9, Institute for Research on Educational Finance and Governance, Stanford University, Palo Alto.

Jackson, G. A., and G. B. Weathersby. 1975. Individual demand for higher education. *Journal of Higher Education* 46: 623–52.

Jacobi, M. 1991. Mentoring and undergraduate academic success: A literature review. *Review of Educational Research* 6: 505–32.

Janasiewicz, B. 1987. Campus leaving behavior. *National Academic Advising Association Journal* 7: 23–30.

Jensen, E. L. 1981. Student financial aid and persistence in college. *Journal of Higher Education* 52: 280–94.

———.1983. Financial aid and educational outcomes: A review. *College and University* 20: 287–302.

Johansson, C., and J. Rossmann. 1973. Persistence at a liberal arts college: A replicated five-year longitudinal study. *Journal of Counselling Psychology* 20: 1–9.

Johnson, D., and R. Johnson. 1987. *Learning together and alone: Cooperative, competitive, and individualistic learning.* Englewood Cliffs, N.J.: Prentice-Hall.

Johnson, D., R. Johnson, and E. Holubec. 1986. *Circles of learning: Cooperation in the classroom.* Edina: Interaction Books.

Johnson, D., R. Johnson, and K. Smith. 1992. *Cooperative learning: Increasing college faculty instructional productivity.* ASHE-ERIC Higher Education Report No.4. Washington, D.C.: George Washington University.

Kamens, D. 1971. The college "charter" and college size: Effects on occupational choice and college attrition. *Sociology of Education* 44: 270–96.

Johnson, R., and C. Rodriguez. 1991. How policy makers address minority student retention: Whose interests are being served? A paper presented at the annual meeting of the Association for the Study of Higher Education. Boston, Massachusetts.

Karabel, J. 1972. Community college and social stratification. *Harvard Educational Review* 42: 521–62.

Kaufman, M. A., and D. G. Creamer. 1991. Influences of student goals for college on freshman year quality of effect and growth. *Journal of College Student Development* 32: 197–206.

Kaun, D. 1974. The college dropout and occupation choice. In *Higher education and the labor market,* edited by M. Gordon. New York: McGraw-Hill Book Company.

Kemerer, F., J. V. Baldridge, and K. Green. 1982. *Strategies for effective enrollment management.* Washington, D.C.: American Association of State Colleges and Universities.

Kendrick, S. A., and C. L. Thomas. 1970. Transition from school to college. *Review of Education Research* 40: 151–79.

Keniston, K. 1968. *Young radicals.* New York: Harcourt Brace Jovanovich.

Kester, D. 1971. *The lesson from the three-year NORCAL attrition study: Many of the potential dropouts can be helped.* Phase III Final Report. Report to the California State Coordinating Council for Higher Education and the Northern California Community College Research Group.

King, A. 1990. Essentials of a minority retention program. A paper presented at the third annual conference on racial and ethnic relations in American higher education. Santa Fe, New Mexico.

Knop, E. 1967. From a symbolic interactionist perspective: Some notes on college dropouts. *The Journal of Educational Research.* 60: 450–52.

Kolstad, A. J. 1981. What college dropout and dropin rates tell us. *American Education* 17: 31–33.

Krebs, R. E., and P. G. Liberty. 1971. *A comparative study of three groups of withdrawal students on ten factor variables derived from a 36-problem self-report inventory.* Austin: University of Texas.

Krotseng, M. 1992. Predicting persistence from the student adaptation to college questionnaire: Early warning or siren song? *Research in Higher Education* 33: 99–111.

Kuh, G. D. 1990. Assessing student culture. *New Directions for Institutional Research,* no. 68 (Winter): 47–60.

Kuh, G. D., and R. E. Andreas. 1991. It's about time: Using qualitative methods in student life studies. *Journal of College Student Development* 32: 397–405.

Kuh, G. D., J. H. Schuh, E. J. Whitt, and Associates. 1991. *Involving colleges.* San Francisco: Jossey-Bass.

Lang, M., and C. A. Ford. 1988. *Black student retention in higher education.* Springfield, Ill.: Charles C. Thomas Publisher.

Lavin, D. E., J. Murtha, and B . Kaufman. 1984. *Long-term graduation rates of students at the City University of New York.* City University of New York, Office of Institutional Research and Analysis. New York.

Lawson, L. 1985. Doctoral student attrition: A role theory approach. Ph.D. dissertation, University of California, Santa Barbara.

Lazarus, R. S. 1980. The stress and coping paradigm. In *Theoretical bases for psychopathology,* edited by C. Elsdorfer, D. Cohen, and A. Kleiman. New York: Spectrum.

Lazarus, R. S., and R. Launier. 1978. Stress related transactions between person and environment. In *Perspectives in interactional psychology,* edited by L. Pervin and M. Lewis. New York: Plenum Press.

Leemon, T. A. 1972. *The rites of passage in a student culture: A study of the dynamics of transition.* New York: Teachers College Press.

Lembesis, A. 1965. A study of students who withdrew from college during their second, third or fourth years. Ph.D. dissertation, University of Oregon.

Lenning. O., P. Beal, and K. Sauer. 1980. *Retention and attrition. Evidence for action and research.* Boulder: National Center for Higher Education Management Systems.

Leslie, L. L., and P. T. Brinkman. 1988. *The economic value of higher education.* New York: Macmillan.

Levin, M. E., and J. R. Levin. 1991. A critical examination of academic retention programs for at-risk minority college students. *Journal of College Student Development* 32: 323–34.

Levinson-Rose, J., and R. Menges. 1981. Improving college teaching: A critical review of research. *Review of Educational Research* 51: 403–34.

Lichtman, C. M., A. R. Bass, and J. W. Ager, Jr. 1989. Differences between Black and White students in attrition patterns from an urban commuter university. *The Journal of College Student Development* 30: 4–9.

Light, R. 1990. *The Harvard seminar on assessment: Final report.* Cambridge: Harvard Graduate School of Education.

Light, R, J. Singer, and J. Willet. 1990. *By design: Planning research in higher education.* Cambridge: Harvard University Press.

Lightfoot, S. 1983. *The good high school.* New York: Basic Books.

London, H. B. 1989. Breaking away: A study of first generation college students and their families. *The American Journal of Sociology* 97: 144–70.

Loo, C. M., and G. Rolison. 1986. Alienation of ethnic minority students at a predominanatly white university. *Journal of Higher Education* 57: 58–77.

Lowe, B. 1981. The relationship between vocational interest differentiation and career undecidedness. *Journal of Vocational Behavior* 19: 346–49.

Lowe, M. 1989. *Chicano students perceptions of their community college-going experience with implications for persistence: A naturalistic inquiry.* An unpublished doctoral dissertation, Arizona State University, Tempe.

McCarthy, M. E., G. M. Pretty, and V. Catano. 1990. Psychological sense of community and student burnout. *Journal of College Student Development* 31: 211–16.

McCool, A. 1984. Improving the admission and retention of Hispanic students: A dilemma for higher education. *College Student Journal* 18: 28–36.

McGowan, A. S. 1977. Vocational maturity and anxiety among vocationally undecided and indecisive students. *Journal of Vocational Behavior* 10: 196–204.

McKeachie, W. 1986. *Teaching tips: A guide for the beginning college teacher.* (8th ed.). Lexington, Mass.: Heath, 1986.

McKeachie, W., P. Pintrich, Y. Lin, and D. Smith. 1986. *Teaching and learning in the college classroom: A review of the research literature.* Ann Arbor: University of Michigan, National Center for Research to Improve Postsecondary Teaching and Learning.

McNeely, J. H. 1937. *College student mortality.* U.S. Office of Education, Bulletin 1937, no. 11. Washington, D.C.: U.S. Government Printing Office.

Magolda, M. B. 1990. The impact of the freshman year on epistemological development: Gender differences. *Review of Higher Education* 13: 259–84.

Malaney, G. 1988. Graduate education as an area of research in higher education. *Higher Education: Handbook of Theory and Research,* vol. 4. New York: Agathon Press.

Mallette, B., and A. Cabrera. 1991. Determinants of withdrawal behavior: An exploratory study. *Research in Higher Education* 32: 179–94.

Manski, C., and D. Wise. 1983. *College choice in America.* Cambridge, Mass.: Harvard University Press.

Marks, E. 1967. Student perceptions of college persistence and their intellective, personality and performance correlates. *Journal of Educational Psychology* 58: 210–11.

Martin, A. D., Jr. 1985. Financial aid. In *Increasing student retention*, edited by L. Noel and R. Levitz. San Francisco: Jossey-Bass.

Martin, O. L. 1990. The college milieu for the 1990's: Increasing black student retention rates on white campuses. A paper presented at the annual meeting of the American Educational Research Association, Boston.

Matchett, William. 1988. *A study of attrition among graduate students at New Mexico State University.* Las Cruces: New Mexico.

Merriam, S. B., T. K. Thomas, and C. P. Zeph. 1987. Mentoring in higher education: What we know now. *The Review of Higher Education* 11: 199–210.

Metzner, B. S. 1989. Perceived quality of academic advising: The effect on freshman attrition. *American Educational Research Journal* 26: 422–42.

Metzner, B. S., and J. Bean. 1987. The estimation of a conceptual model of nontraditional undergraduate student attrition. *Research in Higher Education* 27: 15–38.

Mickey, R. C. 1988. Counseling, advising and mentoring as retention strategies for black students in higher education. In *Black student retention in higher education*, edited by M. Lang and C. A. Ford. Springfield, Ill.: Charles C. Thomas, Publishers.

Miller, R. E., and S. B. Brickman. 1982. Faculty and staff mentoring: A model for improving student retention and service. *National Association of Student Personnel Administrators Journal* 19: 23–27.

Millis, B. J. 1991. Fulfilling the promise of the "Seven Principles" through cooperative learning: An action agenda for the university classroom. *Journal on Excellence in College Teaching* 2: 139–44.

Mincer, J. 1966. Labor force participation and unemployment. In *Prosperity and unemployment*, edited by R. Gordon and M. Gordon. New York: John Wiley and Sons.

Mock, K. R., and G. Yonge. 1969. *Students' intellectual attitudes, aptitude and persistence at the University of California.* Center for Research and Development in Higher Education, University of California, Berkeley.

Moffatt, M. 1989. *Coming of age in New Jersey: College and American culture.* New Brunswick, N.J.: Rutgers University Press.

Moore, W., Jr., and L. C. Carpenter. 1985. Academically underprepared students. In *Increasing student retention*, edited by L. Noel and R. Levitz. San Francisco: Jossey-Bass.

Morrisey. R. J. 1971. Attrition in probationary freshmen. *Journal of College Student Personnel* 12: 279–85.

Mortenson, T. G. 1991. *Equity of higher education opportunity for women, black, hispanic, and low income students.* An American College Testing Program Student Financial Aid Research Report Series 91-1, January.

Muehl, S., and L. Muehl. 1972. A college level compensatory program for educationally disadvantaged black students. *Journal of Negro Education* 41: 65–81.

Munro, B. 1980. Dropouts from nursing education. *Nursing Research* 29: 371–77.

———. 1981. Dropouts from higher education: Path analysis of a national sample. *American Education Research Journal* 81: 133–41.

Murdock, T. A. 1987. It isn't just money: The effects of financial aid on student persistence. *The Review of Higher Education* 11: 75–101.

Murguia, E., R. V. Padilla, and M. Pavel. 1991. Ethnicity and the concept of social integration in Tinto's model of institutional departure. *Journal of College Student Development* 32: 433–39.

Naretto, J. A. 1991. Adult undergraduate student degree completion: The influence of membership in communities external and internal to the college. A Ph. D. dissertation, State University of New York at Buffalow, Buffalo.

Nerad, M. 1990. Doctoral education at the University of California and factors affecting time to degree. A report to the Office of the President, University of California at Berkeley, October 24, 1990.

Nettles, M., et al. 1984. *The causes and consequences of college students' performance.* Nashville: Tennessee Higher Education Commission.

———, ed. 1988. *Toward black undergraduate student equality in American higher education.* New York: Greenwood Press.

Neumann, W. 1985. Persistence in the community college: The student perspective. Ph.D. dissertation, Syracuse University, Syracuse.

Neumann, Y., and E. F. Neumann. 1989. Predicting juniors' and seniors' persistence and attrition: A quality of learning experience approach. *The Journal of Experimental Education* 57: 129–40.

Nicholson, E. 1973. *Predictors of graduation from college.* ACT Research Report No. 56. Iowa City, Iowa: American College Testing Program.

Noel, L., ed. 1978. *Reducing the dropout rate.* New Directions for Student Services, no. 3. San Francisco: Jossey-Bass.

Noel, L., and R. Levitz, eds. 1985. *Increasing student retention.* San Francisco: Jossey-Bass.

Nora, A. 1987. Determinants of retention among chicano college students. *Research in Higher Education* 26: 31–59.

———. 1990. Campus-based aid programs as determinants of retention among hispanic community college students. *Journal of Higher Education* 61: 312–31.

Nora, A., M. Castaneda, and A. Cabrera. 1992. Student persistence: The testing of a comprehensive structural model of retention. A paper presented at the 1992 annual meeting of the Association for the Study of Higher Education, Minneapolis.

Nora, A., and F. Horvath. 1989. Financial assistance: Minority enrollments and persistence. *Education and Urban Society* 21: 299–311.

Nora, A., and L. Rendon. 1990. Determinants of predisposition to transfer among community college students. *Research in Higher Education* 31: 235–55.

Nora, A., and E. Wedham. 1991. Off-campus experiences: The pull factors affecting freshman-year attrition on a commuter campus. A paper presented at the 1991 annual meeting of the American Educational Research Association, Chicago.

Olivas, M. A. 1986. Financial aid and self-reports by disadvantaged students: The importance of being earnest. *Research in Higher Education* 25: 245–52.

Oosterbeek, H. 1989. An economic analysis of educational dropouts. An unpublished manuscript. Department of Economics, University of Amsterdam.

Ory, J. C. and L. A. Braskamp. 1988. Involvement and growth of students in three academic programs. *Research in Higher Education* 28: 116–29.

Ostrow, E., S. Paul, V. Dark, and J. Berhman. 1986. Adjustment of women on campus: Effects of stressful life events, social support, and personal competencies. In S. E. Hobfoll, ed., *Stress, social support, and women.* Washington, D.C.: Hemisphere.

Ott, M., T. Markewich, and N. Ochsner. 1984. Logit analysis of graduate student retention. *Research in Higher Education,* 21: 439–59.

Pace, C. R. 1980. *Measuring the quality of student effort.* Los Angeles: Laboratory for Research in Higher Education, University of California.

———. 1984. *Measuring the quality of college student experience.* Los Angeles: University of California, Higher Education Research Institute.

Padilla, R. 1991. Using dialogical research methods with Chicano college students. A paper presented at the annual meeting of the American Educational Research Association, Chicago.

Padilla, R., and D. M. Pavel. 1986. *Successful hispanic community college students: An exploratory qualitative study.* Tempe: Hispanic Research Center, Arizona State University.

Panos, R. J., and A. W. Astin. 1968. Attrition among college students. *American Education Research Journal* 5: 57–72.

Pantages, T. J., and C. F. Creedon. 1978. Studies of college attrition: 1950–1975. *Review of Educational Research* 48: 49–101.

Pappas, J. P., and R. K. Loring. 1985. Returning students. In *Reducing the dropout rate,* edited by L. Noel and R. Levitz. San Francisco: Jossey-Bass.

Parker, J., and J. Schmidt. 1982. Effects of college experience. In H. Mitzel, ed., *Encyclopedia of Educational Research* (5th ed.). New York: Free Press.

Pascarella, E. T. 1980. Student-faculty informal contact and college outcomes. *Review of Educational Research* 50: 545–95.

———. 1985a. Racial differences in the factors influencing bachelor's degree completion: A nine-year follow-up. Paper presented to the annual meeting of the American Educational Research Association, Chicago.

———. 1985b. College environmental influences on learning and cognitive development: Critical review and synthesis. In *Higher Education: Handbook of Theory and Research. Vol. 1,* edited by J. Smart. New York: Agathon Press.

———. 1985c. Racial differences in factors associated with bachelor's degree completion: A nine-year follow-up. *Research in Higher Education* 23: 351–73.

———. 1985d. Students' affective development within the college environment. *Journal of Higher Education* 56: 640–63.

———. 1989. The development of critical thinking: Does college make a difference? *Journal of College Student Development* 30: 10–26.

Pascarella, E. T., and D. Chapman. 1983. A multi-institutional, path analytic validation of Tinto's model of college withdrawal. *American Educational Research Journal* 20: 87–102.

Pascarella, E. T., P. B. Duby, and B. Iverson. 1983. A test and reconceptualization of a theoretical model of college withdrawal in a commuter institution setting. *Sociology of Education* 56: 88–100.

Pascarella, E. T., P. Duby, V. Miller, and S. Rasher. 1981. Preenrollment variables and academic performance as predictors of freshman year persistence, early withdrawal and stopout behavior in an urban, nonresidential university. *Research in Higher Education* 15: 329–49.

Pascarella, E. T., C. A. Ethington, and J. C. Smart. 1988. The influence of college on humanitarian/civic involvement variables. *Journal of Higher Education* 59: 412–37.

Pascarella, E. T., J. C. Smart, and C. A. Ethington. 1985. Tracing the long-term persistence/withdrawal behavior of two-year college students: Tests of a causal model. Paper presented to the annual meeting of the American Educational Research Association, Chicago.

Pascarella, E. T., J. C. Smart, C. A. Ethington, and M. Nettles. 1987. The influence of college on self-concept: A consideration of race and gender differences. *American Educational Research Journal* 24: 49–77.

Pascarella, E. T., and P. T. Terenzini. 1977. Patterns of student-faculty informal interaction beyond the classroom and voluntary freshman attrition. *Journal of Higher Education* 5: 540–52.

———. 1979. Interaction effects in Spady's and Tinto's conceptual model of college dropout. *Sociology of Education* 52: 197–210.

———. 1980. Predicting freshman persistence and voluntary dropout decisions from a theoretical model. *Journal of Higher Education* 51: 60–75.

———. 1983. Predicting voluntary freshman year persistence/withdrawal behavior in a residential university: A path analytic validation of Tinto's model. *Journal of Educational Psychology* 75: 215–26.

———. 1991. *How college affects students.* San Francisco: Jossey-Bass.

Pascarella, E. T., P. T. Terenzini, and J. Hibel. 1978. Student faculty interactional settings and their relationship to predicted academic performance. *Journal of Higher Education* 49: 450–63.

Pascarella, E. T., P. T. Terenzini, and L. Wolfle. 1985. Orientation to college as anticipatory socialization: Indirect effects of freshman year persistence/ withdrawal decisions. Paper presented at the annual meeting of the American Educational Research Association, Chicago.

Pascarella, E. T., and L. M. Wolfle. 1985. Persistence in higher education: A nine-year test of a theoretical model. Paper presented at the annual meeting of the American Educational Research Association, Chicago.

Patton, M. J. 1991. Qualitative research on college students: Philosophical and methodological comparisons with the quantitative approach. *Journal of College Student Development* 32: 389–96.

Pearson, R. E. 1990. *Counselling and social support: Perspectives and practices.* Newbury Park, Calif.: Sage.

Peng, S. S., and W. B. Fetters. 1977. College student withdrawal: A motivational problem. Paper presented at the annual meeting of the American Educational Research Association, New York.

Perry, W. G. 1970. *Forms of intellectual and ethical development in the college years.* New York: Holt, Rinehart & Winston.

Pervin, L. A., and D. B. Rubin. 1967. Student dissatisfaction with college and the college dropout: A transactional approach. *The Journal of Social Psychology* 72: 285–95.

Peterson, S. L. 1992. *The relationship between career decision-making self-efficacy and dimensions of institutional integration among underprepared college students.* An unpublished doctoral dissertation, University of Minnesota.

Peters, D., and M. Peterson. 1987. Rites of passage for doctoral students in higher education. Paper presented at the annual meeting of the Association for the Study of Higher Education, Baltimore, Maryland, November.

Pincus, F. 1980. The false promise of community colleges: Class conflict and vocational education. *Harvard Educational Review* 50: 332–61.

Pollard, D. 1990. Black women: Interpersonal support and institutional change. In *Women and Change in Education,* edited by J. Antler and S. Biklin. Albany: State University of New York.

Porter, O. F. 1990. *Undergraduate completion and persistence at four-year colleges and universities: Detailed findings.* Washington, D.C.: National Institute of Independent Colleges and Universities.

Prager, C., ed. 1988. *Enhancing articulation and transfer.* New Directions for Community Colleges, no. 61. San Francisco: Jossey-Bass.

Price, J. L. 1977. *The study of turnover.* Ames, Iowa: Iowa State University Press.

Price, J. L., and C. W. Mueller. 1981. A causal model of turnover for nurses. *Academy of Management Journal* 24: 543–65.

Pruitt, A., and P. Isaac. 1985. Discrimination in recruitment, admission, and retention of minority graduate students. *Journal of Negro Education* 54: 526–36.

Raimst, L. 1981. *College student attrition and retention.* College Board Report No. 81-1, New York: College Entrance Examination Board.

Research Triangle Institute. 1975. *Report on special services programs.* Research Triangle Park, N.C.

Richardson, R. C., Jr. 1987. *Fostering minority access and achievement in higher education.* San Francisco: Jossey-Bass.

Richardson, R. C., Jr., H. Simmons, and A. G. de los Santos, Jr. 1987. Graduating minority students. *Change* 19: 20–27.

Rist, R. 1970. Student social class and teacher expectations: The self-fulfilling prophecy in ghetto education. *Harvard Educational Review* 40: 411–51.

Robinson, L. 1967. Relation of students in college with "environment" factors. Ph.D. dissertation, University of Arkansas.

Rodgers, B. H., and L. Pratt. 1989. The relationship between freshman intentions, motivations, academic aptitude, and college performance to persistence in college. Paper presented at the annual meeting of the Association for Institutional Research, Baltimore, Maryland.

Rootman, I. 1972. Voluntary withdrawal from a total adult socializing organization: A model. *Sociology of Education* 45: 258–70.

Rose, R. A., and C. F. Elton. 1966. Another look at the college dropout. *Journal of Counseling Psychology* 13: 242–45.

———. 1971. Attrition and the vocationally undecided student. *Journal of Vocational Behavior* 1: 99–103.

Rosenbaum, J. 1976. *Making inequality.* New York: John Wiley and Sons.

Rossmann, J. E., and B. A. Kirk. 1970. Factors related to persistence and withdrawal among university students. *Journal of Counseling Psychology* 17: 55–62.

Roth, M. 1985. Immigrant students in an urban commuter college: Persistors and dropouts. Ph.D. dissertation. Adelphi University, Garden City.

Rumberger, R. 1982a. *The changing economic benefits of couege graduates.* Institute for Research on Educational Finance and Governance, Stanford University, Palo Alto.

———. 1982b. *The job market for college graduates, 1960–1990.* Institute for Research on Educational Finance and Governance, Stanford University, Palo Alto.

Russo, P., and V. Tinto. 1992. Expanding one's vision: The impact of collaborative learning upon student intent to transfer. Unpublished manuscript. Syracuse University.

St. John, E. P, R. J. Kirshstein, and J. Noell. 1991. The effects of student financial aid on persistence: A sequential analysis. *The Review of Higher Education* 14: 383–406.

Sanchez, A. R., and M. King. 1986. Mexican Americans' use of counseling services: Cultural and institutional factors. *Journal of Counseling Psychology* 30: 215–20.

Schlossberg, N. K., A. Q. Lynch, and A. W. Chickering. 1989. *Improving higher education environments for adults: Responsive programs and services from entry to departure.* San Francisco: Jossey-Bass.

Schwartz, S. 1990. Application of a conceptual model of college withdrawal of technical college students. Paper presented at the annual meeting of the American Education Research Association, Boston.

Scott, M. M. 1991. Naturalistic research: Applications for research and professional practice with college students. *Journal of College Student Development* 32: 416–23.

Sedlacek, W., and D. W. Webster. 1978. Admission and retention of minority students in large universities. *Journal of Couege Student Personnel* 19: 242–46.

Seidman, A. 1992. Integrated admission counseling: Impact on enrollment. *The Freshman Year Experience Newsletter* 4: 6.

Sewell, W., and R. Hauser. 1975. *Education, occupation and earnings.* New York: Academic Press.

Shaffer, P. E. 1973. Academic progress of disadvantaged minority students: A two-year study. *Journal of College Student Personnel* 14: 41–46.

Sharp, L. F., and L. R. Chason. 1978. Use of moderator variables in predicting college student attrition. *Journal of College Student Personnel* 19: 388–93.

Sheffield, W., and V. P. Meskill. 1974. What can colleges do about student attrition? *College Student Journal* 8: 37–45.

Shils, E. 1961. *Center and periphery: Essays in macrosociology.* Chicago: University of Chicago Press.

Shulman, L. S. 1985. Paradigms and research programs in the study of teaching: A contemporary perspective. In *The handbook of research on teaching,* 3d ed., edited by M. Wittrock. New York: Macmillan.

Simpson, C., K. Baker, and G. Mellinger. 1980. Conventional failures and unconventional dropouts: Comparing different types of university withdrawals. *Sociology of Education* 53: 203–14.

Skaling, M. M. 1971. Review of the research literature. In *An investigation of entrance characteristics related to types of college dropouts,* edited by R. Cope et al. U.S. Office of Education, Final Research Report, pp. 17–60. Washington, D.C.: U.S. Government Printing Office.

Slaney, R. 1980. Expressed vocational choices and vocational indecision. *Journal of Counseling Psychology* 27: 122–29.

Slavin, R. 1990. *Cooperative learning: Theory, research, and practice.* Englewood Cliffs: Prentice-Hall.

Smith, L., et al. 1981. *Mobilizing the campus for retention.* Iowa City: American College Testing Program.

Snyder, F. A., and C. E. Blocker. 1970. *A profile of non-persisting students: A description of educational goals and achievements, activities, and perceptions of non-graduates, Spring 1969.* Research Report No. 3. Harrisburg Area Community College, Harrisburg, Pennsylvania.

Spady, W. 1970. Dropouts from higher education: An interdisciplinary review and synthesis. *Interchange* 1: 64–85.

———. 1971. Dropouts from higher education: Toward an empirical model. *Interchange* 2: 38–62.

Staats, S., and C. Partio. 1990. Predicting intent to get a college degree. *Journal of College Student Development* 31: 245–49.

Stage, F. 1989a. Motivation, academic and social integration and the early dropout. *American Educational Research Journal* 26: 385–402.

———. 1989b. Reciprocal effects between the academic and social integration of college students. *Research in Higher Education* 30: 517–30.

Stampen, J. O., and A. F. Cabrera. 1986. Exploring the effects of student aid on attrition. *The Journal of Student Financial Aid* 16: 28–40.

———. 1988. The targeting and packaging of student financial aid and its effects on attrition. *Economics of Education Review* 7: 29–46.

Stampen, J. O., and R. H. Fenske. 1988. The impact of financial aid on ethnic minorities. *The Review of Higher Education* 11: 337–53.

Steele, M. W. 1978. Correlates of undergraduate retention at the University of Miami. *Journal of College Student Personnel* 19: 349–52.

Stein, E., and J. Weidman. 1990. The socialization of doctoral students to academic norms. Paper presented at the annual meeting of the American Educational Research Association, Boston.

Stinson, M. S., M. J. Scherer, and G. G. Walter. 1987. Factors affecting persistence of deaf college students. *Research in Higher Education* 27: 244–58.

Stoecker, J., E. Pascarella, and L. Wolfle. 1988. Persistence in higher education: A nine-year test of a theoretical model. *Journal of College Student Development* 29: 196–209.

Stroup, H. 1966. *Bureaucracy in higher education*. New York: Free Press.

Study Group on the Conditions of Excellence in American Higher Education. 1984. *Involvement in learning: Realizing the potential of American higher education*. A report to the National Institute of Education, U.S. Department of Education. Washington, D.C.: U.S. Government Printing Office.

Suczek, R. F., and E. Alfert. 1966. *Personality characteristics of college dropouts*. Berkeley: Department of Psychiatry, University of California.

Suen, H. K. 1983. Alienation and attrition of Black college students on a predominantly White campus . *Journal of Couege Student Personnel* 24: 117–21.

Summerskill, J. 1962. Dropouts from colleges. In *The American college: A psychological and social interpretation of higher learning*, edited by N. Sanford. New York: John Wiley and Sons.

Swift, J. S., Jr. 1987. Retention of adult college students. *National Academic Advising Association Journal* 7: 7–19.

Systems Development Corporation. 1981. *Progress report on the evaluation of special services in higher education*. Santa Monica, Calif.: Systems Development Corporation.

Taubman, P., and T. Wales. 1972. *Mental ability and higher educational attainment in the 20th century*. Berkeley, Calif.: Carnegie Commission on Higher Education.

Taylor, R., and G. Hanson. 1970. Interest and persistence. *Journal of Counseling Psychology* 17: 506–9.

Terenzini, P. T., W. G. Lorang, and E. T. Pascarella. 1981. Predicting freshman persistence and voluntary dropout decisions: A replication. *Research in Higher Education* 15: 109–27.

Terenzini, P. T., and E. T. Pascarella. 1977. Voluntary freshman attrition and patterns of social and academic integration in a university: A test of a conceptual model. *Research in Higher Education* 6: 25–43.

———. 1978. The relation of students' precollege characteristics and freshman year experience to voluntary attrition. *Research in Higher Education* 9: 347–66.

———. 1980. Toward the validation of Tinto's model of college student attrition: A review of recent studies. *Research in Higher Education* 12: 271–82.

Terenzini, P. T., and T. Wright. 1987a. Influences on students' academic growth during four years of college. *Research in Higher Education* 26: 161–79.

———. 1987b. Students' personal growth during the first two years of college. *Review of Higher Education* 10: 259–71.

Terkla, D. G. 1985. Does financial aid enhance undergraduate persistence? *Journal of Student Financial Aid* 15: 11–18.

Theophilides, C., and P. T. Terenzini. 1981. The relation between nonclassroom contact with faculty and students' perceptions of instructional quality. *Research in Higher Education* 15: 255–69.

Thomas, G., B. Clewell, and W. Pearson. 1987. Case study of major doctoral producing institutions in recruiting, enrolling, and retaining Black and Hispanic graduate students. A report to the Graduate Record Examination Board, Princeton, New Jersey. September.

————. 1991. The role and activities of American graduate schools in recruiting, enrolling, and retaining U.S. Black and Hispanic students. Draft Research Report of the Minority Graduate Education Project, jointly sponsored by the Graduate Record Examination Board and Educational Testing Service, Princeton, New Jersey.

Thompson, C. E., and B. R. Fretz. 1991. Predicting the adjustment of Black students at predominantly white institutions. *Journal of Higher Education* 62: 437–50.

Tierney, M. L. 1980. The impact of financial aid on student demand for public/private higher education. *Journal of Higher Education* 51: 527–45.

————. 1984. Letter to author, 14 April.

Tierney, W. 1992. An anthropological analysis of student participation in college. *Journal of Higher Education* 63: 603–18.

Tinto, V. 1975. Dropout from higher education: A theoretical synthesis of recent research. *Review of Educational Research* 45: 89–125.

————. 1981. The limits of theory and practice in student attrition. *Journal of Higher Education* 45: 687–700.

————. 1985a. Rites of passage and the stages of student withdrawal from higher education. Paper presented to the annual meeting of the American Educational Research Association, Chicago.

————. 1985b. Dropping out and other forms of withdrawal from college. In *Increasing student retention*, edited by L. Noel and R. Levitz. San Francisco: Jossey-Bass.

————. 1986. Theories of student departure revisited. In *Higher Education: Handbook of Theory and Research*, vol. 2, edited by J. Smart. New York: Agathon Press.

————. 1987. *Leaving college: Rethinking the causes and cures of student attrition.* Chicago: University of Chicago Press.

————. 1989. Stages of student departure: Reflections on the longitudinal character of student leaving. *Journal of Higher Education* 59: 438–55.

Tinto, V., and R. Froh. 1992. Deconstructing social theory: Translating research on student persistence into policy. Paper presented at the annual meeting of the Association for the Study of Higher Education, Chicago.

Tinto, V., and B. Lentz. 1986. Rates of system departure from higher education: 1890–1980. Paper presented to the annual meeting of the American Educational Research Association, San Francisco.

Tinto, V., and D. Wallace. 1986. Retention: An admissions concern. *College and University* 61: 290–93.

Tinto, V., A. Goodsell, and P. Russo. 1993. Gaining a voice: The impact of collaborative learning on student experience in the first year of college. Unpublished manuscript. Syracuse University, Syracuse, New York.

Titley, R., B. S. Titley, and W. Wolff. 1976. The major changers: Continuity and discontinuity in the career decision process? *Journal of Vocational Behavior* 8: 105–11.

Tobias, S. 1982. When do instructional methods make a difference? *Educational Research* 11: 4–10.

Tomlinson, L. 1989. *Postsecondary developmental programs: A traditional agenda with new imperatives.* Report No.3, ASHE-ERIC Higher Education Reports, George Washington University.

Tracey, T., and W. Sedlacek. 1985. The relationship of noncognitive variables to academic success: A longitudinal comparison by race. *Journal of College Student Personnel* 26: 405–10.

———. 1987. A comparison of white and black student academic success using noncognitive variables: A Lisrel analysis. *Research in Higher Education* 27: 333–48.

Trent, J., and J. Ruyle. 1965. Variation, flow and patterns of college attendance. *College and University* 41: 61–76.

Trippi, J., and H. Cheatham. 1991. Counseling effects on African American college student graduation. *Journal of College Student Development* 32: 342–49.

Tuckman, H. 1990. The rise in doctoral completion time. *Higher Education: Handbook of Theory and Research, Volume VI.* New York: Agathon Press.

Tuckman, H., S. Coyle, and Y. Bae. 1990. *On time to the doctorate.* Washington, D.C.: National Academy Press.

Turner, R. 1961. Modes of social ascent through education: sponsored and contest mobility. In *Education, economy, and society,* edited by Halsey et al. Glencoe: Free Press.

Upcraft, M. L., J. Gardner, and Associates. 1989. *The freshman year experience.* San Francisco: Jossey-Bass.

U.S. Department of Education, National Center for Educational Statistics. 1977. *Withdrawal from institutions of higher education.* Washington, D.C.: U.S. Government Printing Office.

———. 1980. *High school and beyond, first follow-up.* Washington, D.C.: U.S. Government Printing Office.

———. 1983a. *Digest of educational statistics.* Washington, D.C.: U.S. Government Printing Office.

———. 1983b. *Participation of black students in higher education: A statistical profile from 1970–71 to 1980–81.* Washington, D.C.: U.S. Government Printing Office.

———. 1985. Many college freshman take remedial course. *National Center for Education Statistics Bulletin.* Washington, D.C.: U.S. Government Printing Office.

———. 1990. *Projections of education statistics to 2001: An update.* Washington, D.C.: U.S. Government Printing Office.

———. 1991a. *Digest of educational statistics, 1991.* Washington, D.C.: U.S. Government Printing Office.

———. 1991b. *The condition of education, 1991.* Washington, D.C.: U.S. Government Printing Office.

Valadez, J. R., and R. P. Duran. 1991. Mentoring in higher education. Paper presented at the annual meeting of the American Educational Research Association, Chicago.

Valverde, L. 1985. Low-income students. In *Increasing student retention*, edited by L. Noel and R. Levitz. San Francisco: Jossey-Bass.

Van Gennep, A. 1960. *The rites of passage*. Translated by M. Vizedon and G. Caffee. Chicago: University of Chicago Press. Originally published as *Les rites de passage*. Paris: Nourry, 1909.

Varner, S. 1967. *School dropouts*. Washington, D.C.: National Education Association.

Vaughan, R. P. 1968. College dropouts: Dismissed vs. withdrew. *Personnel and Guidance Journal* 46: 685–89.

Voorhees, R. A. 1984. Financial aid and new freshman persistence: An exploratory model. Paper presented at the annual meeting of the Association for Institutional Research, Fort Worth, Texas.

———. 1987. Toward building models of community college persistence: A logit analysis. *Research in Higher Education* 26: 115–29.

Waterman, A. S., and C. K. Waterman. 1972. Relationship between freshman ego identity status and subsequent academic behavior: A test of the predictive validity of Marcia's categorization system of identity status. *Developmental Psychology* 6: 179.

Webb, M. W.. 1990. Development and testing of a theoretical model for predicting student degree persistence at a four-year communter college. Paper presented at the American Education Research Association, Boston.

Wechsler, H. 1989. *Meeting the transfer challenge: Five partnerships and their model*. The report of the Vassar/AAC National project on Community College Transfer. Washington D.C.: Association for Junior Colleges and Vassar College.

Weidman, J. 1985. Retention of non-traditional students in postsecondary education. Paper presented at the annual meeting of the American Educational Research Association, Chicago.

Weidman, J., and R. Friedmann. 1984. The school-to-work transition for high school dropouts. *Urban Review* 16: 25–42.

Weil, R. 1989. Factors affecting doctoral students' time to degree. Ph.D. dissertation. Claremont Graduate School.

Weimer, M. 1989. *Teaching large classes well*. New Directions for Teaching and Learning No. 32. San Francisco: Jossey-Bass.

———. 1990. *Improving college teaching*. San Francisco: Jossey-Bass.

Weingartner, C. 1981. The past is prologue. *The Review of Education* 7: 127–33.

Wenc, L. M. 1977. The role of financial aid in attrition and retention. *The College Board Review* 104: 17–21.

Wilder, M. A., Jr., and S. E. Kellams. 1987. Commitment to college and student involvement. Paper presented at the annual meeting of the American Educational Research Association, Washington, D.C..

Wilkerson, D. W. 1988. The black collegian advisement program at Kennesaw College: A comprehensive black student retention model. In *Black student retention in higher education*, edited by M. Lang and C. A. Ford. Springfield, Ill.: Charles C. Thomas Publishers.

Williamson, D., and D. Creamer. 1988. Student attrition in 2 and 4-year colleges: Application of a theoretical model. *Journal of College Student Development* 29: 197–217.

Williamson, M., and R. Fenske. 1992. Mentoring factors in doctoral programs of Mexican American and American Indian students. Paper presented at the American Educational Research Association, San Francisco.

Wilson, R., J. Gaff, R. Dienst, L. Wood, and J. Bavry. 1975. *College professors and their impact on students.* New York: Wiley-Interscience.

Wilson, R., L. Wood, and J. Gaff. 1974. Social-psychological accessibility and faculty-student interactions beyond the classroom. *Sociology of Education* 1: 74–92.

Wiseman, R. L., R. A. Emry, and D. Morgan. 1988. Predicting academic success for disabled students. *Research in Higher Education* 28: 255–70.

Wittrock, M., ed. 1985. *The handbook of research on teaching,* 3d ed. New York: Macmillan.

Wright, B. 1985. Programming success: Special student services and the American Indian college student. *Journal of American Indian Education* 24: 1–7.

Wright, D. J., ed. 1987. *Responding to the needs of today's minority students.* New Directions in Student Services, No. 38. San Francisco: Jossey-Bass.

Young, R. B., R. Backer, and G. Rogers. 1989. The impact of early advising and scheduling on freshman success. *Journal of College Student Development* 30: 309–12.

Yuker, H. E., et al. 1972. Who leaves Hofstra for what reasons? Hempstead, N.Y.: Center for the Study of Higher Education, Hofstra University.

Zaccaria, L., and J. Creaser. 1971. Factors relating to persistence in an urban commuter university. *Journal of College Student Personnel* 12: 256–61.

Zemsky, R., and P. Oedel. 1983. *The structure of college choice.* New York: College Entrance Examination Board.

Zwick, R. 1991. Factors contributing to persistence in graduate school. Paper presented at the annual meeting of the American Educational Research Association, Chicago.

— Index —

Chacon, M. A., 65, 77, 78
Chaney, B., 13, 16
Chapman, D., 27, 78
Chase, C. I., 247 n.1, 247 n.2
Chason, L. R., 44–45, 85
Cheatham, H., 185
Chesapeake College, 169–70
Chicanos. *See* Mexican Americans
Chickering, A. W., 63, 64, 135, 187, 247 n.5
Christie, N. G., 46, 62–63, 126, 127
Churchill, W. D., 87, 88
City University of New York, 26, 63, 198
Clark, B., 59
Classroom learning: assessment of, 216, 222; large lecture classes, 200; student involvement in, 132–34, 210–11
Clemson University, 158, 164
Cleveland State University, 173–74
Clewell, B., 182, 184, 231, 232, 237, 256 n.16
Coast Guard Academy, 81
Cohen, E. G., 65, 77, 78
Coker, D., 246 n.1
Coleman, J. S., 49, 90–91
Collaborative learning, 168–69, 177, 189–90, 193
College choice: expectations, role of, 54–55; finances, role of, 65–66; studies of, 249 n.16
College entry: cohort analysis, value of, 245 n.4; composition of entrant pool, 9–11; delayed, 20, 26–27, 246 n.13; external events, impact of, 129; finances, impact of, 88; retention assessment data collection at, 220; retention programs at, 154–58. *See also* Admissions; Recruitment
College of New Rochelle, 173
College of Notre Dame of Maryland, 179, 188
Color, students of. *See* Blacks; Hispanics; Native Americans; Race/ethnicity
Colorado State University, 166
Commitment, institutional: and educational mission, 206–7; importance, 204–6, 212; paradox of, 207–9; and retention program effectiveness, 144, 146–47, 149, 154
Commitment, student: goal, 43, 44; gradu-

ate persistence, impact on, 236, 239; incongruence and lack of, 52; institutional commitment, relation to, 208; to institutions, 43–44; in longitudinal model of departure, 113–15, 120, 130, 136, 137; of older students, 76–77; and retention program effectiveness, 145–48; as root of departure, 37, 41–45, 48, 82, 110–12; and stress of adjustment, 46–47
Communities, college/university: academic/social systems, 106–9; building social/intellectual, as retention program principle, 147–48; external impacts on, 126–27; incorporation into, 98–99, 125; learning and persistence, link between, 130–35, 210–11; multiple, and persistence, 59–62, 121–26, 132; society likened to, 104–6, 121, 146, 204–6. *See also* Academic systems; Social systems; Student subcultures
Communities, external: college communities likened to, 104–6, 121, 146, 204–6; college persistence, impact on, 38, 62–65, 109, 214; gap between nonresidential institutions and, 194–95; graduate persistence, impact on, 233–34, 237, 242, 256 n.11; in longitudinal model of departure, 115, 116, 126; students' separation from, 94–97
Communities, learning. *See* Learning communities
Community-building programs, 165–68, 177–78, 186, 192–93
Community College of Philadelphia, 189
Community colleges. *See* Two-year colleges
Commuting students/institutions. *See* Nonresidential students/institutions
Computers, 171, 196, 201
Conflict theory, 87
Conformity, 105
Contact. *See* Faculty-student contact; Integration; Isolation; Peer contact
Contracts, 156
Cook, M., 231
Cooperative learning, 64, 168, 169, 177, 189, 193
Cope, R., 35, 43, 54, 85, 251 n.3
Cornell University, 173, 185
Cosgrove, T. J., 70

Scholastic Aptitude Test (SAT) scores, 15–
16, 19, 21. *See also* Selectivity
Schuh, J. H., 58, 104, 119, 132, 177–78
Schwartz, S., 78
Scott, M. M., 217, 218
Screening, pre-entry, 160–62
Seattle Central Community College, 168,
189, 198
Sedlacek, W., 51, 53, 73
Seidman, A., 157
Selectivity: and admissions, 160–61; and
attrition rates, 15–17, 86; and degree
completion, 19, 21–22, 230
Separation: as college career stage, 94–97,
220; in rites of passage, 92–93
Sewell, W., 87
Sex differences: degree completion, 27–29;
departure process, 76–77; entry patterns,
11–12, 28; family responsibilities, 64–
65; graduate persistence, 237, 239, 256
Shaffer, P. E., 73
Sharp, L. F., 44–45, 85
Sheffield, W., 247 n.5
Shelby State Community College, 164
Shils, E., 248 n.14
Shulman, L. S., 248 n.11
Simmons, H., 184, 243
Simpson, C., 59, 248 n.10
Singer, J., 221
Size of institution: and departure process,
80–81; in organizational retention the-
ory, 89; retention programs at large
public universities, 198–201
Skaling, M. M., 35
Skenes, R., 77, 188
Skills, academic. *See* Ability
Slaney, R., 247 n.5
Slavin, R., 169
Smart, J. C., 69, 73, 79
Smith, B., 168
Smith, D., 248 n.11
Smith, K., 169
Snyder, F. A., 247 n.2
Social class. *See* Socioeconomic back-
ground
Social integration. *See* Integration
Socialization, 233. *See also* Integration;
Membership
Social-support theory, 122
Social systems: academic systems, inter-

play with, 108; defined, 106–8; graduate
school, 239; involvement in, and learning, 131–35; in longitudinal model of
departure, 113–26, 135–37
Social theories of departure, 86–87
Socioeconomic background: and academic
difficulty, 49; and college career stages,
96–97; and degree completion, 27, 29–
32; departure process variations, 73–76;
in environmental departure theories, 86–
87; and external obligations, 63; and financial aid, 68–69; and graduate
persistence, 239; in longitudinal model
of departure, 115; urban college students, 198
Sociology: and Durkheim, 100, 102; organizational, 88
Sororities, 99, 124, 199–200
South Carolina State College, 164
Southern University, 169–70
Spady, W., 35, 91, 100, 250 n.3
Special Service Programs, 61, 74
Sponsored mobility, 256 n.15
Sports, intramural, 99
Staats, S., 78
Staff, institutional: retention program as-
sessment, role in, 153, 218; retention
programs, role in, 148, 159, 167, 173,
178, 201; student contact with, 53, 206,
208, 214. *See also* Faculty
Stage, F., 56, 57, 70, 77, 78, 108, 119
Stampen, J. O., 65, 68, 75, 88, 116
Stanford University, 165, 177
Staten Island Continuum of Education, 158
State University of New York, 169–70,
172, 173, 194
Steele, M. W., 52
Stein, E., 254 n.3
Stinson, M. S., 249 n.17
Stockton State College, 164
Stoecker, J., 53, 56
Stopout(s), 129; defined, 8, 25–26; exter-
nal obligations, 65; retention programs,
178–79
Strommer, D. W., 168, 200, 201, 248 n.11
Strover, S., 65, 77, 78
Student departure: data sources, 13–14; di-
mensions and consequences, 1–2, 244
n.1; high schools, 91; limits to current
knowledge, 2–3; misestimation of, 9,

Western New Mexico University, 166
Whitt, E. J., 58, 104, 119, 132, 177–78
Wilder, M. A., Jr., 38
Wilkerson, D. W., 185
Willet, J., 221
Williamson, D., 39, 78
Williamson, M., 242
Wilson, R., 57, 69
Winthrop College, 164
Wise, D., 30, 66, 87, 88, 249 n.16
Wiseman, R. L., 249 n.17
Wittrock, M., 248 n.11
Wolff, W., 247 n.5
Wolfle, L., 53, 56–57, 78, 80, 159
Women. *See* Sex differences
Wood, L., 57, 69
Work. *See* Employment
Work-study programs, 64, 68–69, 108, 119, 179–80

Work turnover model, 89
Wright, B., 249 n.17
Wright, D. J., 185
Wright, T., 57, 69

Xavier University, 177, 185

Yakima Valley Community College, 164
Yonge, G., 247 n.1
York University, 173
Young, R. B., 160, 172
Yuker, H. E., 247 n.2

Zaccaria, L., 78
Zemsky, R., 54, 249 n.16
Zeph, C. P., 70
Zwick, R., 231, 232, 236, 256 n.14